AF506023

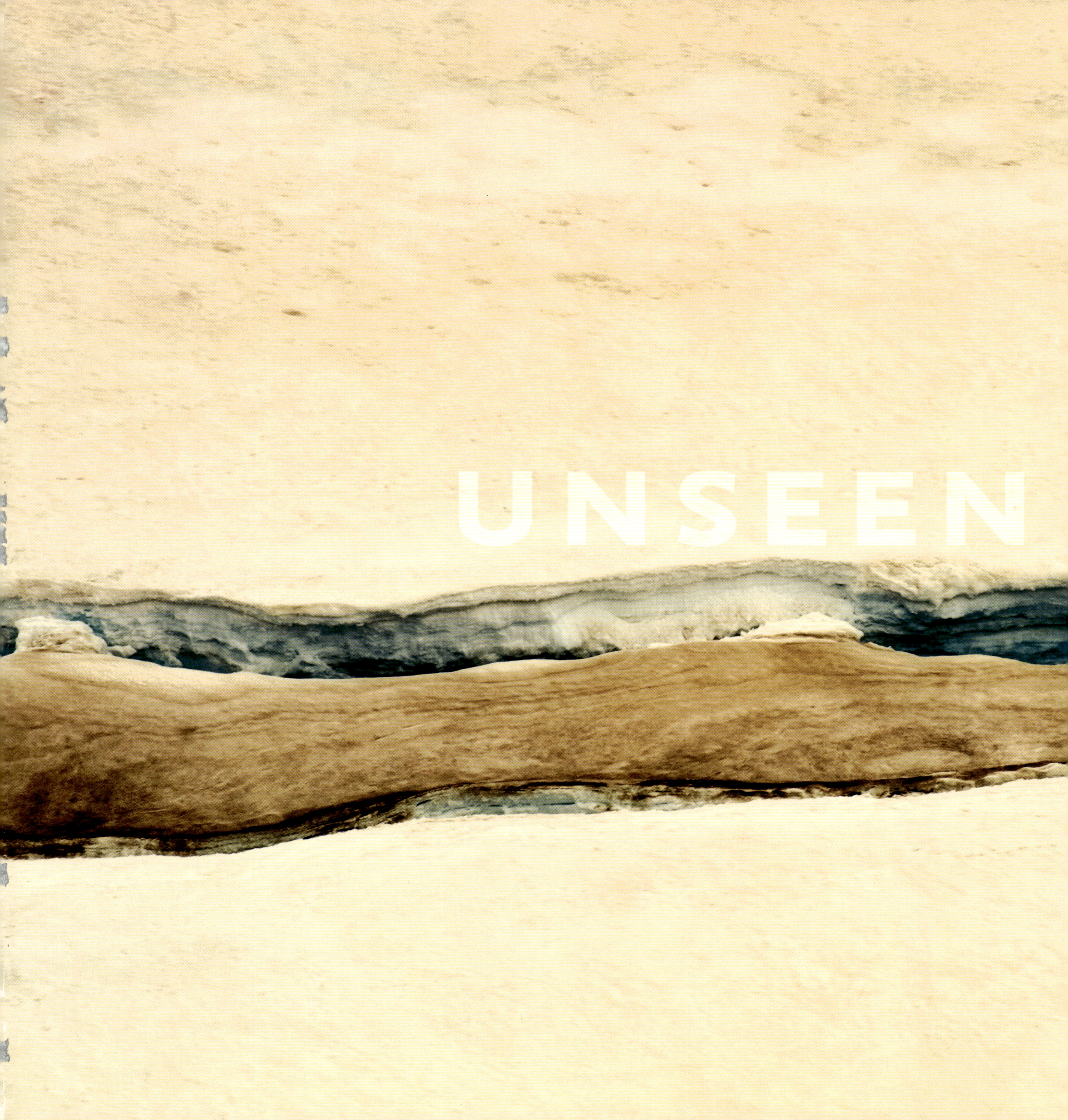

UNSEEN

PHOTOGRAPHS BY DIANE TUFT

Text by William L. Fox

UNSEEN

Ameringer & Yohe Fine Art
New York

Ameringer & Yohe Fine Art
20 West 57th Street
New York, NY 10019
tel: 212 445 0051 fax: 212 445 0102

AMERINGER
YOHE
FINE ART

Page 1: "Eyvindor's Crevasse," from the Icelandic Sagas series

Library of Congress Cataloging-in-Publication Data is available.
ISBN: 978-0-9820810-1-3

10 9 8 7 6 5 4 3 2 1

Designed by Zach Hooker
Color management by iocolor, Seattle
Produced by Marquand Books, Inc., Seattle
   www.marquand.com
Printed and bound in the United States of America

SOURCES

Cartmell, Robert. Invisible Light. Washington, D.C.: Smithsonian Institution, 1981. Catalog for SITES
   exhibition.

Coppola, Regina. Beyond Light: Infrared Photography by Six New England Artists. Amherst: University
   Gallery, University of Massachusetts, 1987. Essays in both this and the Cartmell catalog provided
   invaluable historical context for this essay.

Paternite, Stephen, & David Paternite, eds. American Infrared Survey. Akron, Ohio: Photo Survey Press
   Publishing, 1982.

Ruechardt, Eduard. Light: Visible and Invisible. Ann Arbor: University of Michigan Press, 1958.

Thompson, Silvanus P. Light, Visible and Invisible: A Series of Lectures Delivered at the Royal Institution
   of Great Britain. New York: The MacMillan Company, 1897.

To my wonderful family—Tom, Erica, Scott, and Jen—who have stood by my passion for travel and have remained patient while accompanying me to the most remote places in the world.

acknowledgments

Unseen would not have been possible without the guidance of Lesley Martin and Michelle Dunn of the Aperture Foundation; the expertise of Donna Wingate and Zach Hooker of Marquand Books; and Alan Rapp, whose editing coordinated these elements.

I am grateful to William Fox who understood my passion for nature and was able to capture this in his writing.

Special thanks to my husband, Tom, whose unconditional love has allowed me the freedom to explore, and to Scott and Jen, who have trekked with me for hours in pursuit of the best image.

My gratitude also extends to the numerous people and galleries who have believed in my vision and encouraged me to pursue my work, including: Dale and Doug Anderson, Satish Joshi, Stacey Epstein, Alberto Magnan, Neil Watson, Graham Leader, Melva Bucksbaum, Ray Learsy, Celso Gonzalez-Falla, Sondra Gillman, Elisabeth Sussman, Bippy Siegel, Hollis Taggart Gallery, and Miles McEnery and everyone at Ameringer & Yohe Fine Art.

And to all who feel that Nature has an unseen spirit.

The entire cosmos vibrates—from the tiniest of subatomic particles buzzing in and out of existence like frenzied bees far beyond our hearing, to the universe itself tolling like a bell beyond imagining, likewise far outside the reach of our senses. We call that continuum of activity the electromagnetic spectrum, which includes everything from radio waves to visible light to X-rays. Just as artists travel to the far reaches of the world in search of images that might reveal the nature of our universe, so they also now foray into the electromagnetic spectrum beyond visible light to make apparent the invisible. Diane Tuft is a photographer who has combined both kinds of journeys in her quest to uncover the deep linkages between physical and spiritual ways of apprehending the world.

Scientists, in order to penetrate ever more remote knowledge about how the world works, continue to probe those realms of the spectrum beyond our unaided senses, but until relatively recently artists have tended to be more conservative, dwelling mostly in the realm of what we can hear, touch, taste, smell, and see. Until well into the twentieth century, many critics and curators did not consider photography a serious artistic medium. Its scientific applications reinforced that bias; when artists followed the work of researchers and extended our perceptions with other technologies (such as stroboscopic photography and electron microscopy), the results were dismissed as mere tricks—as if only our unaugmented senses give us the one true version of the world. As if painters during the late Renaissance never used a *camera obscura*. As if the flight of a bullet revealed through high-speed photography or a hydrophonic recording of a whale song could not be legitimate subjects for artistic interpretation. As if contemporary artists were meant to forswear the innumerable possibilities inherent in digital imaging or work within the confines of the visible light spectrum.

Computers had a huge role in changing all that, making images so malleable that we had no choice but to enlarge our capacity to understand and accept what was previously thought of as impossible. As more and more chunks of the electromagnetic spectrum were probed, scientists revealed entirely new realms as relevant to our lives, and thus art. And so it is that the works of Diane Tuft, photographing at the near-infrared and near-ultraviolet ends of the spectrum—those wavelengths just above and below our visual range—seem less like a bag of tricks and more like logical extensions of our experience. Tuft's work now seems a necessary engagement with a world that we understand to be far larger and stranger than we had imagined.

The visible or optical spectrum extends to wavelengths in air from about 400 to 700 "nm"— namometers, or a billionth of a meter. That's the part of the spectrum our sun emits the most in, which is believed to be why we're adapted to see within that range. At the shorter end of the visible spectrum, nearly 64,000 violet 400 nm waves would line up along a one-inch line. At the longer end, only about 36,000 red 700 nm waves could fit along that one-inch line. Sir William Herschel discovered infrared (IR) radiation in 1800 while measuring how sunlight heats surfaces. He found that a thermometer reacted more strongly to red light than to violet or blue, and even more strongly when placed beyond the red end of the spectrum of the light that had passed through his prism. Subsequently, the IR spectrum has been found to extend to wavelengths of about 1.0 mm, about the size of a pinhead—only about 25 wavelengths to the inch. The year after Herschel's discovery of infrared radiation, the German physicist Johann Wilhelm Ritter discovered ultraviolet (UV) radiation, the much shorter (higher energy) wavelengths of radiation now known to be responsible for sunburns and genetic damage.

In 1910 the American physicist Robert W. Wood, who explored both ends of the spectrum, made the first successful infrared photograph. In the 1930s, with the invention of faster films and other technical advances, IR photography became possible for most serious photographers, and by the time World War II had started, the militaries of the world were aware that aerial photos made at that end of the spectrum could distinguish between live plants and camouflage paint. Postwar, Kodak made black-and-white infrared film widely available commercially, and it seems as if every photographer of note at the time experimented with it. Edward Steichen, Ansel Adams, and Weegee tried infrared film in the 1940s and 1950s, but it wasn't until Minor White's 1958 photograph "Cobblestone House, Avon, New York" was published in the Time-Life book Light and Film in 1970 that infrared gained more widespread attention with the general public. In the 1980s several survey exhibitions were mounted, and then its novelty status died down. Interest in infrared photography continues among artists, however. Chlorophyll reflects strongly in that part of the spectrum, while transparent media such as air and water do not. Plants and people give off an unearthly glow, while skies appear almost black. Artists use this steep gradient of contrast to make the quotidian slightly less familiar, a way of intimating a larger reality.

Diane Tuft, born in rural Connecticut, wanted to be a biochemist but ended up graduating in 1969 with a major in mathematics and a minor in philosophy. She first worked as an actuarial assistant and as a relatively early computer programmer, and ended up selling computers before marrying and starting a family. She had, however, always been interested in making art and did her own self-directed work. This combination of interests positioned her in such a way that in 1969, the year after she purchased her first camera, she continued her education by enrolling in both photography and painting classes at the New School in New York City.

Tuft was at first more interested in painting, sculpture, and printmaking than photography; she managed to continue her studies while raising a family, earning credits toward a masters degree at Pratt Institute in 1989 with a major in Graphic Arts. She admired work by painters such as the early abstractionists Arthur Dove and Helen Frankenthaler. While Dove had a strong graphic style that turned landscapes into abstracts, Frankenthaler's techniques often created allusions to natural landscapes. Both painters were seeking to reach a reality beyond that which was merely visible. The influence of Frankenthaler's palette is evident in Tuft's canvases, as is Dove's selection of forms found in nature as formal shapes to balance against one another. As with Dove, Tuft's compositions of seemingly organic shapes tempt the viewer to decipher a represented place, when in fact she is manifesting what is at least in part an imaginary landscape.

By the time her youngest daughter turned fifteen in 1994, she had decided to devote herself full-time to art but by 1998 found that she was working mostly in photography. She had been drawn to the work of Edward Weston and Man Ray, which likewise provides clues for the photography to come. Weston's work with nudes and sand dunes yielded shapes so abstract that at times they seemed almost interchangeable, a transformation of natural forms that was an astonishing feat at the time for a photographer, and one that revealed a unity of physical purpose in the world akin to that found in Dove's paintings. Man Ray was a photographer known for his photograms, compositions made directly on paper with light, without a camera. Tuft simplified the shapes she was photographing and paid close attention to negative spaces, concerns more typical of painters and sculptors than most photographers. She is, in fact, the only photographer handled by her New York gallery, which otherwise represents painters.

Tuft's love of travel is the other key factor in her work. She took her first camera with her to Europe, and extended her journeys to places as exotic as New Guinea, and she began to frequent the world's great empty quarters of sand and ice, such as Tunisia and Greenland. These are landscapes where nature has carved itself down to physiographic forms, betraying the dynamics of geomorphology—in short, abstractions of natural powers such as wind and rain. She was already prowling the edge of the visible, where natural structures implied patterns that extended into the unseen.

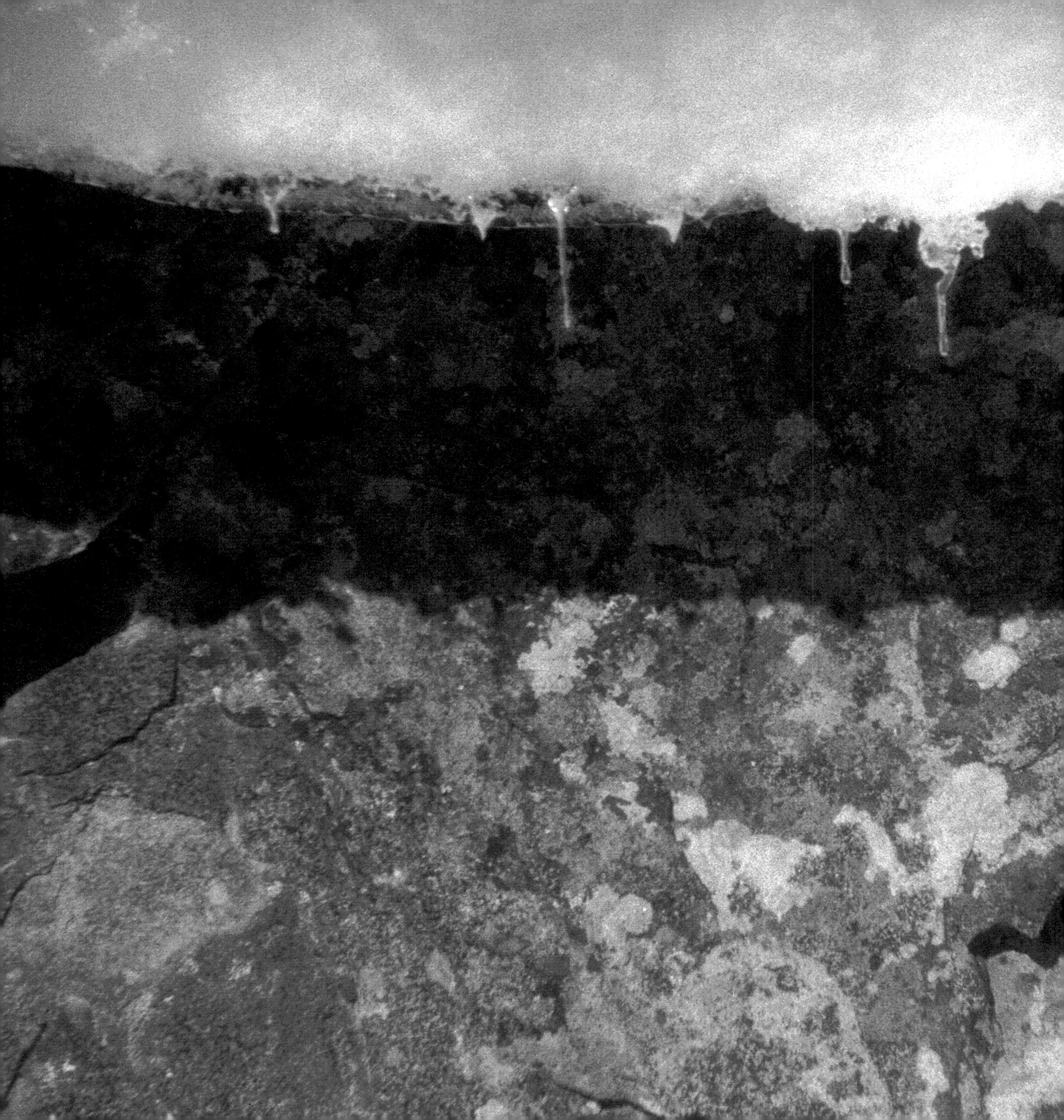

Tuft is an artist by inclination and training, but she is also schooled in the scientific formalities of how to question what we know. She had taken classes for several years at the International Center of Photography in New York, including some on alternative processes, when she began experimenting with black-and-white infrared film in 1998, a technique that extended her ability to query the world. By making visible what is normally invisible to humans—accepting that she therefore could not previsualize the results in a traditional manner—she derived a series of abstractions from close-up shots of ice and snow. Her images, taken from nature and transformed into compositions that at times could read as earth or body, bespeak their lineage to Dove, Weston, and other modernists of the period. Those abstracts also begin to hint at what we sometimes define as spiritual matters, patterns that we perceive to be greater than visible reality.

Infrared light goes through things that are transparent, such as water, and when it hits a solid, you can't predict how it's going to reflect. Furthermore, objects that are warmer appear relatively light in infrared photos compared to cooler surfaces. Small pieces of ice in water show up as dark spots, a phenomenon invisible in the optical spectrum. The photographs in the appropriately titled Distillations series, which Tuft prints in platinum, take a moment to decipher; "17" is a good example. This is also apparent in Tuft's photographs of sand dunes in Tunisia, which owe a stylistic debt to Weston's 1936 photograph "Wind Erosion, Dunes, Oceano," but her framing is even tighter and more disorienting, and the graininess of the infrared throws off our sense of scale. Platinum printing is a process well suited to the infrared, unlike printing in silver. Platinum chemicals soak into the paper itself, allowing the greatest tonal range in printing of any chemical process. Again, Tuft was pushing the boundary of what photographic technology could make visible.

distillations

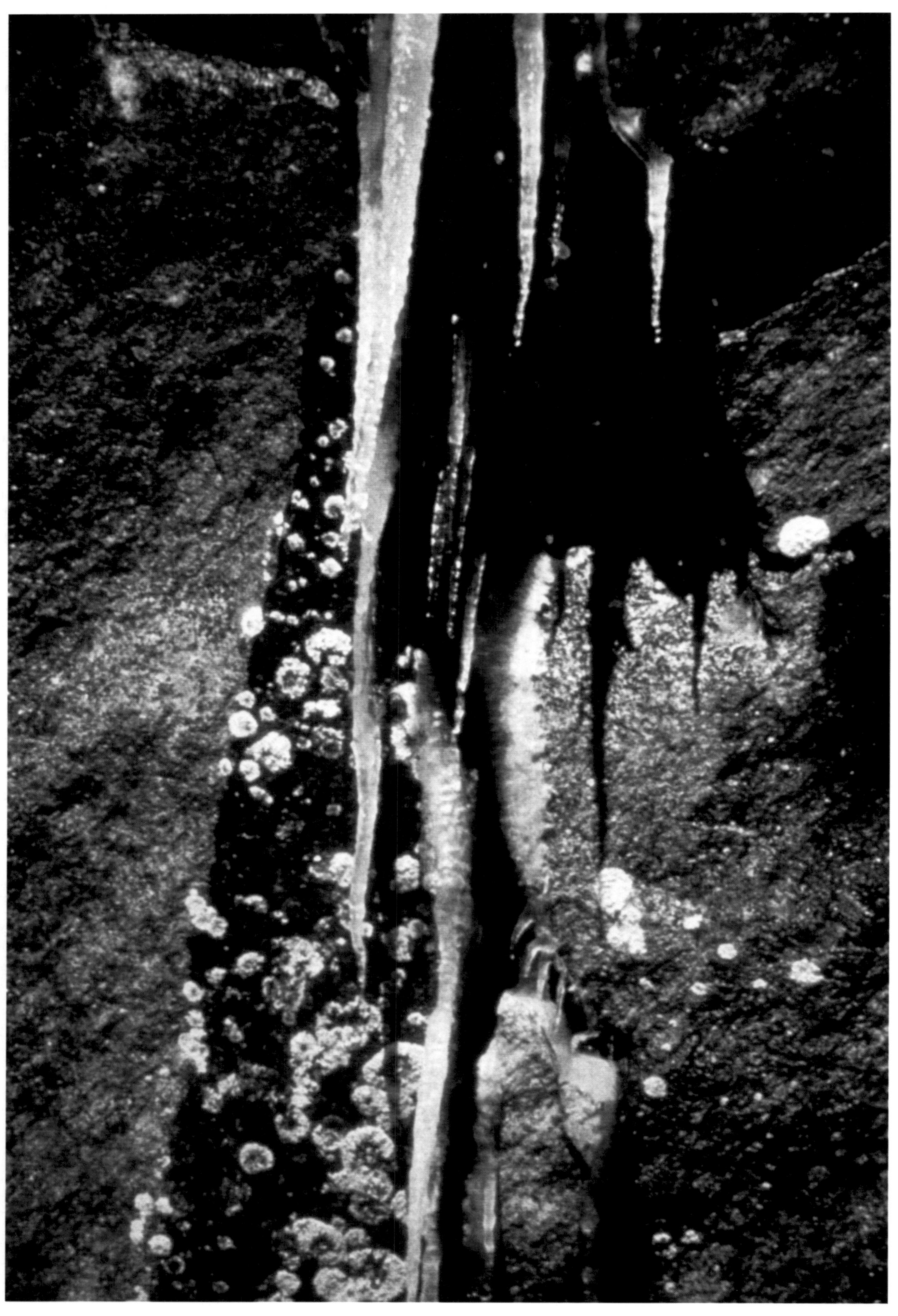

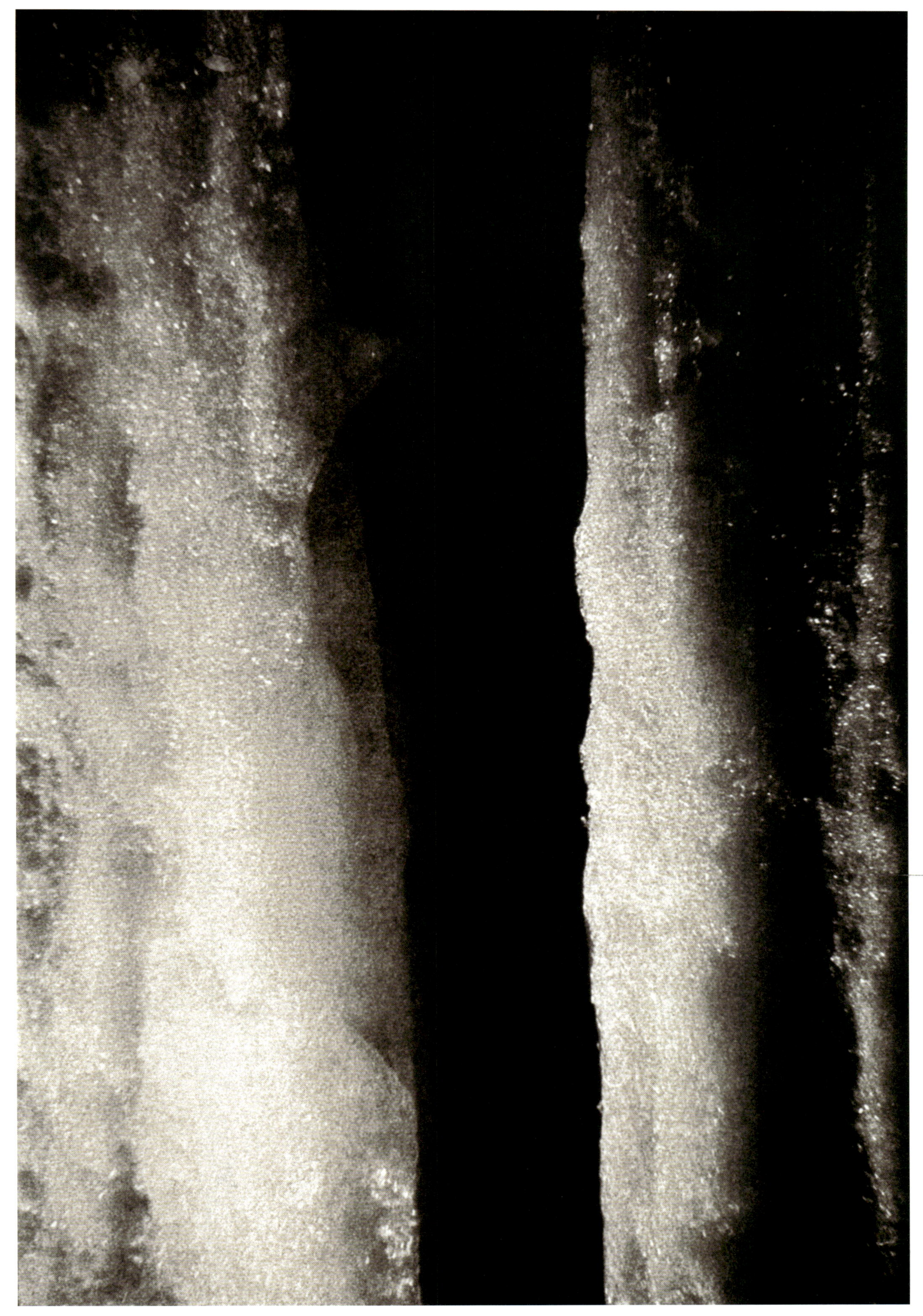

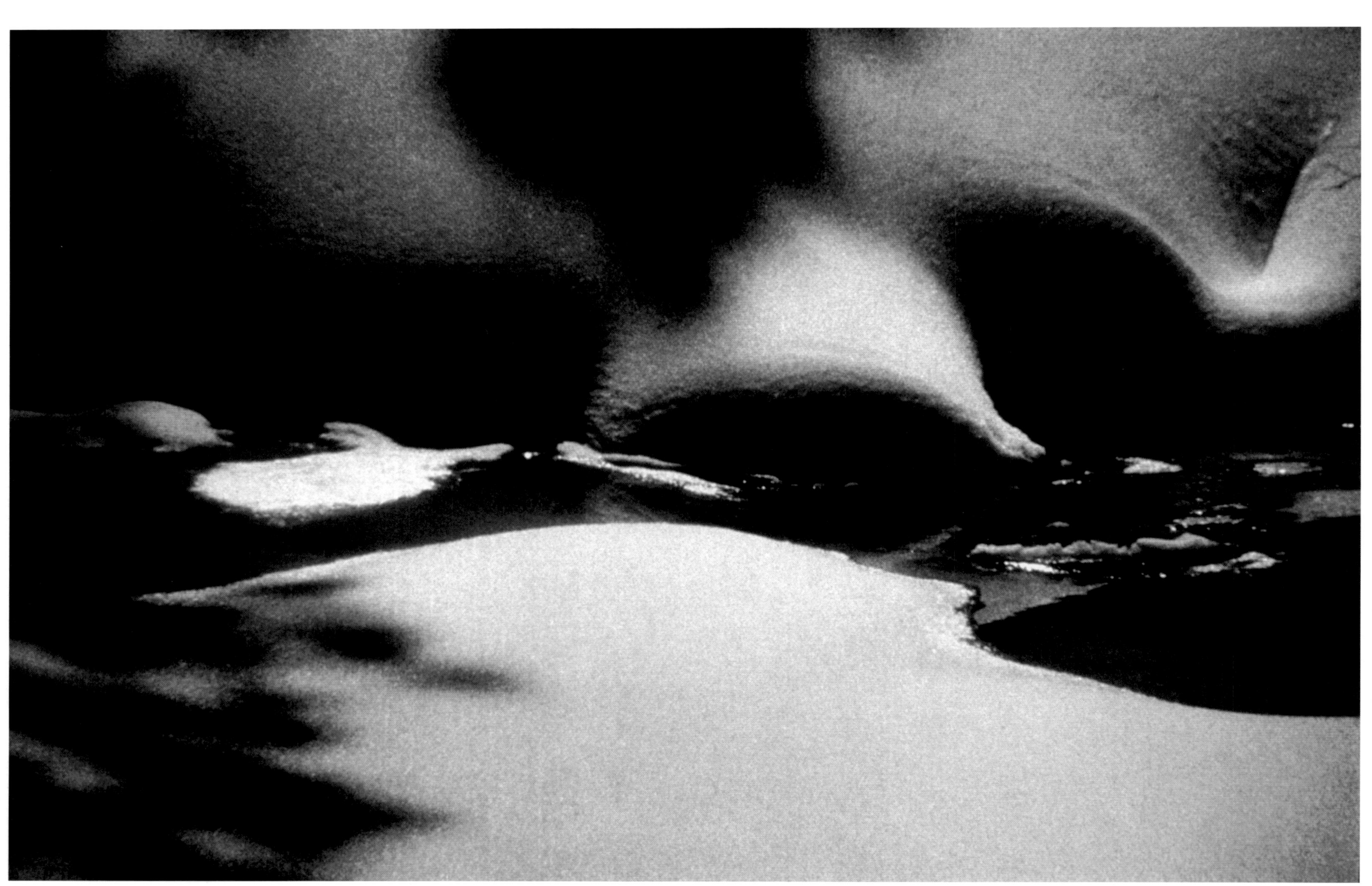

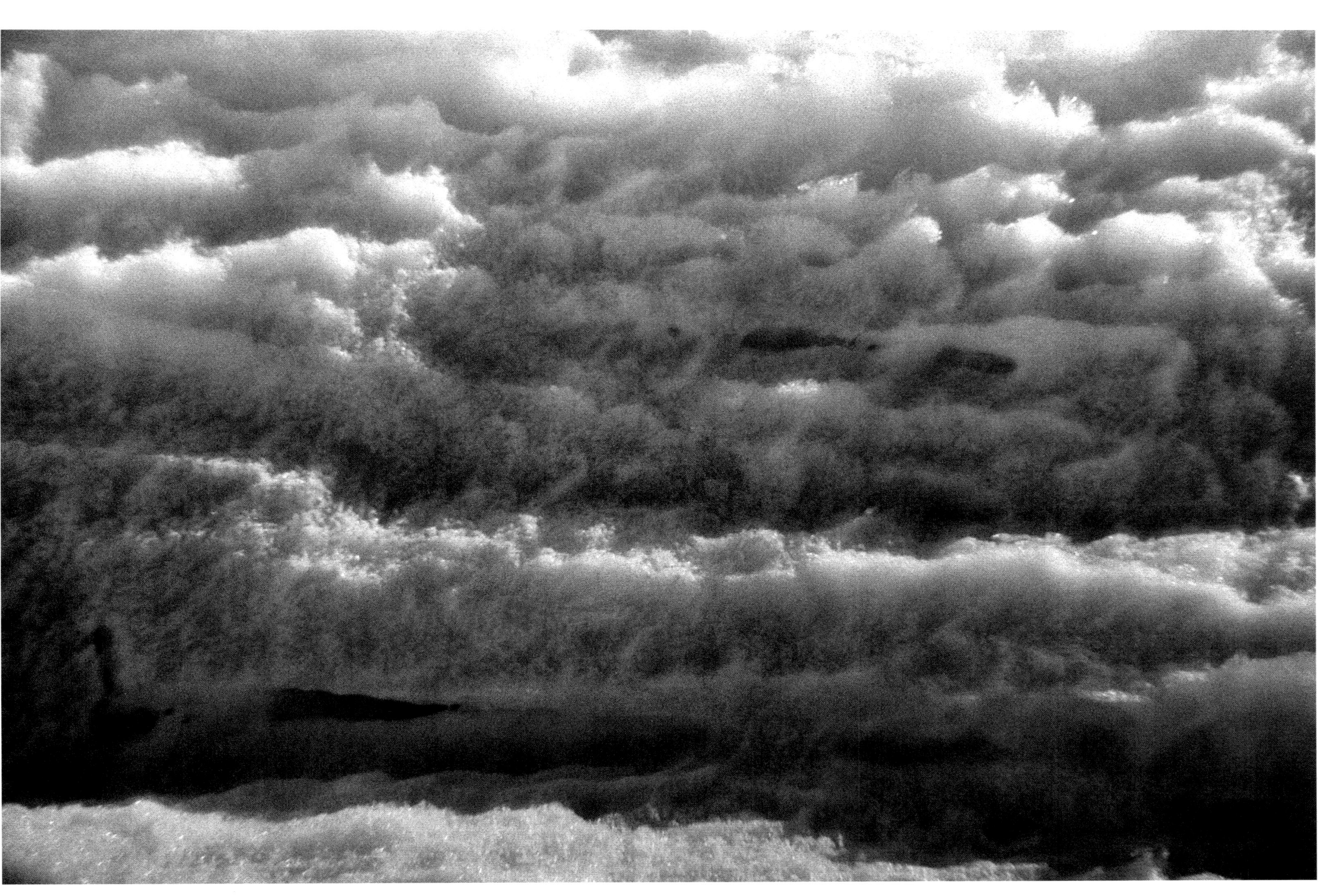

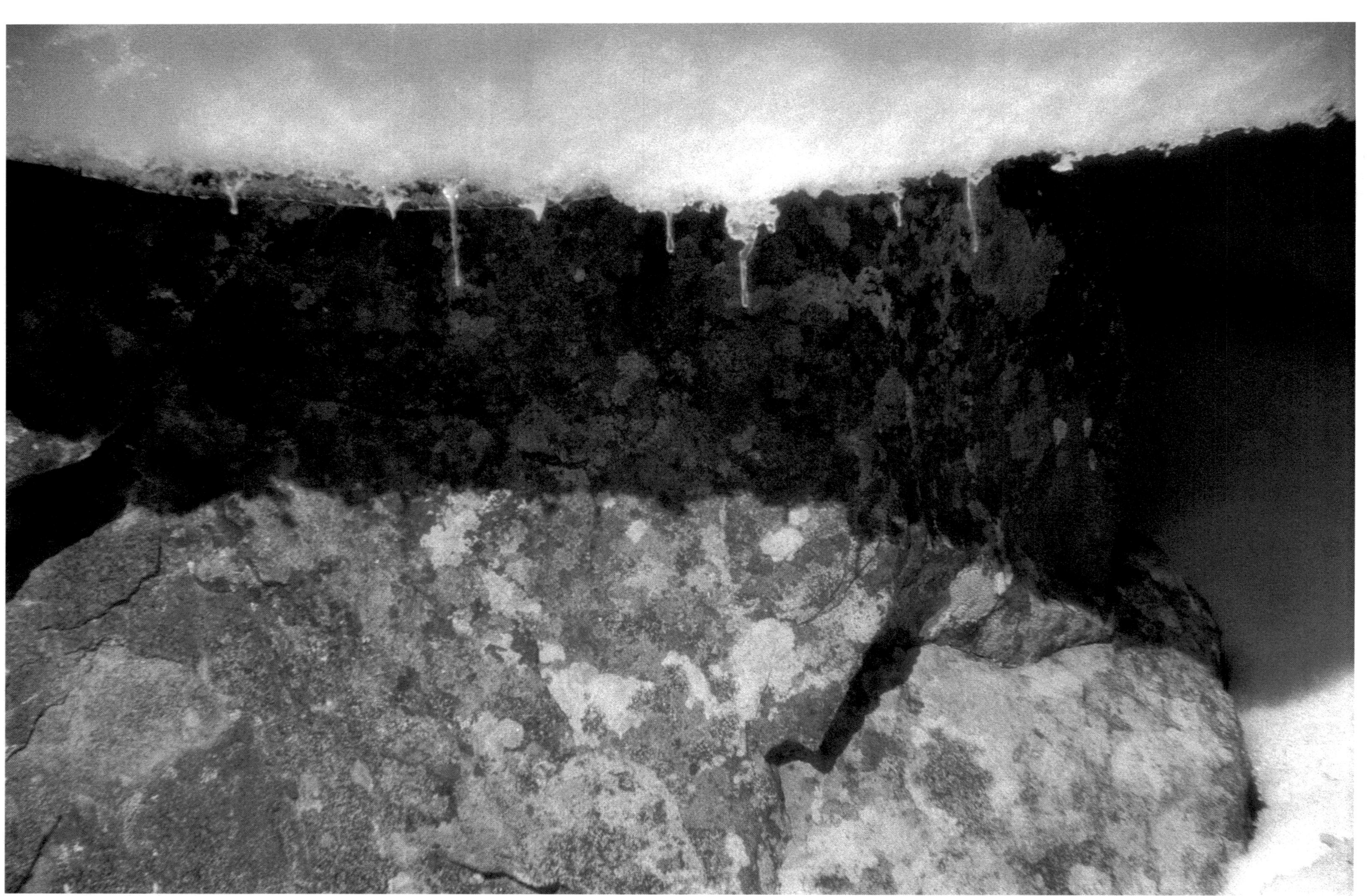

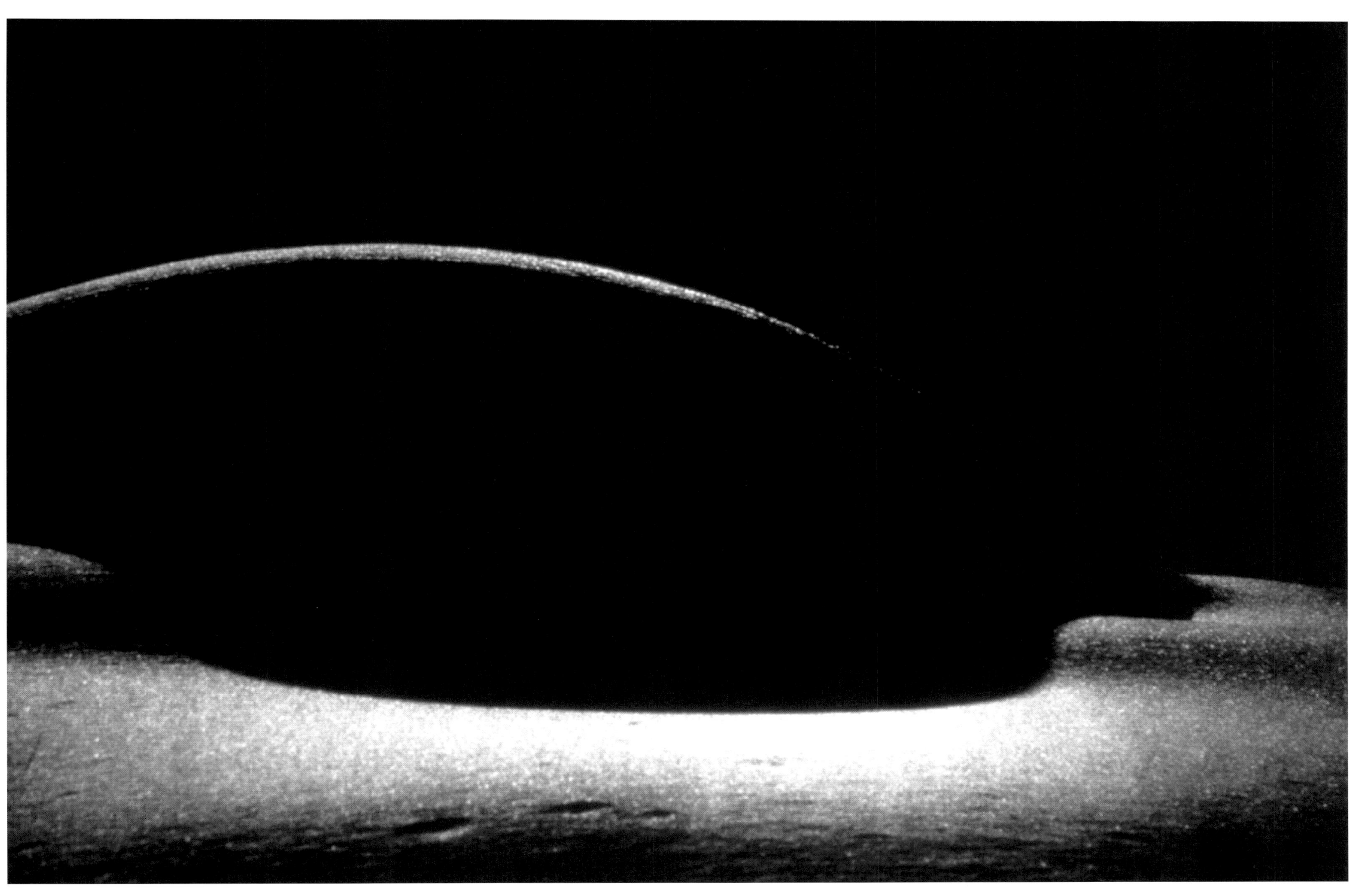

abstractions

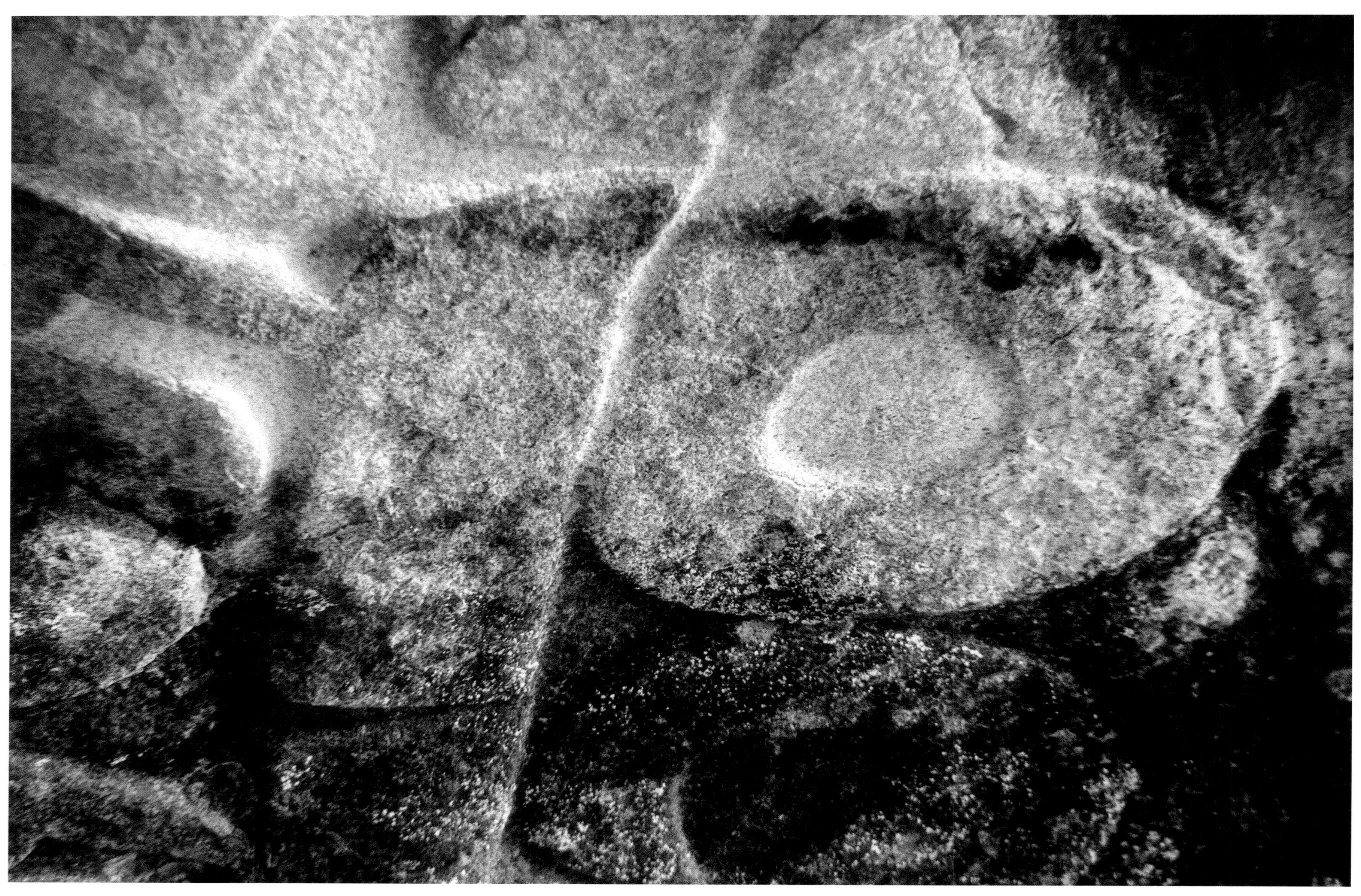

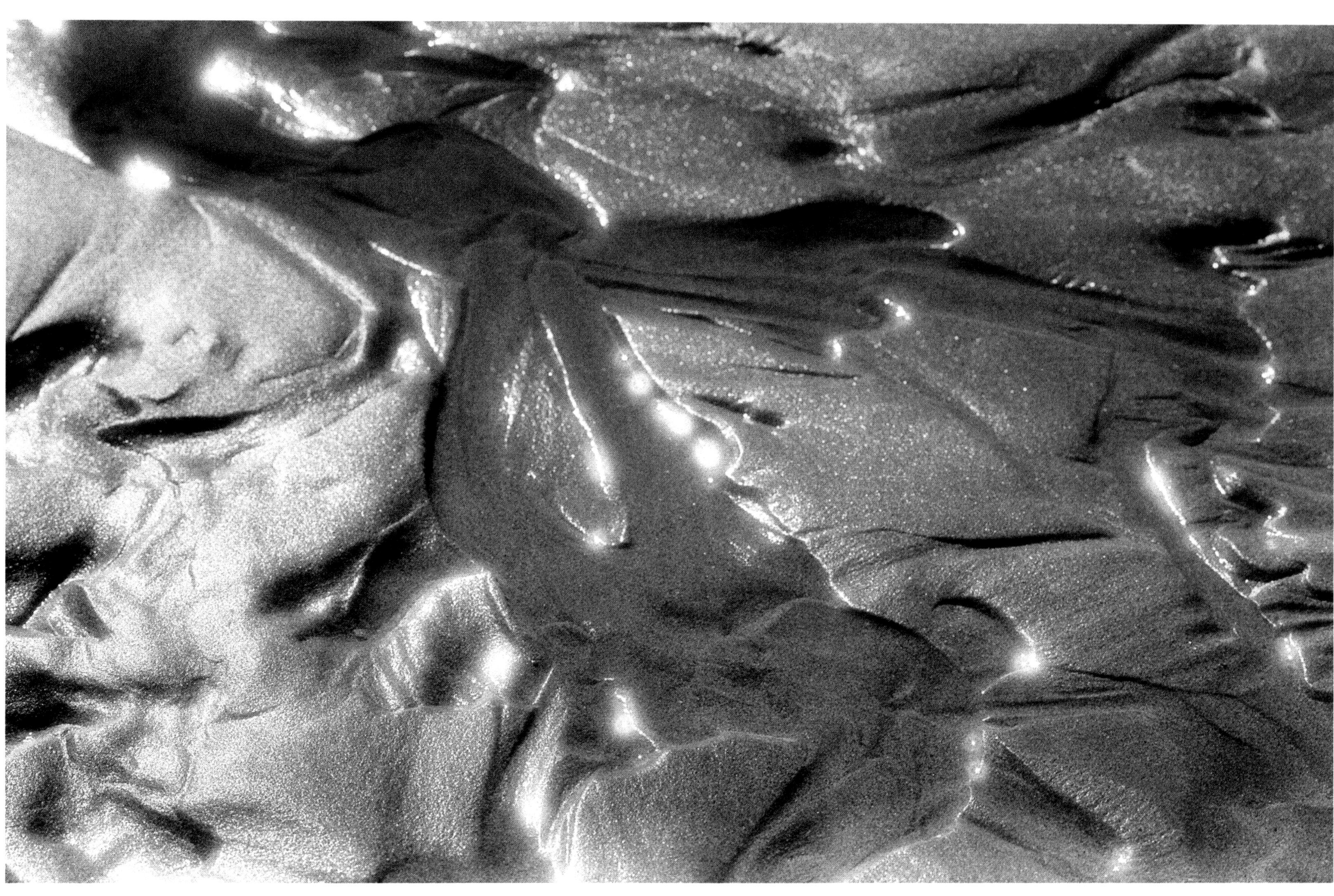

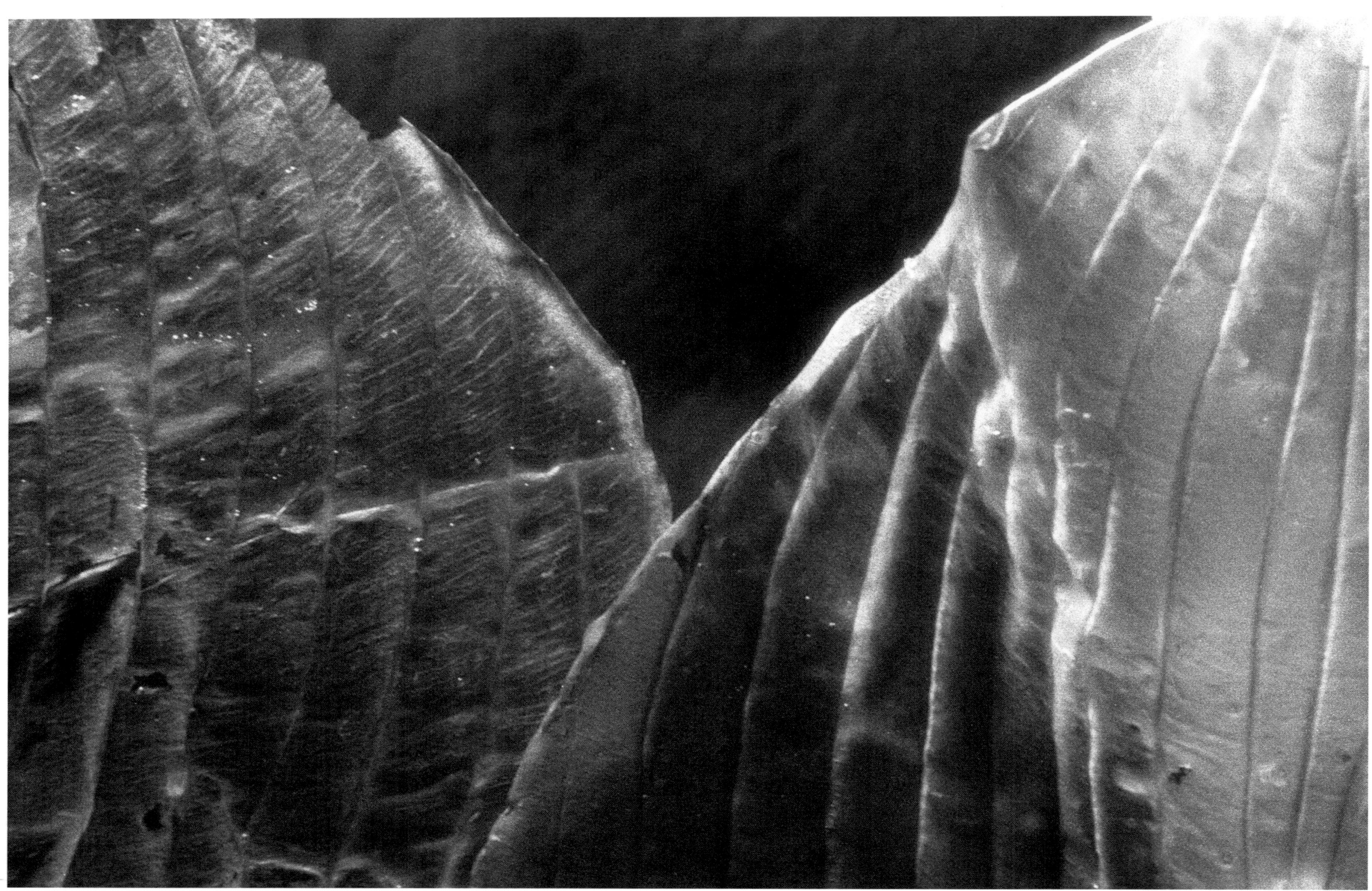

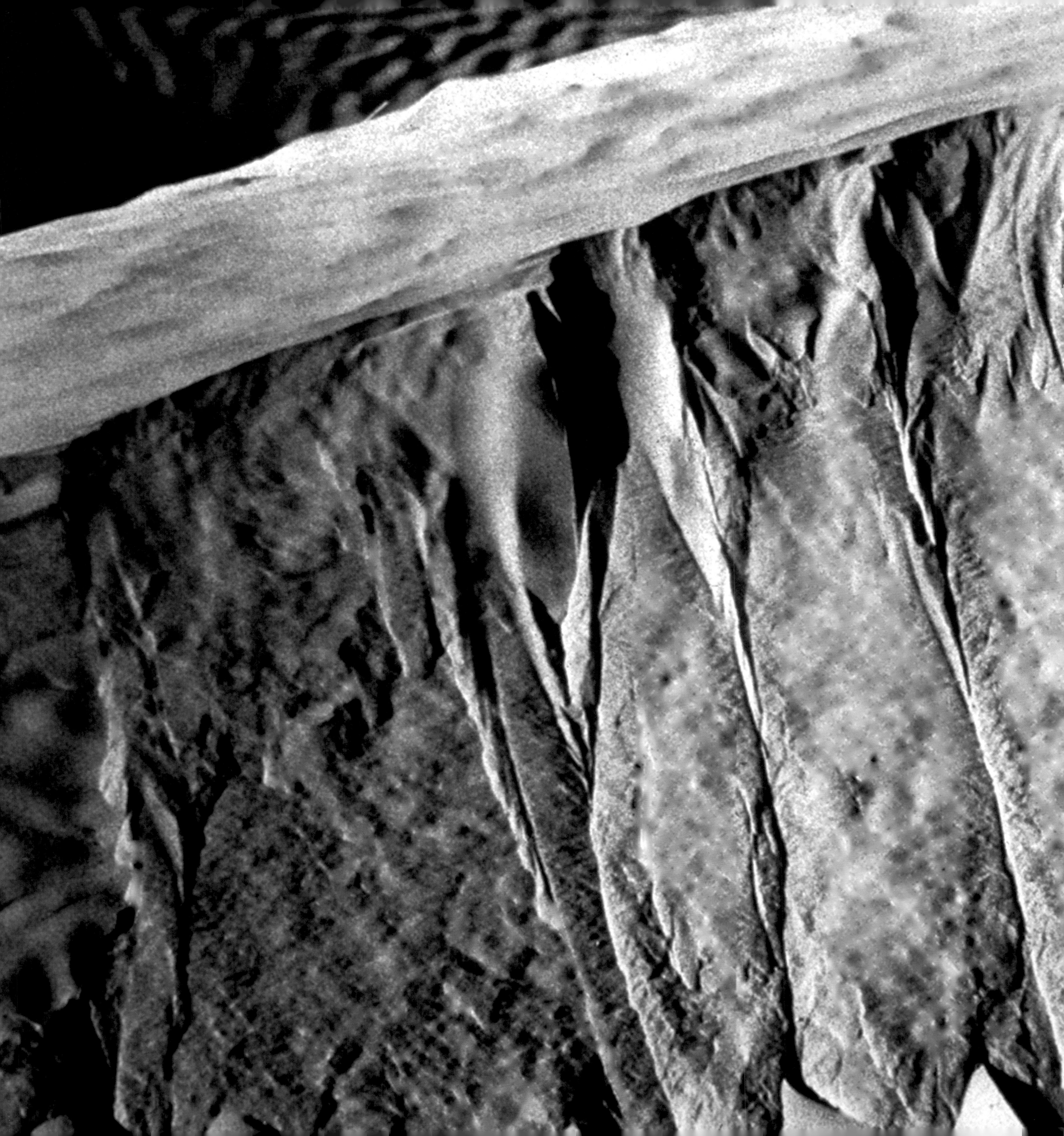

tunisian fantasy

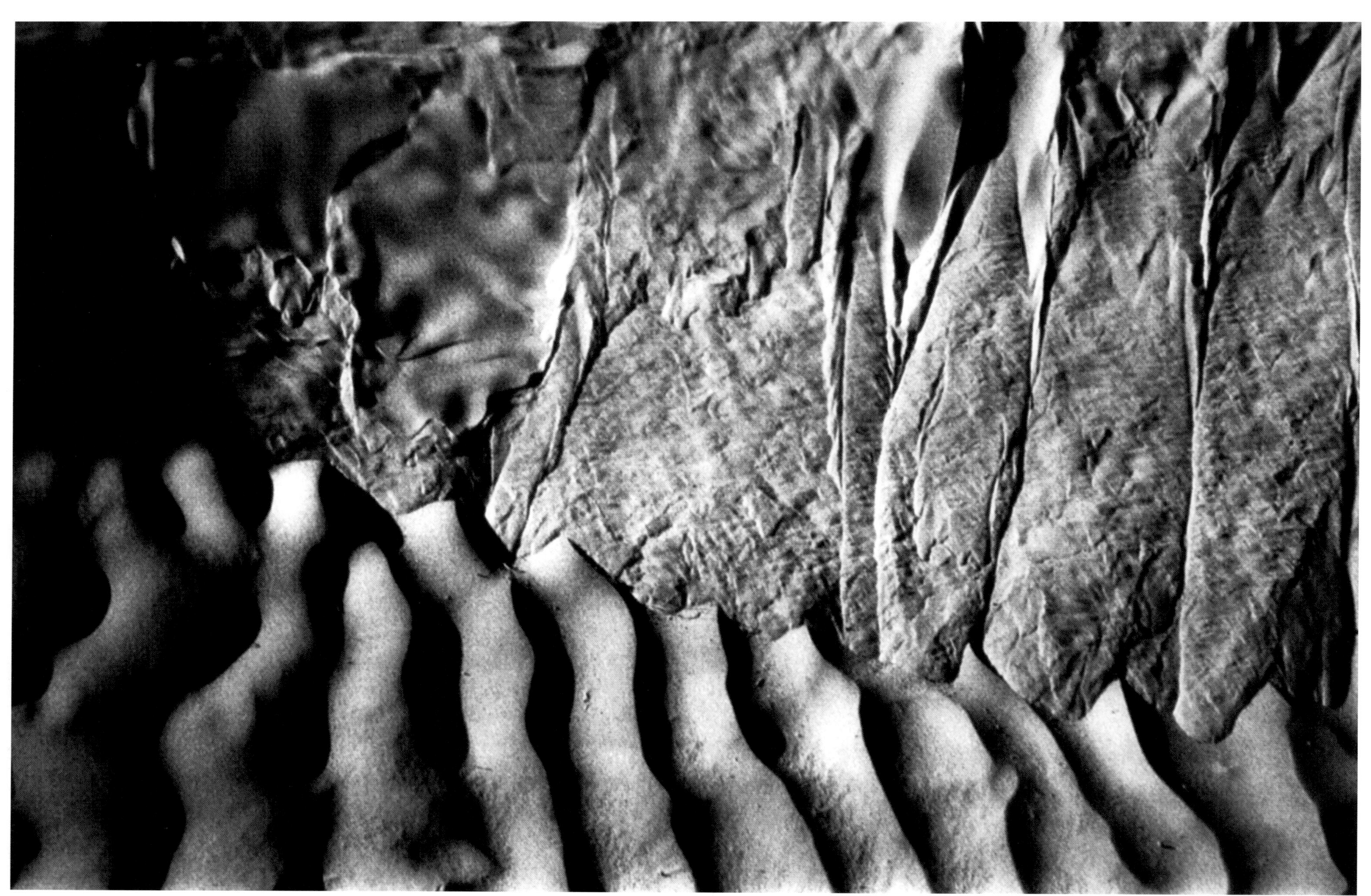

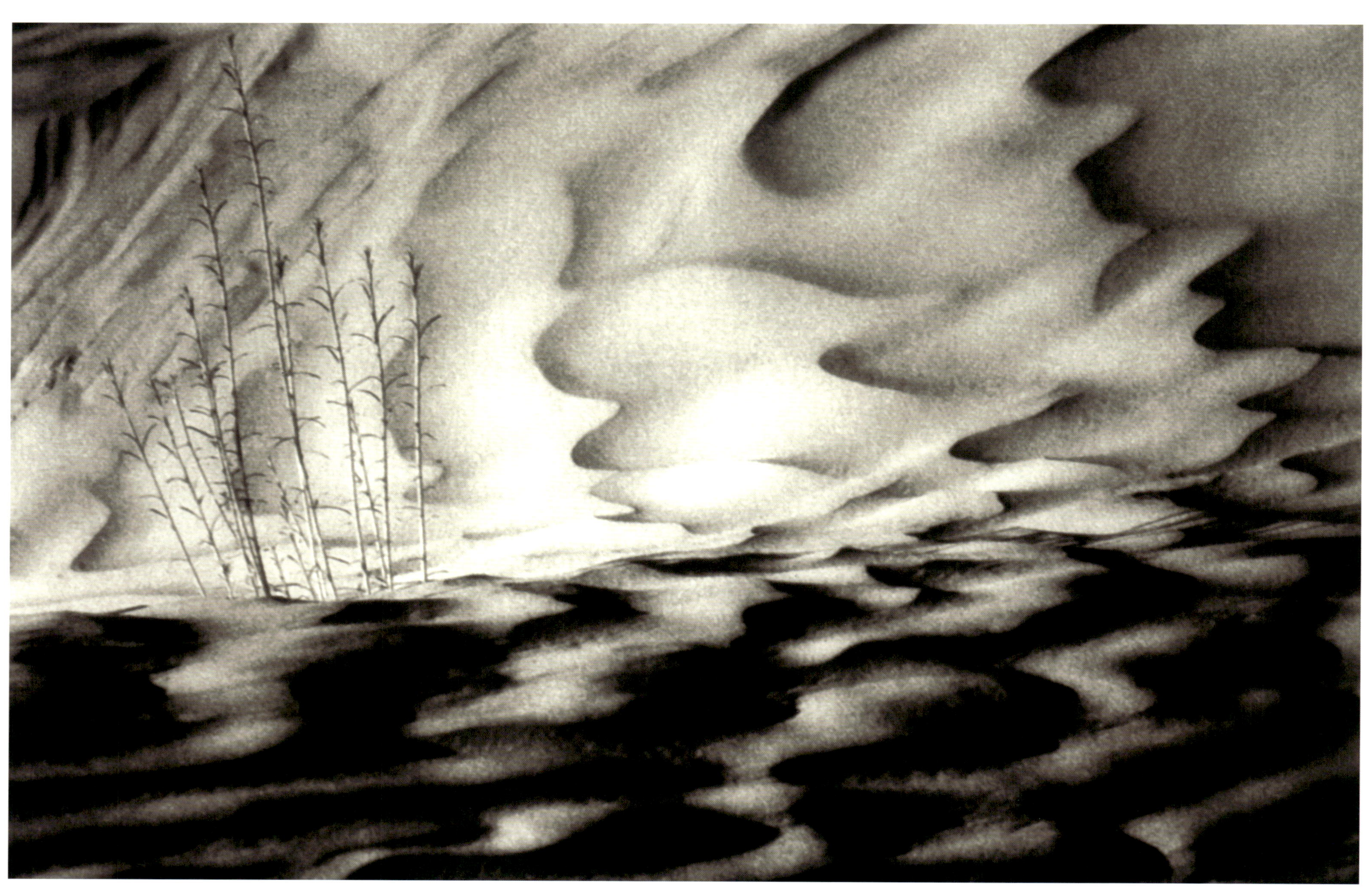

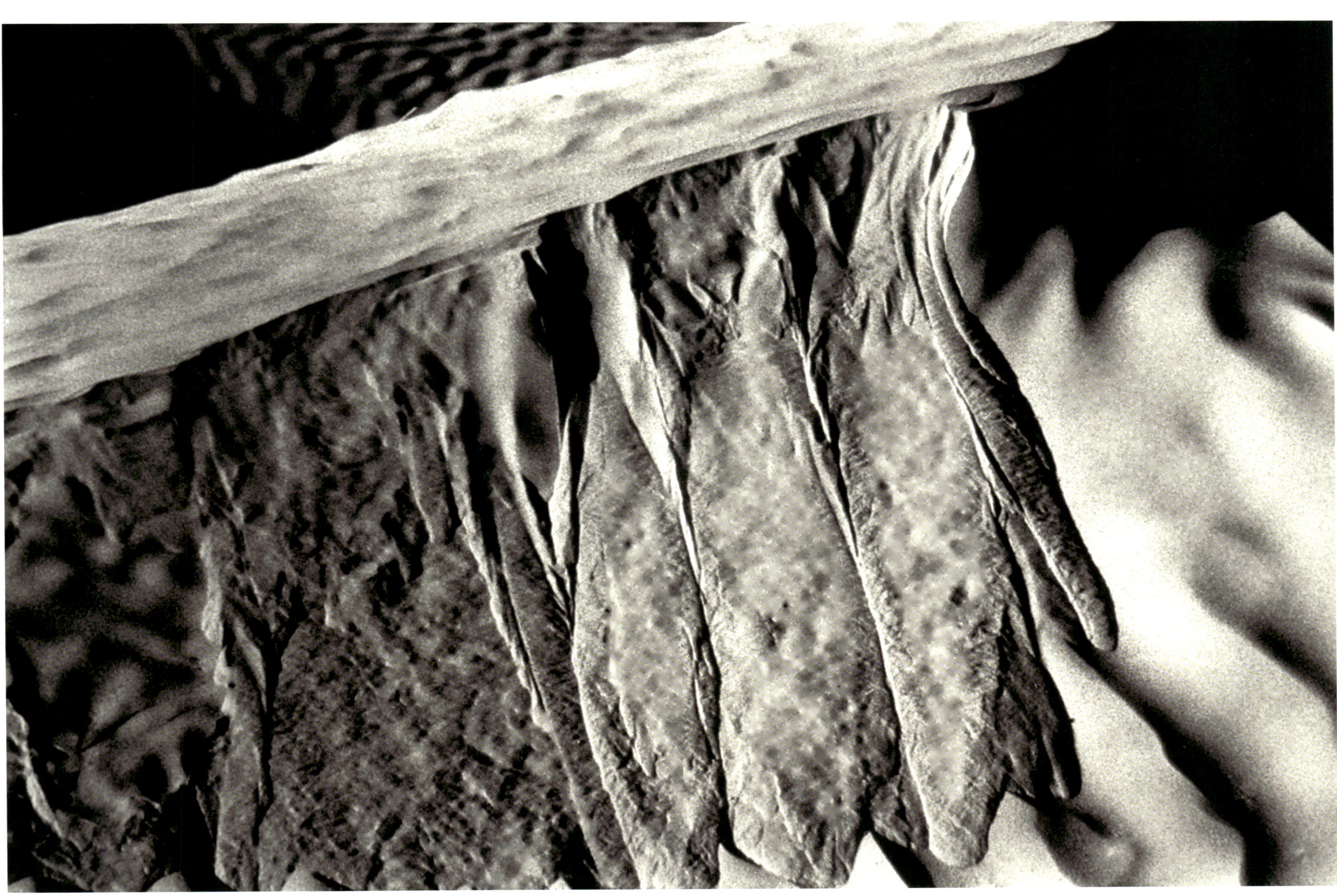

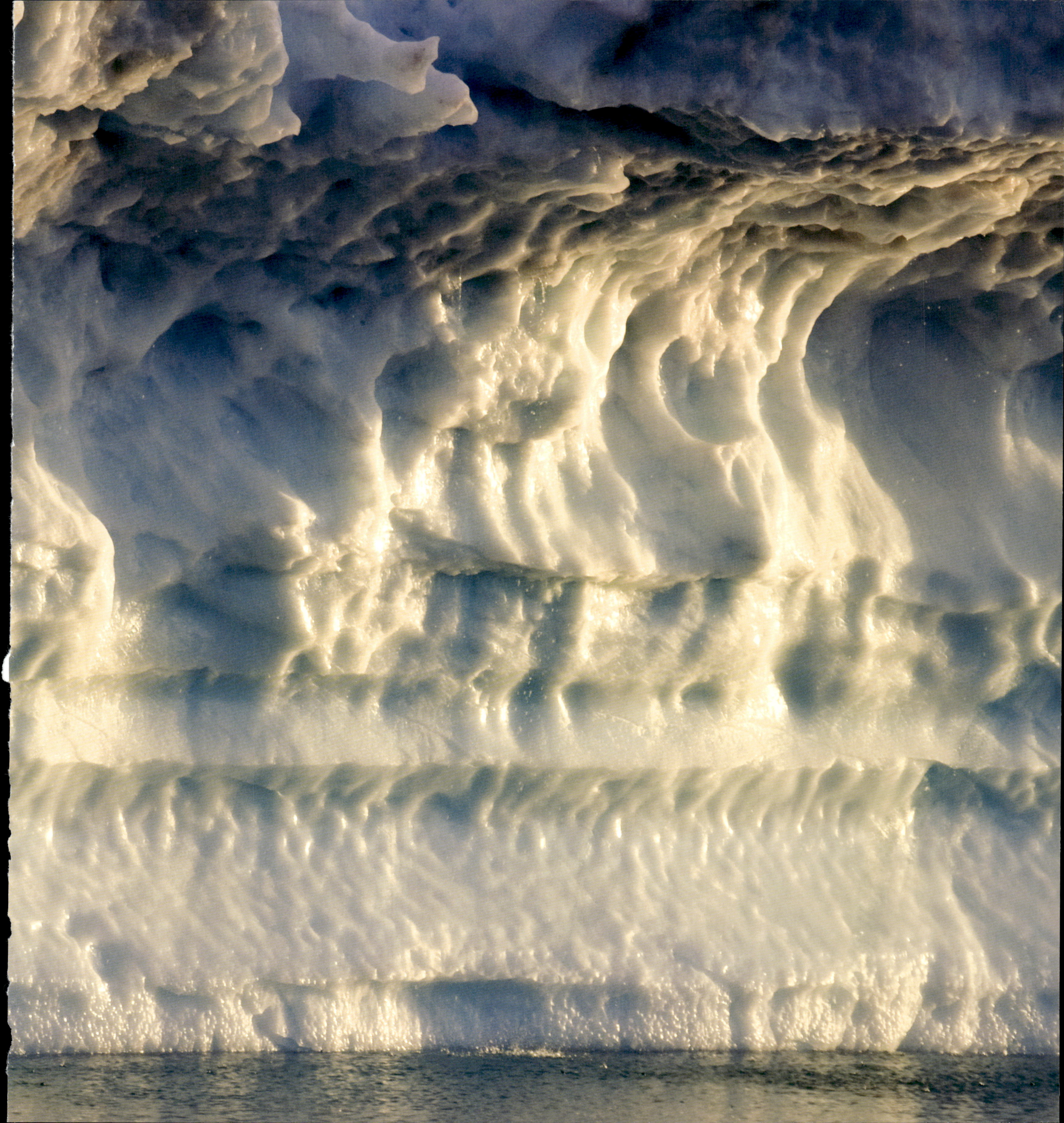

Tuft's travels increased in range and extremity as she took on the glaciers and ice fields of Iceland in 2002 and Greenland in 2007. Both locations are challenging, not only for their remoteness and harsh weather, but also because her subject—the ice—is disappearing. Glaciers have retreated and some recently accessed on foot are now far enough away to necessitate a helicopter trip. In Iceland she worked at an intimate scale, but in Greenland she took advantage of the more available large ice faces and frozen seascapes. "13" in the black-and-white *Greenland* series, an Arctic Ocean scene, presents us with a tonal range that is far more balanced with darks than we could see with the unaided eye, and it's a gothic vision worthy of a novel. Sunlight glints from above, casting a shadow on an iceberg frozen in place at upper left, while to the right a glacial wall is all dark grays, more a function of temperature in the infrared than of light. The photograph casts a palpable chill toward the viewer.

Tuft has also worked in Greenland in color at the ultraviolet end of the spectrum. To photograph in the infrared, she loads infrared film into her Leica camera and shoots through a red filter, which diminishes visible light and allows the longer end of the spectrum to be captured. Because there is no such thing as ultraviolet film, when working in that shorter wavelength she uses a digital camera, which because of its sensitivity across the spectrum can record information in the near ultraviolet. The slightly soft image that ultraviolet tends to produce, the striated colors in nature, and Tuft's careful proportioning of those vertical and horizontal lines—whether at the intimate scale of "Dendritic Impulse" or more widely in "Akna's Embrace" and "Sedna's Refuge" (titles based on Inuit mythology)—could be mistaken for modernist paintings.

greenland

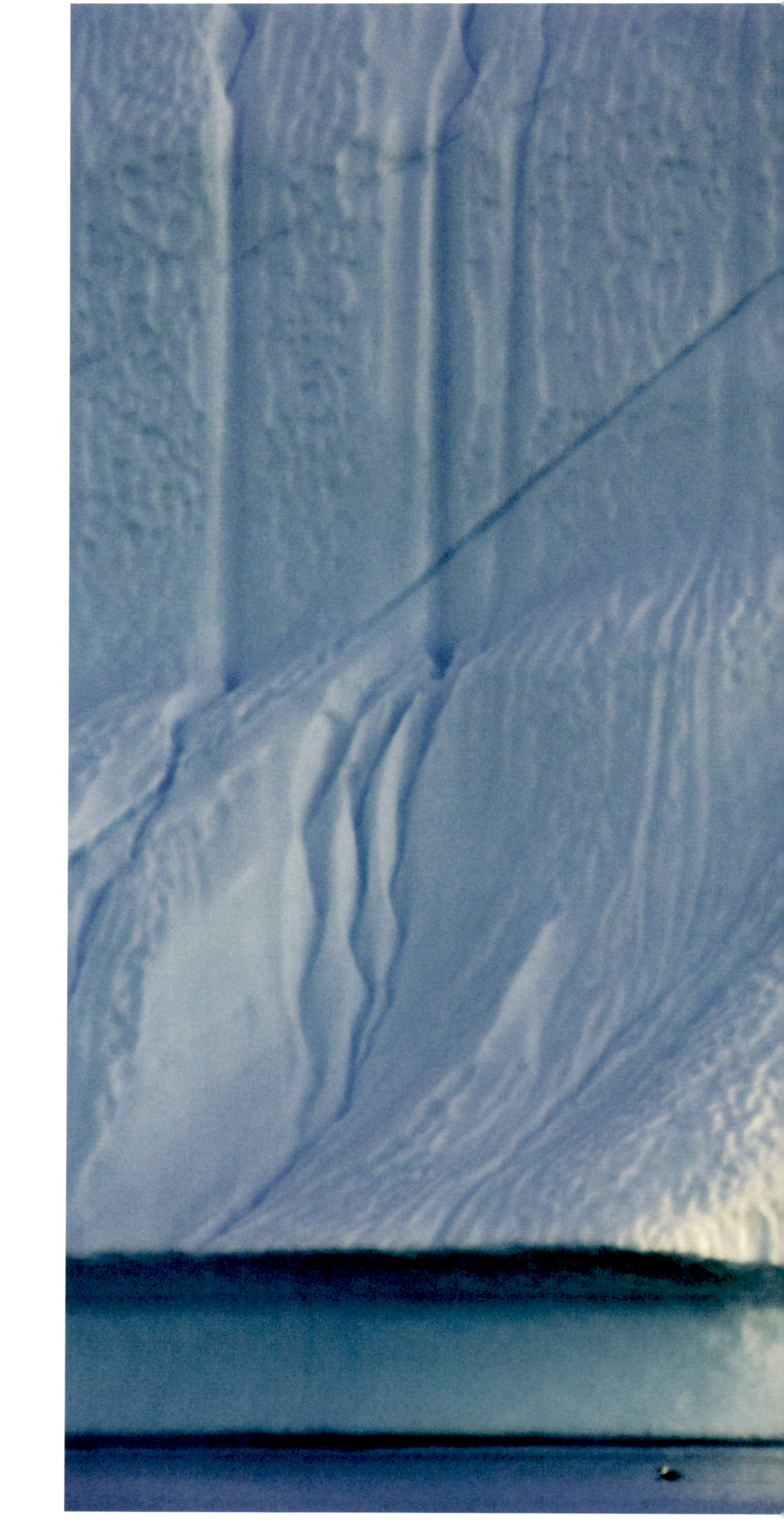

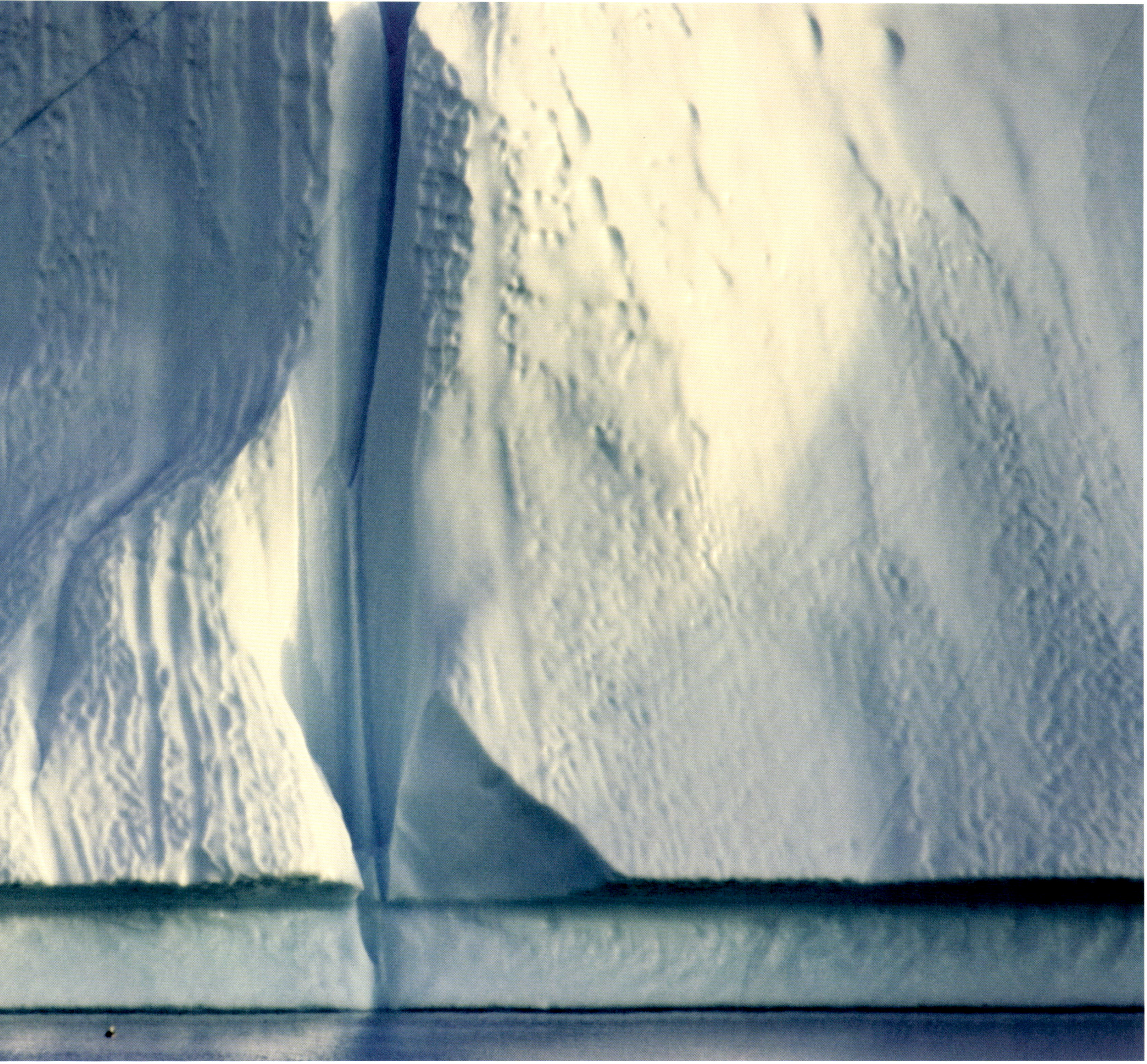

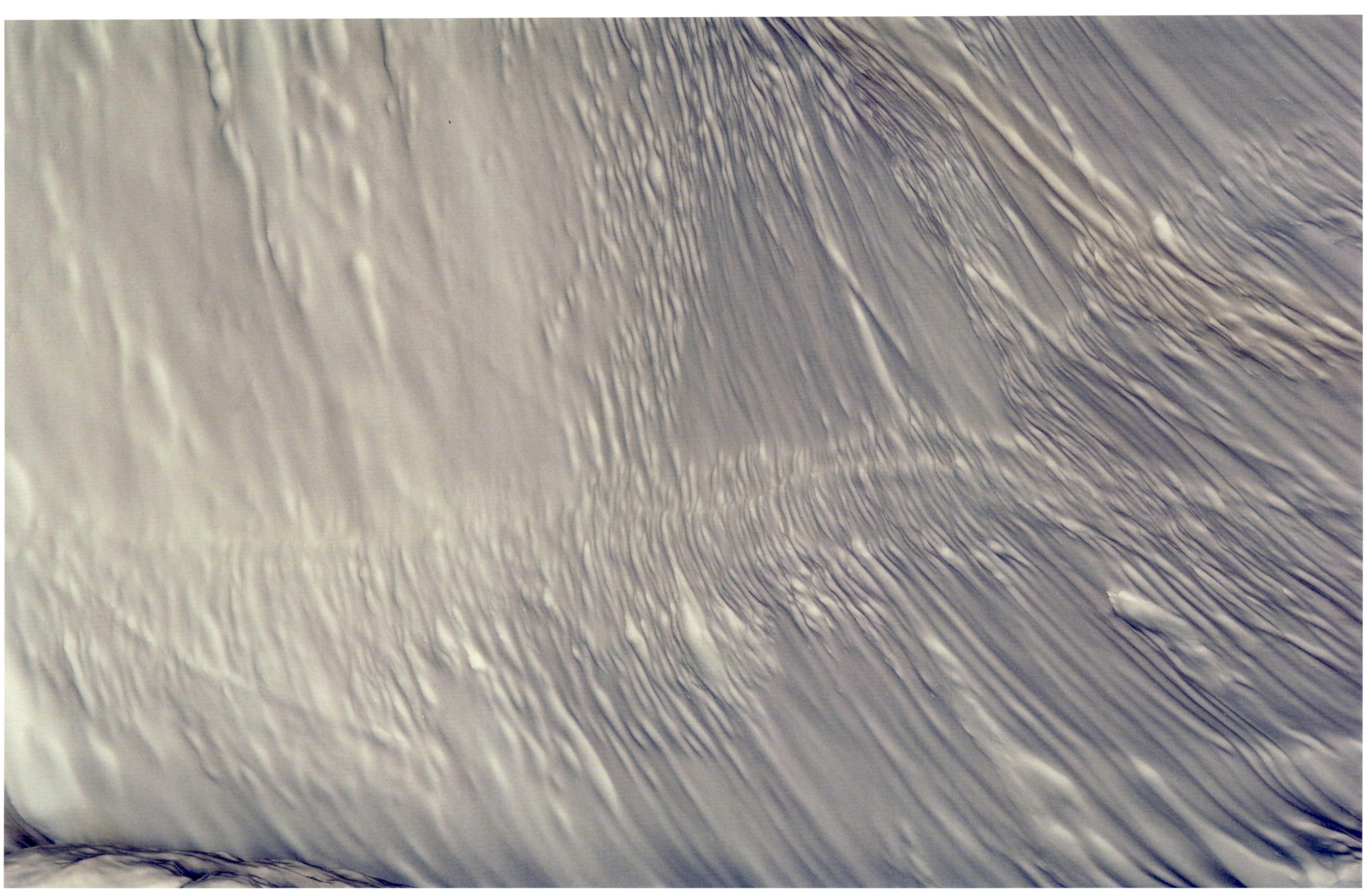

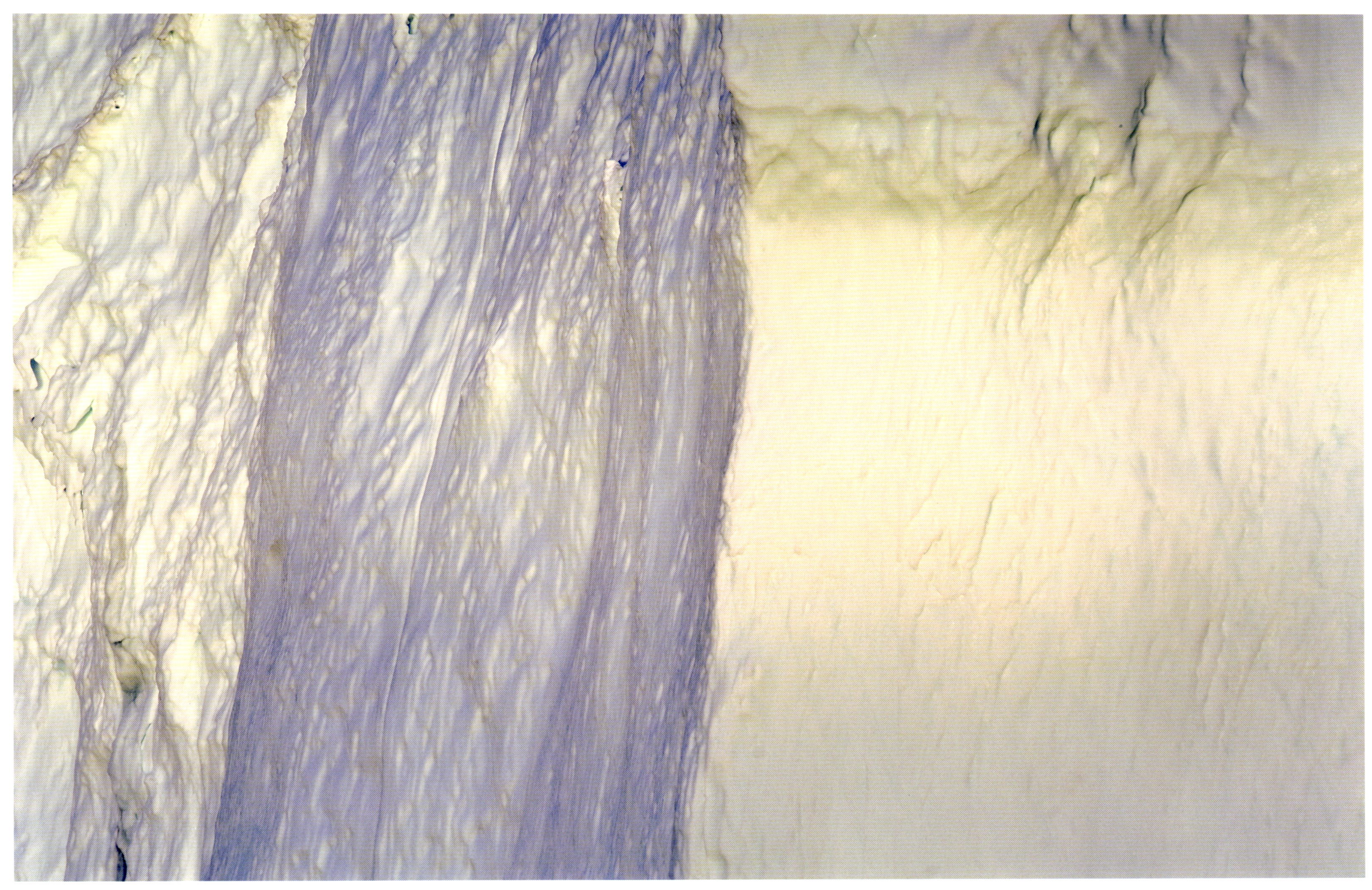

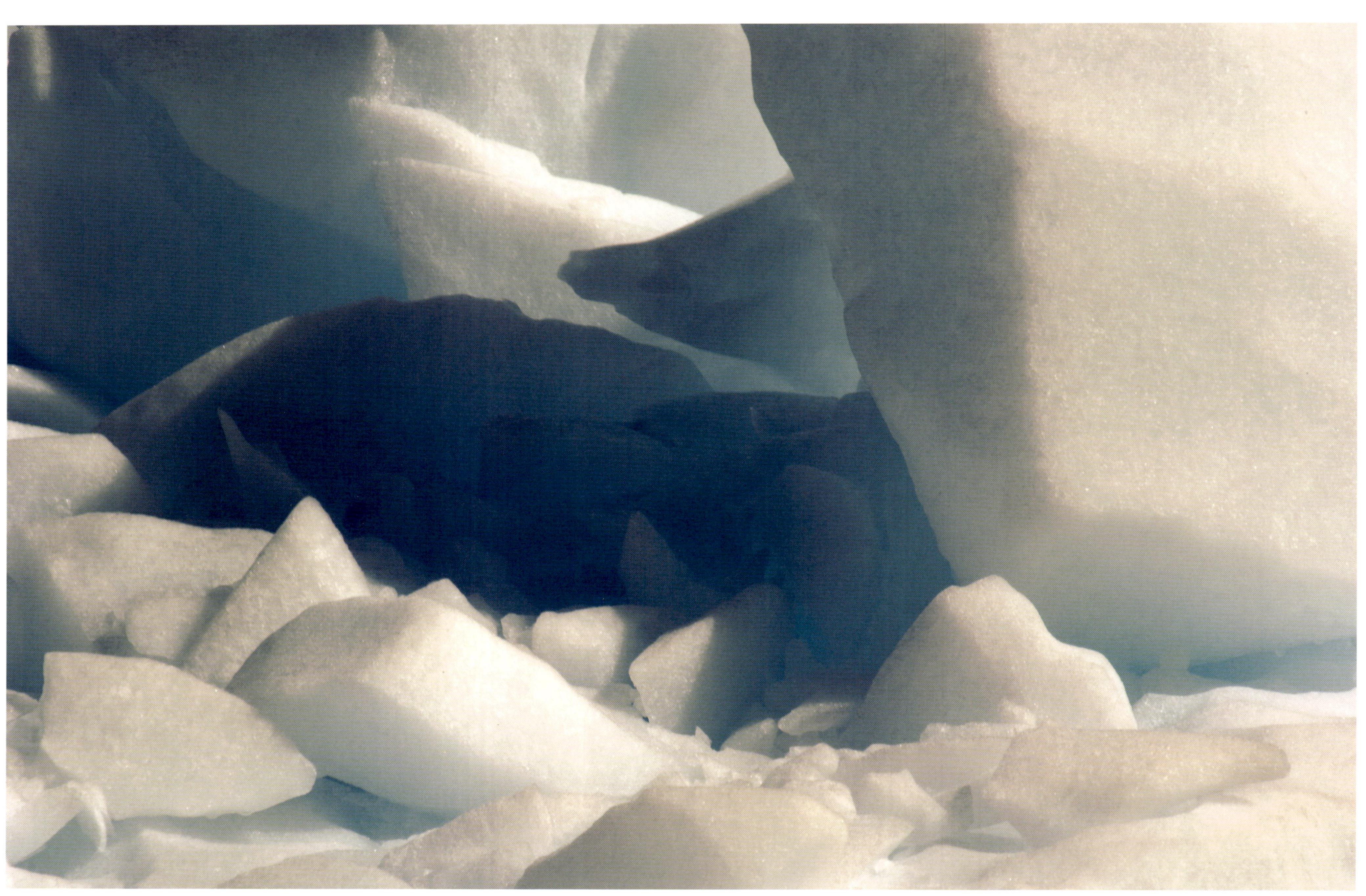

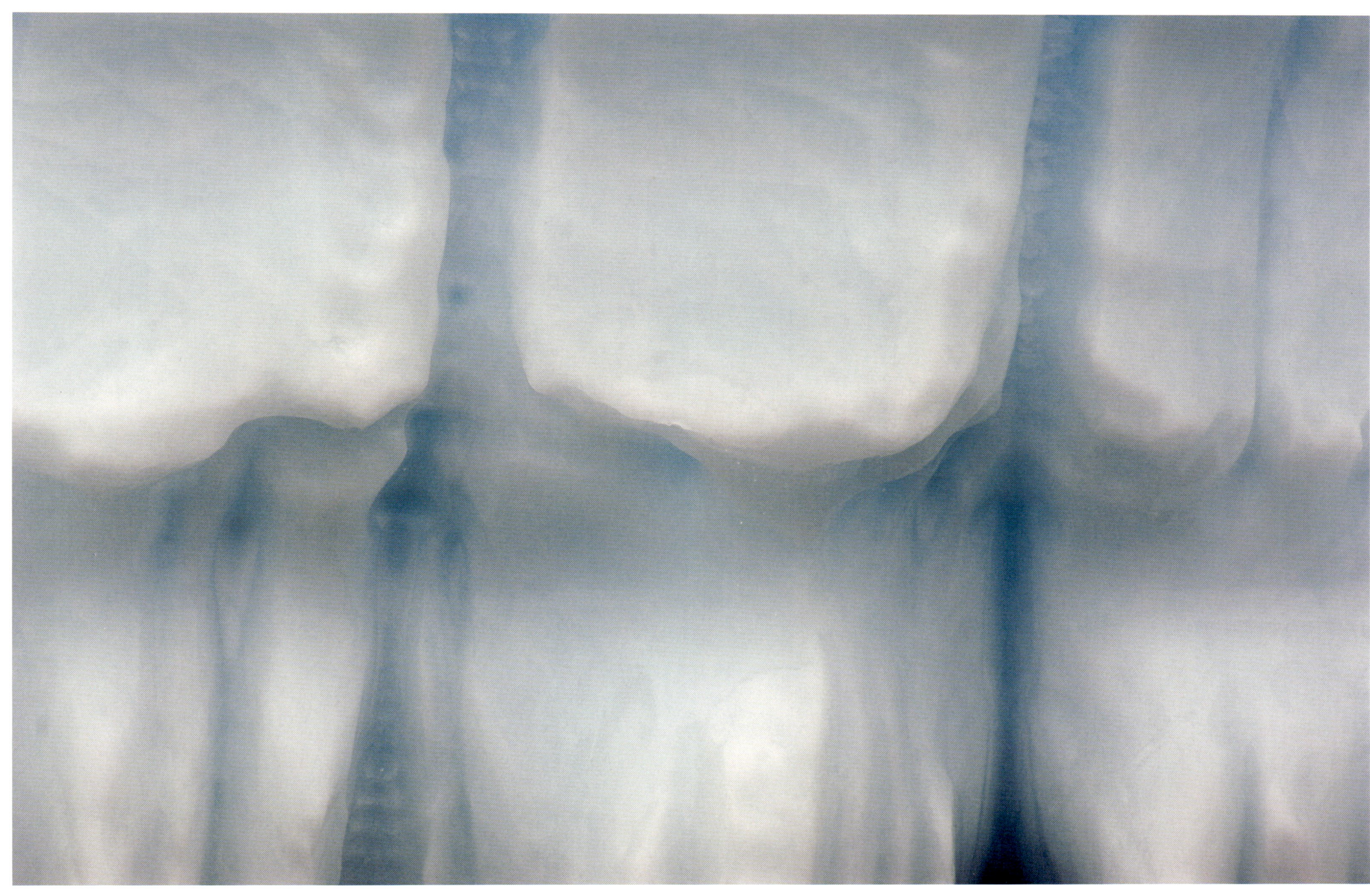

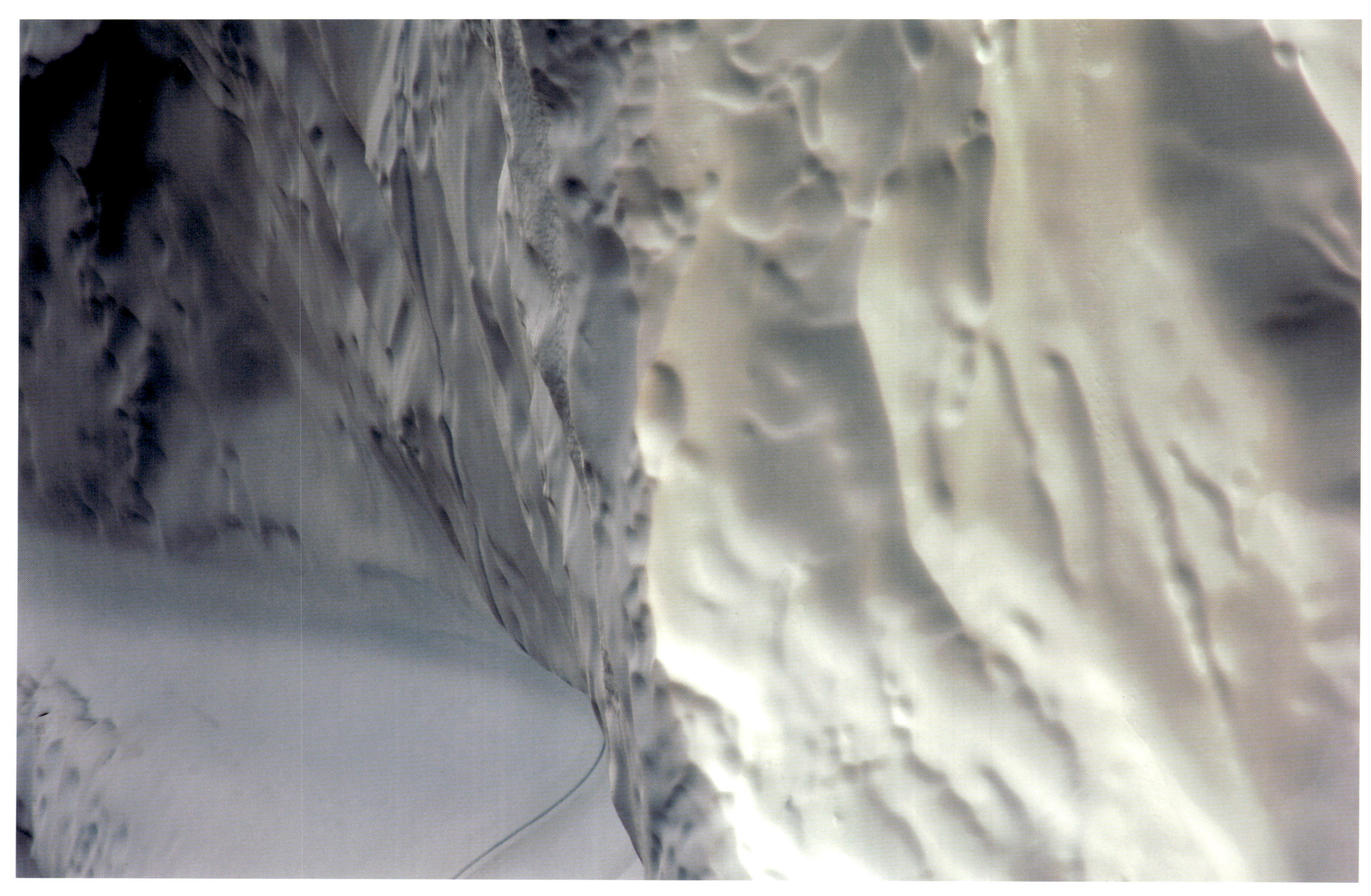

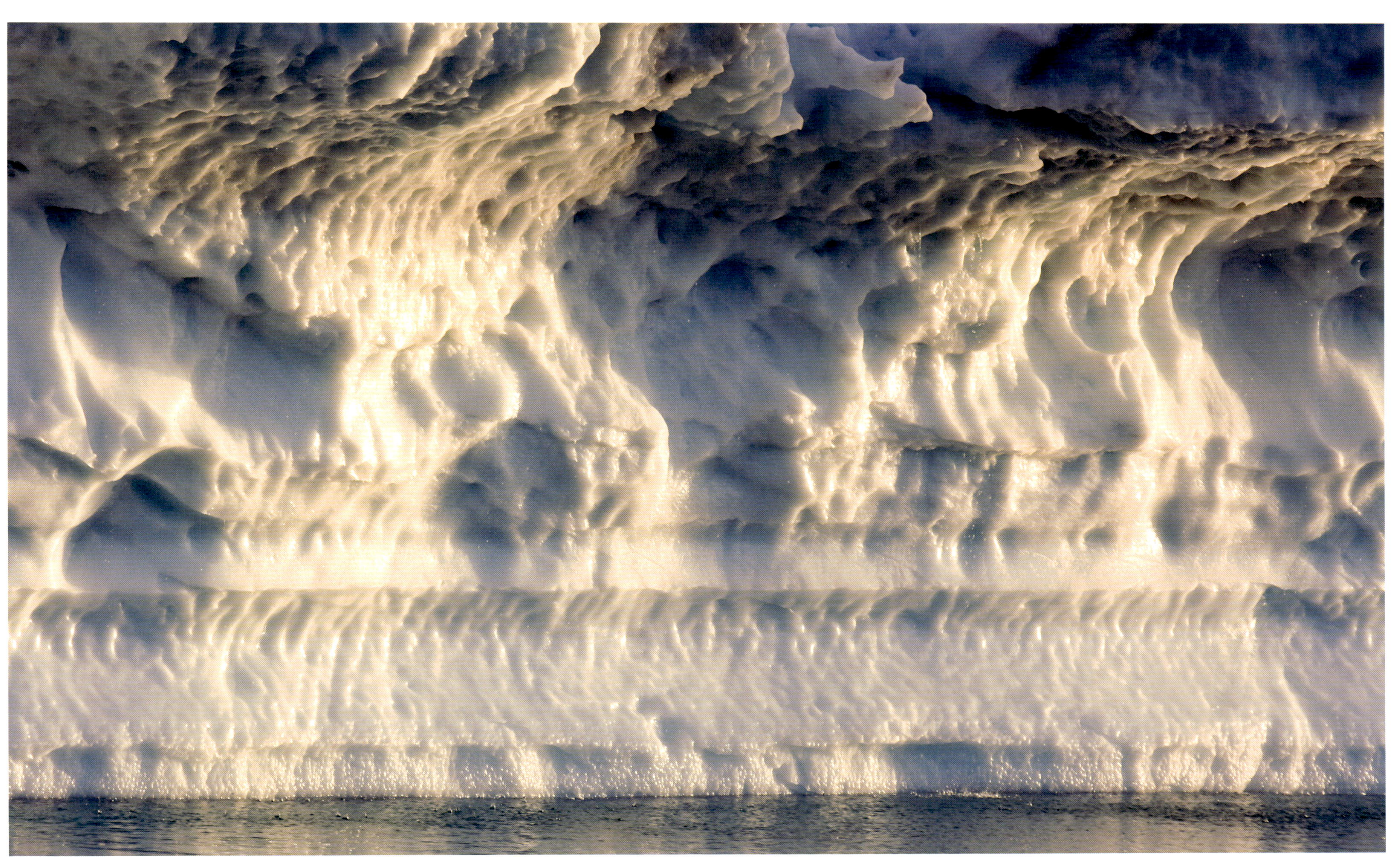

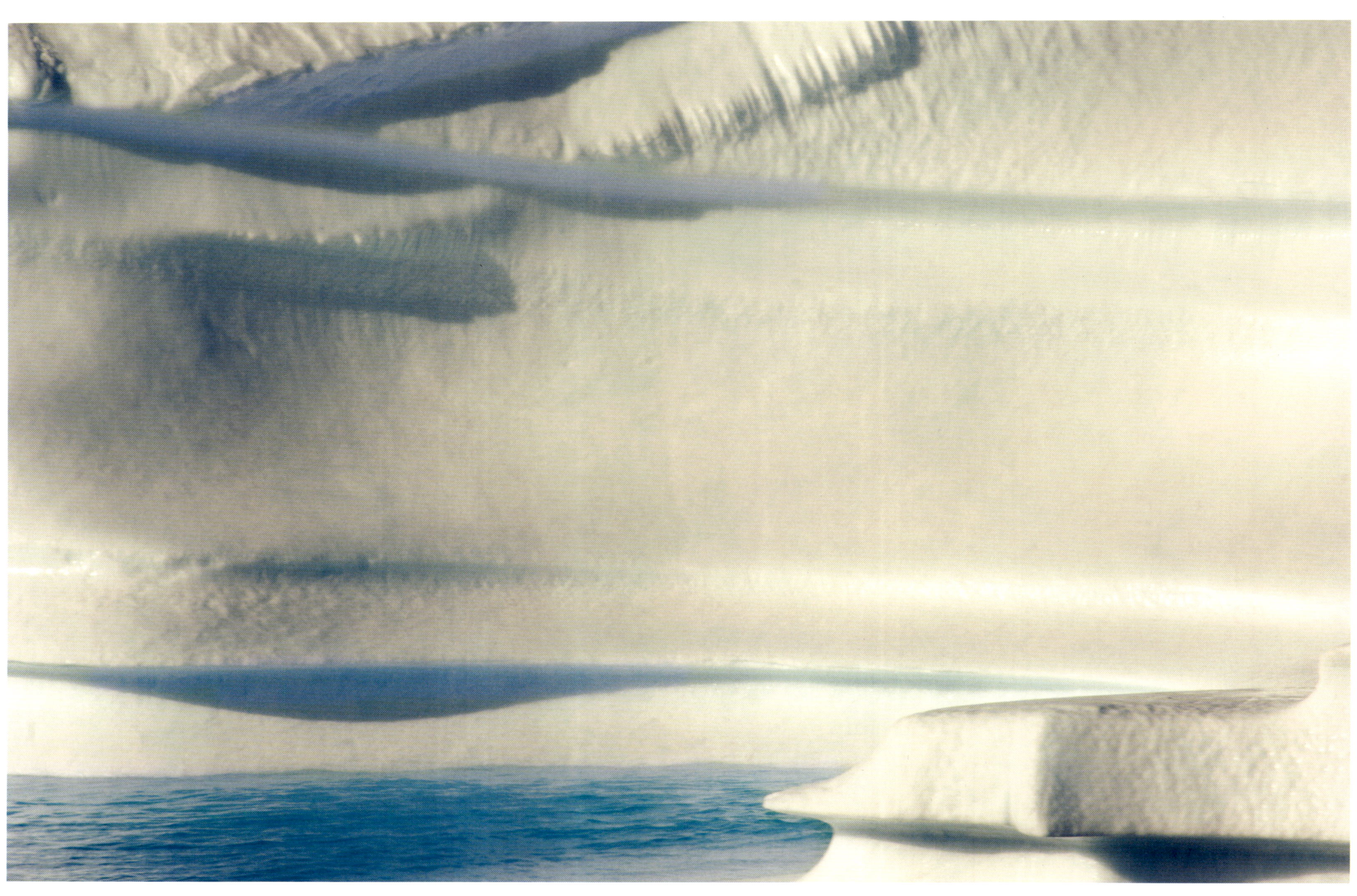

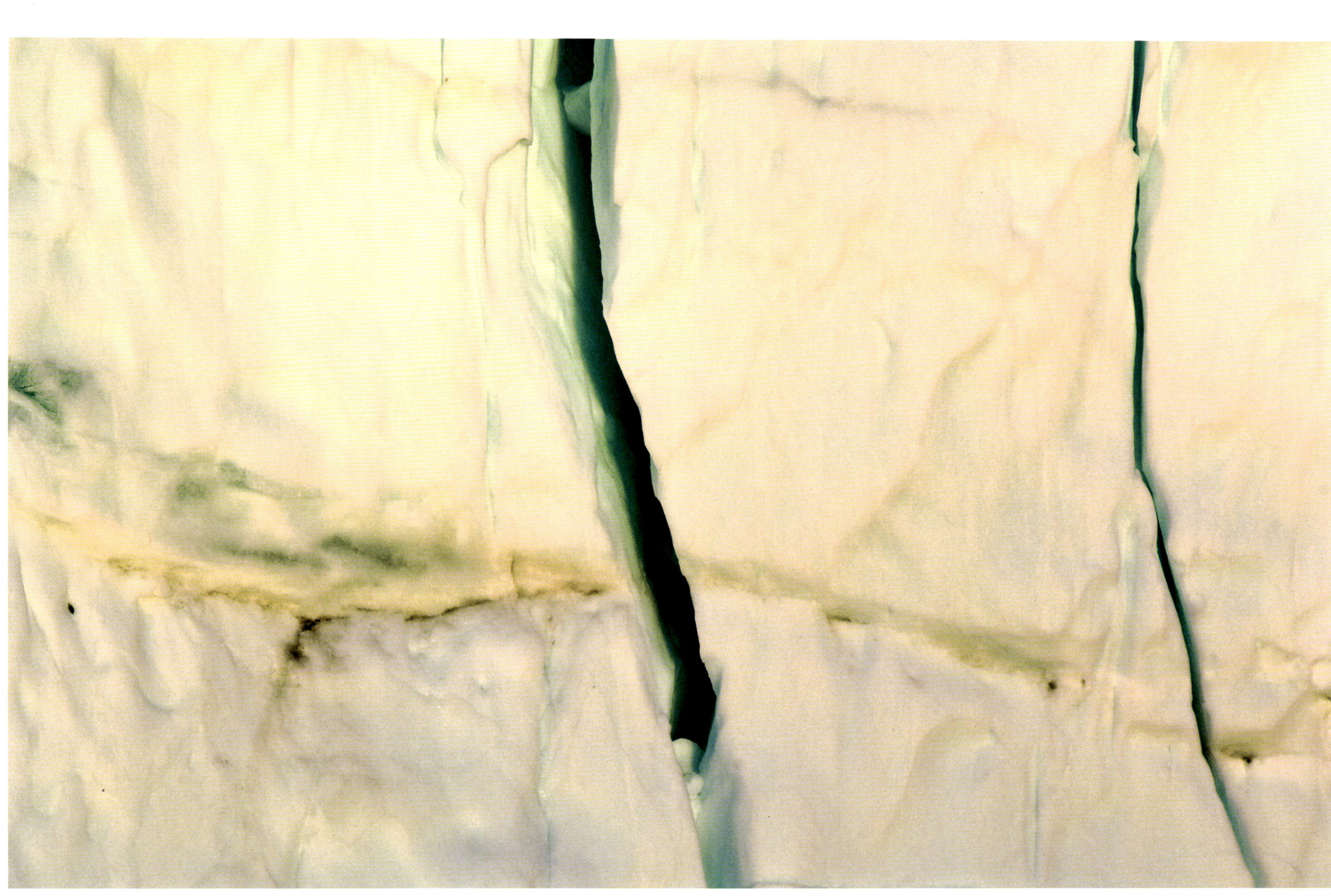

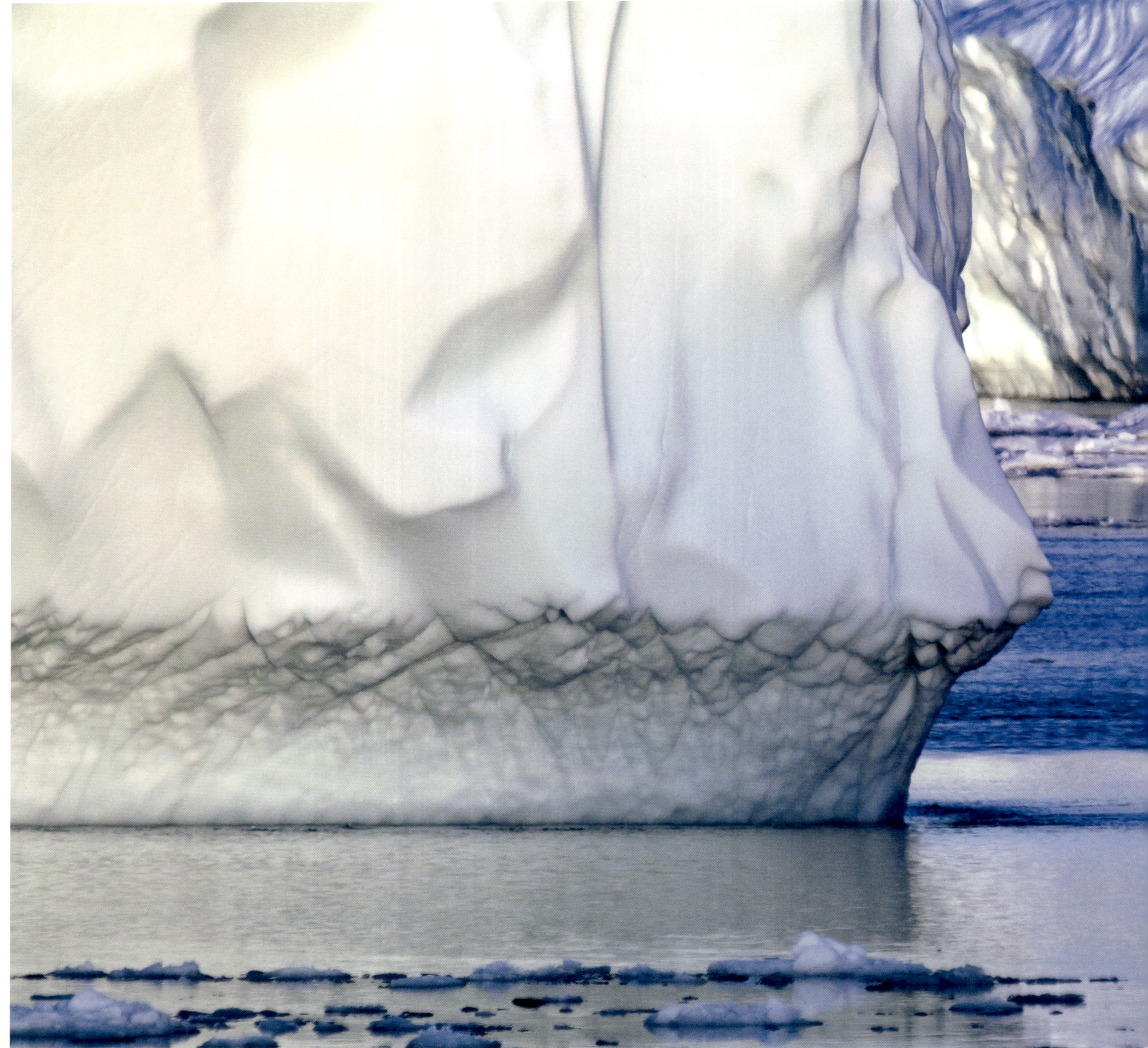

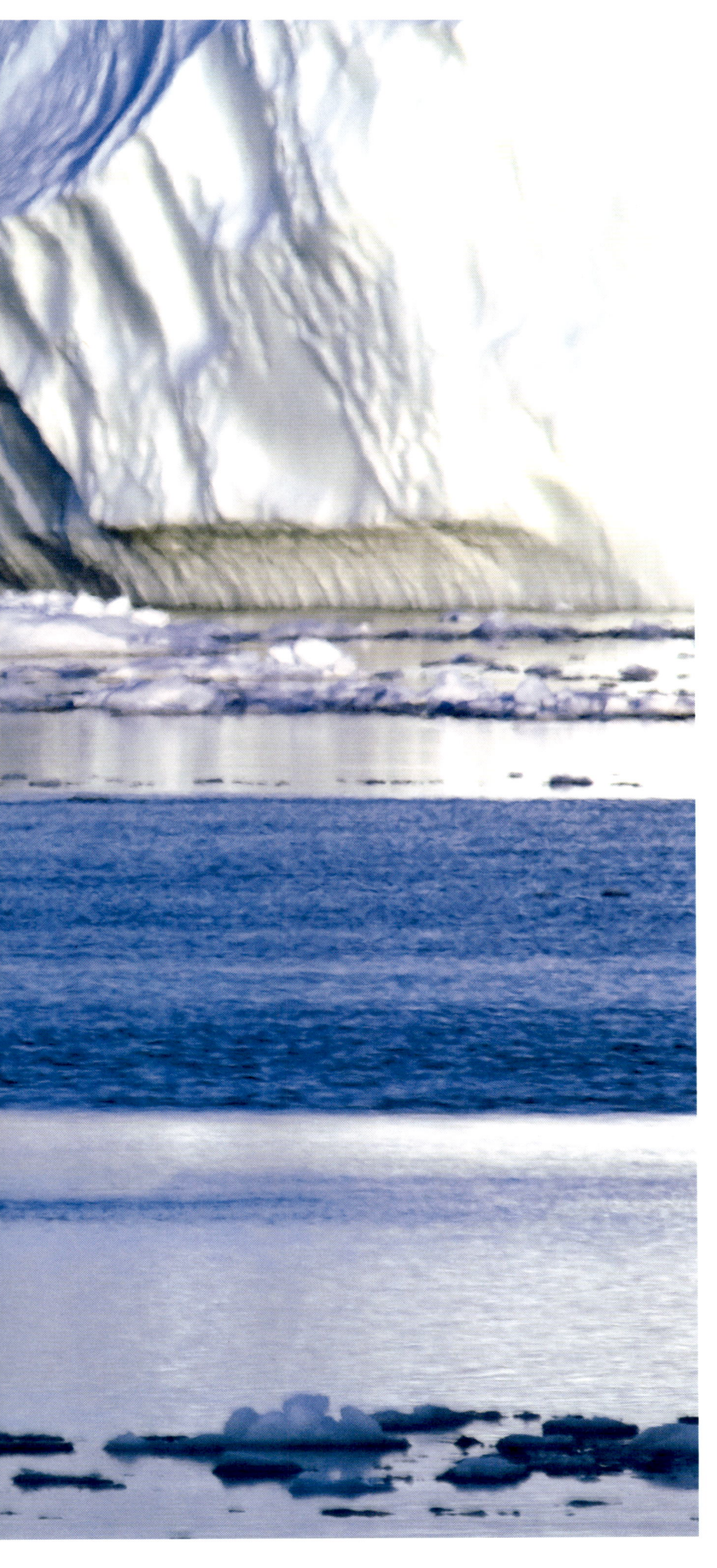

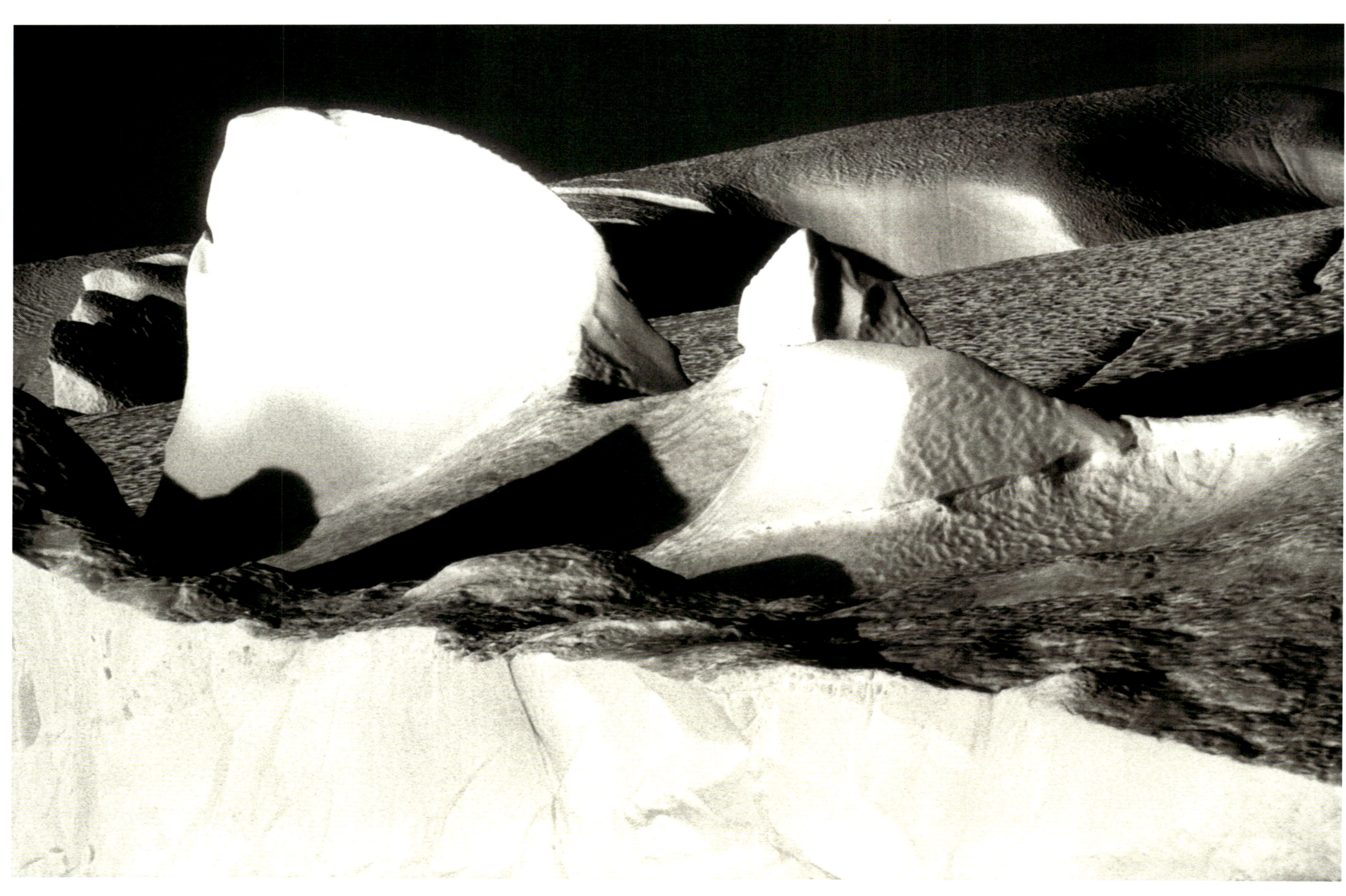

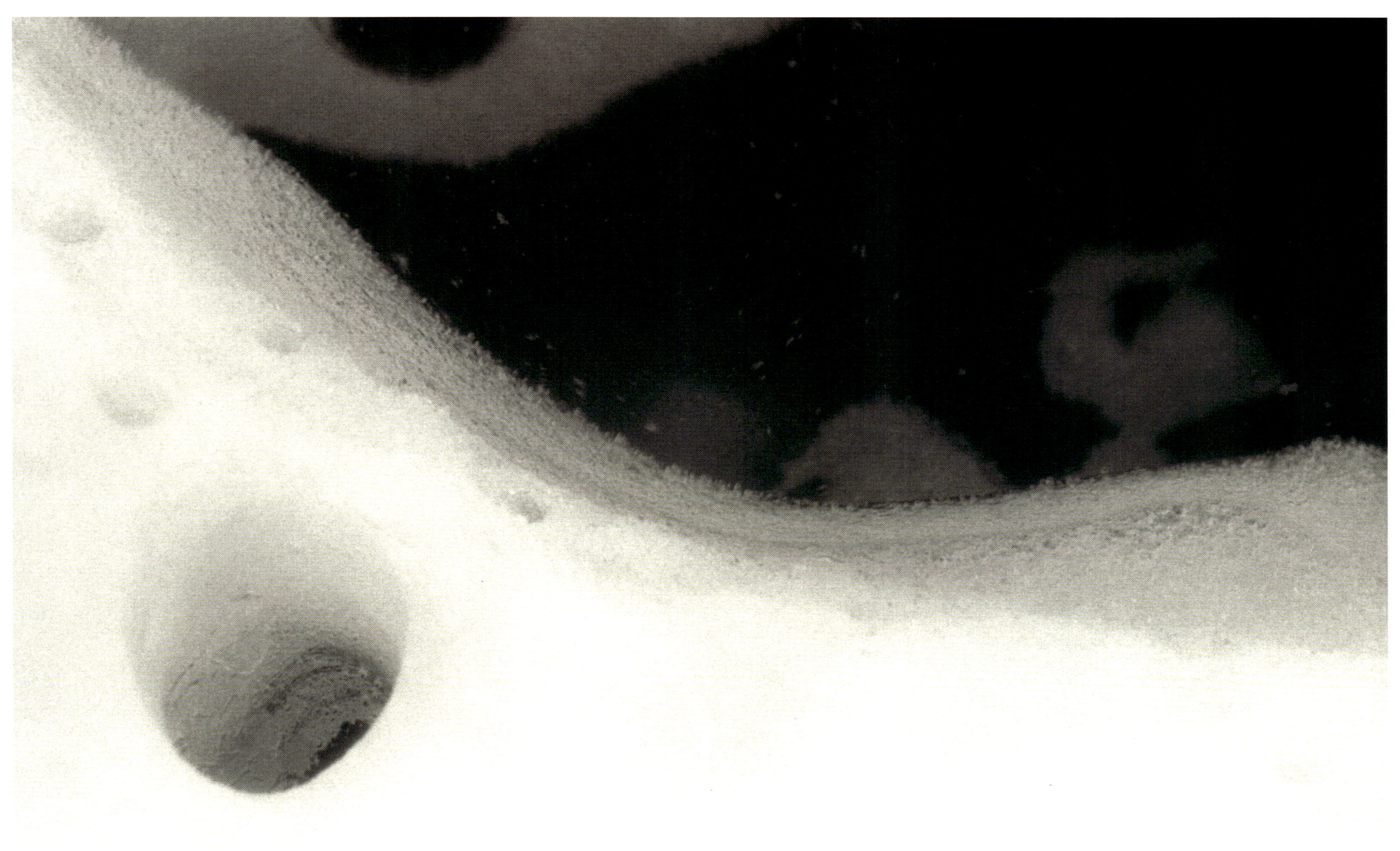

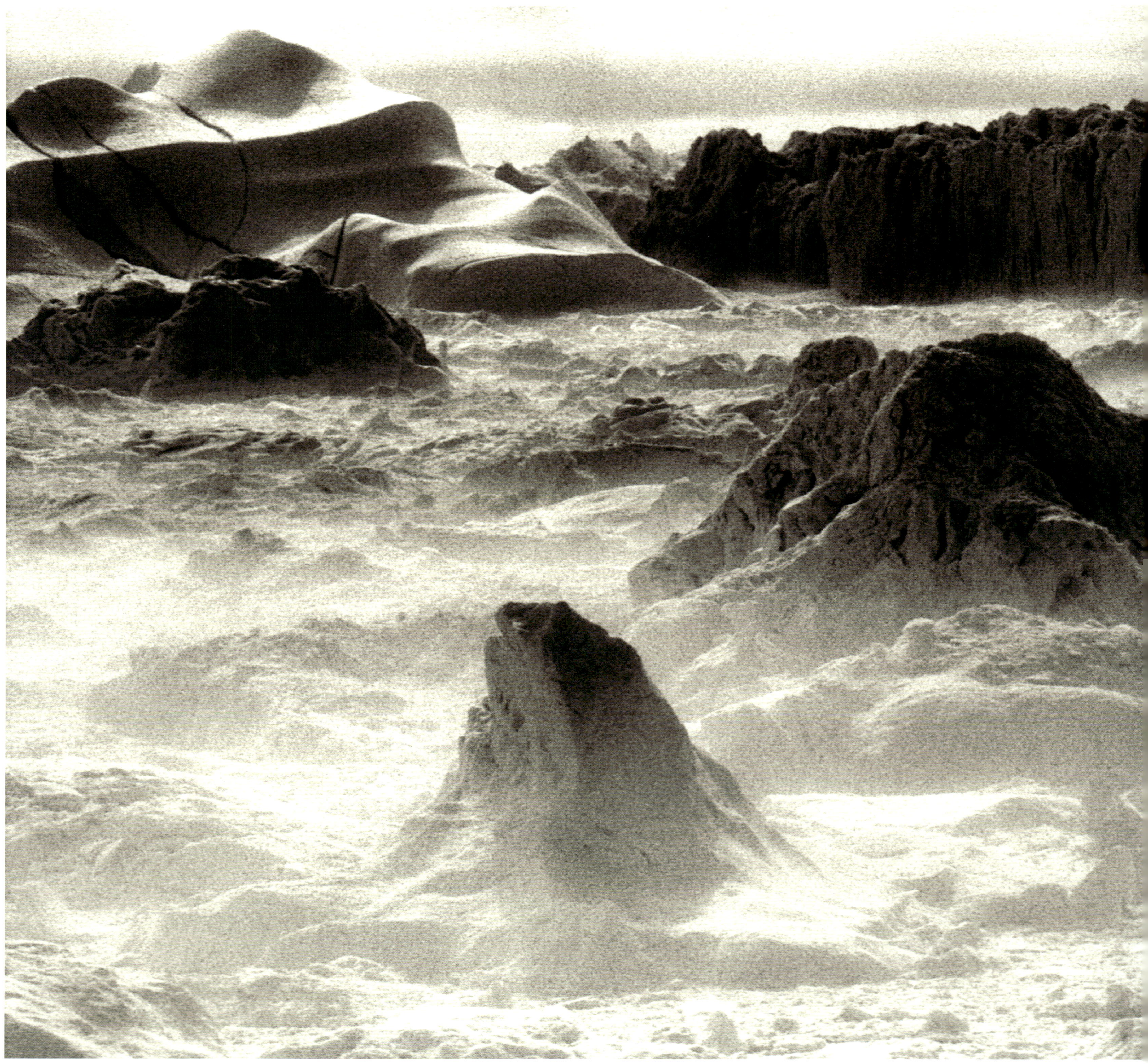

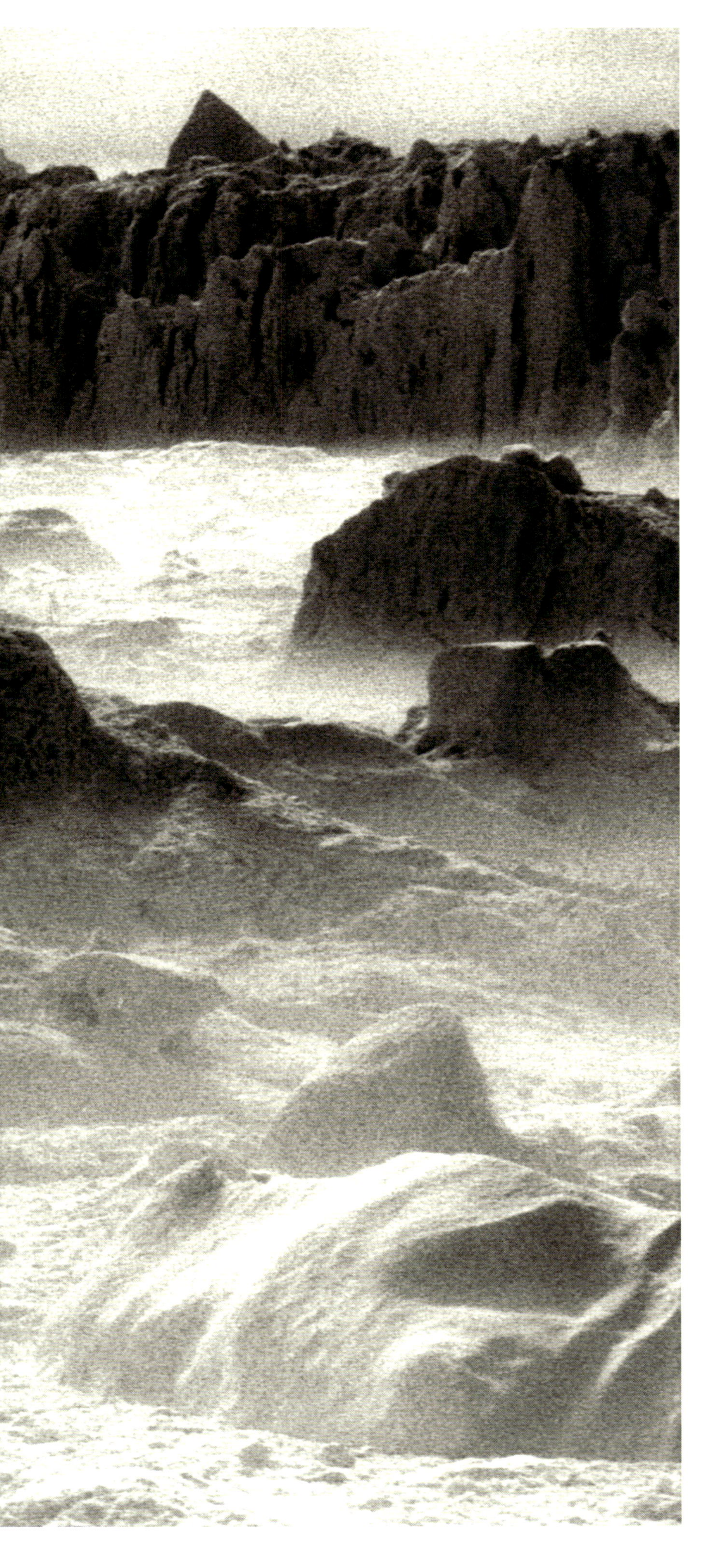

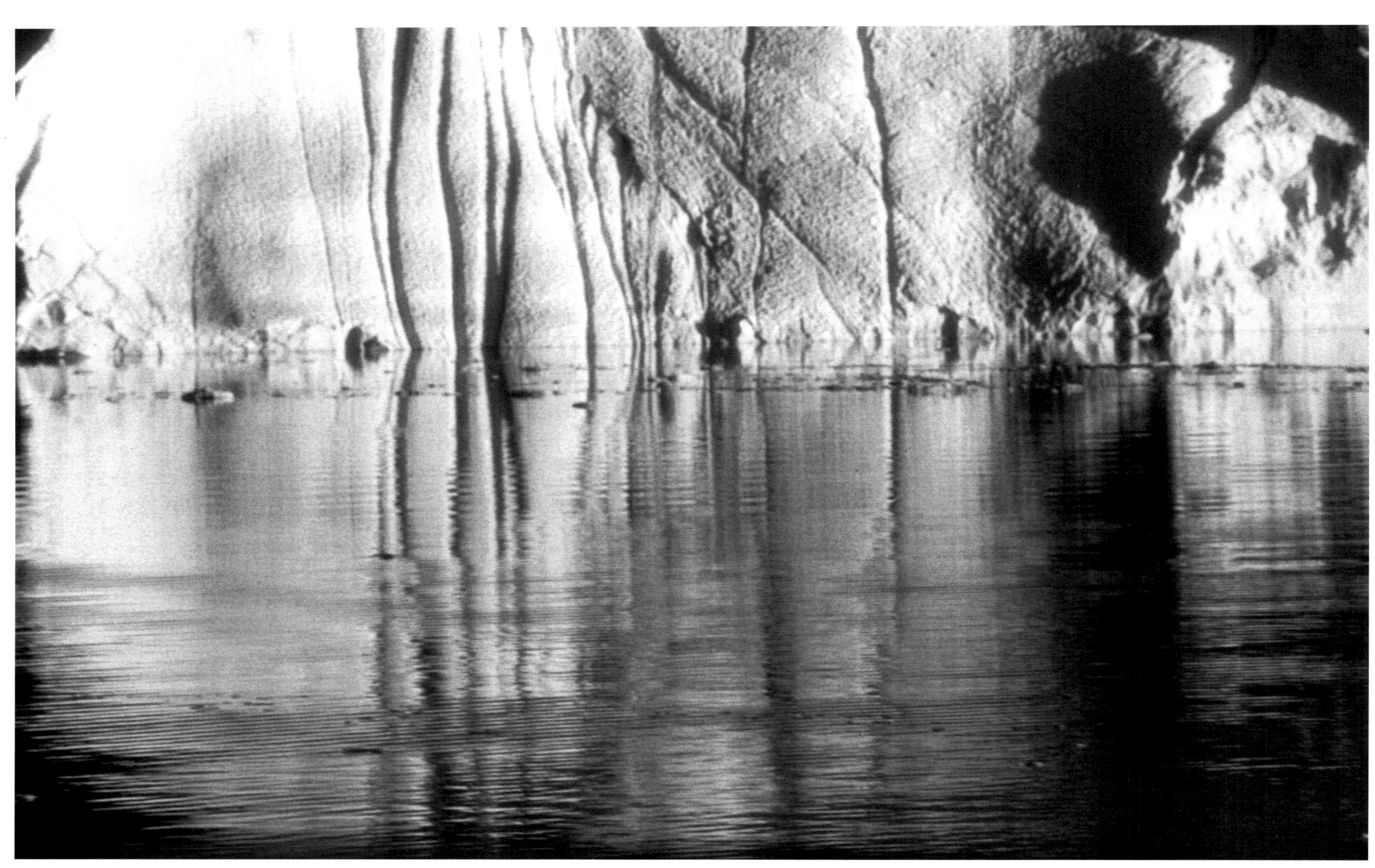

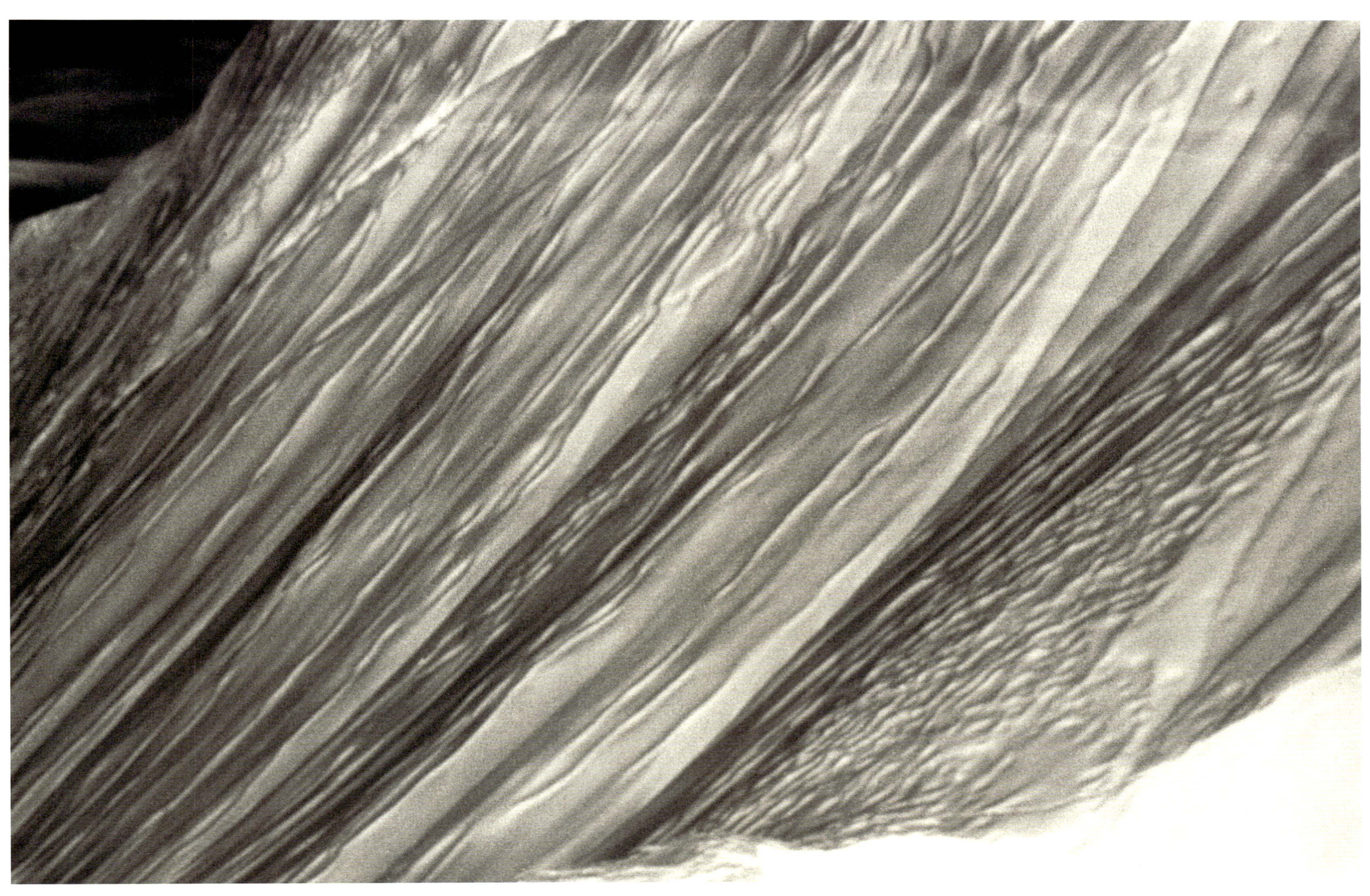

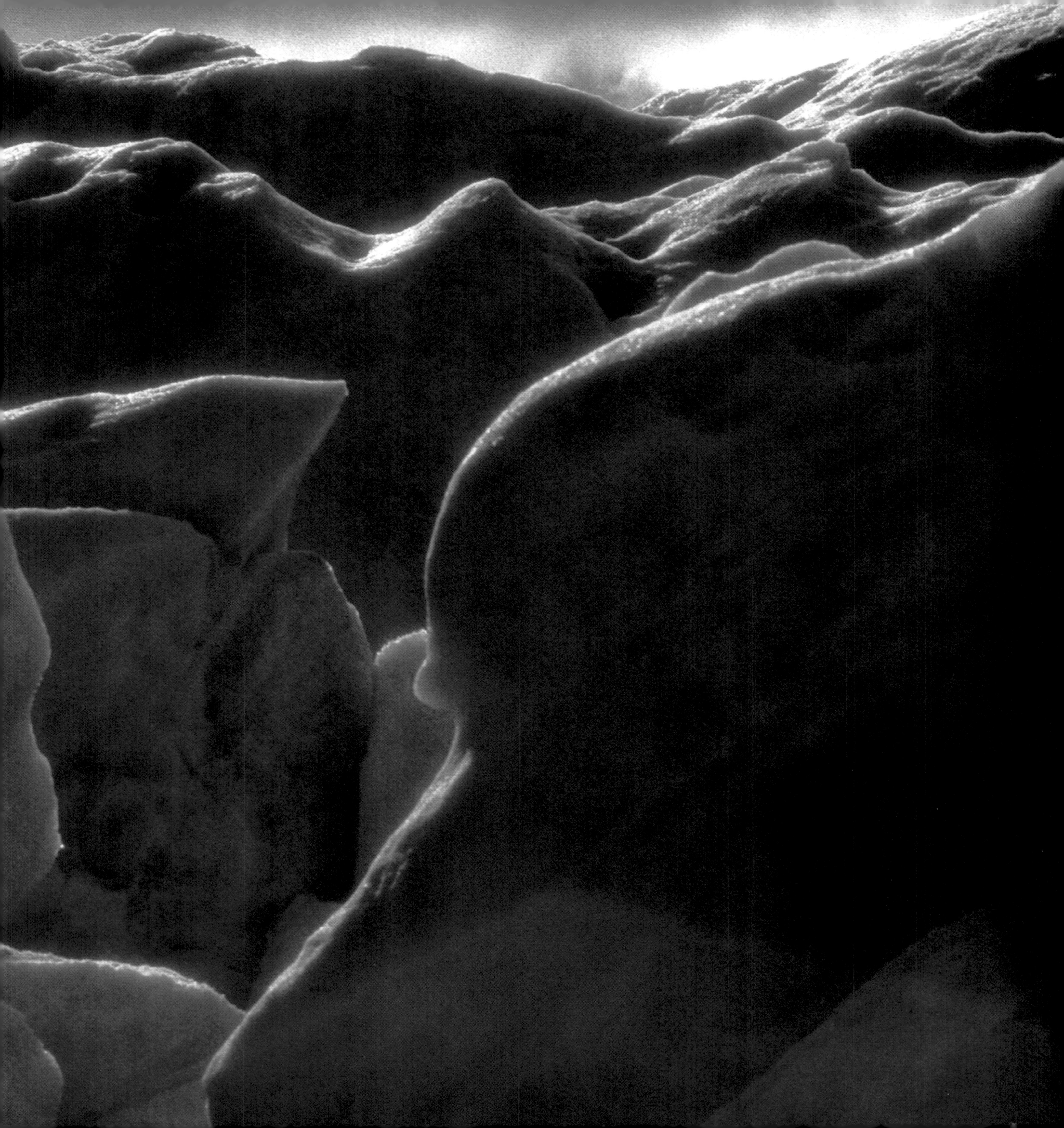

icelandic glaciers

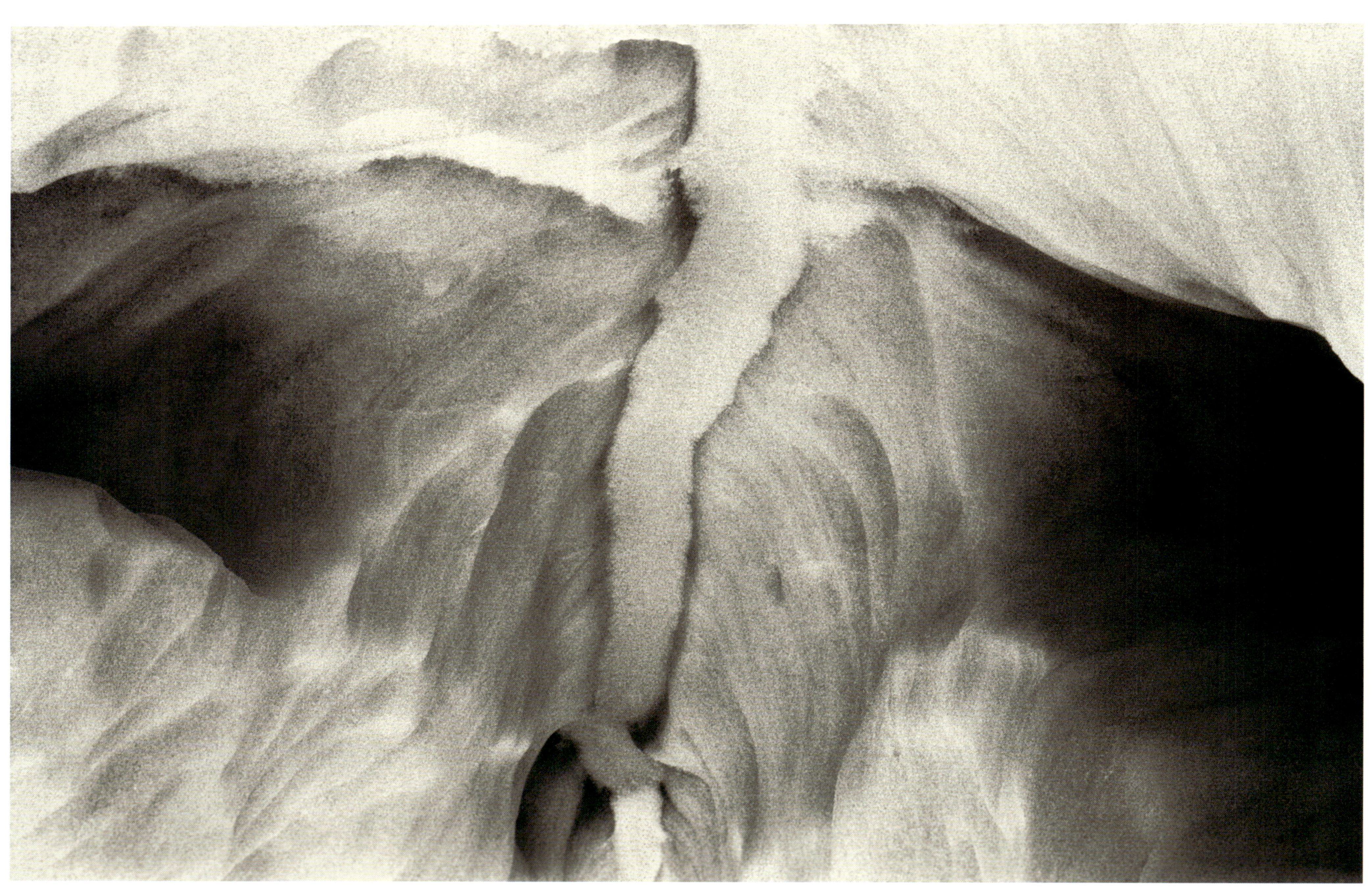

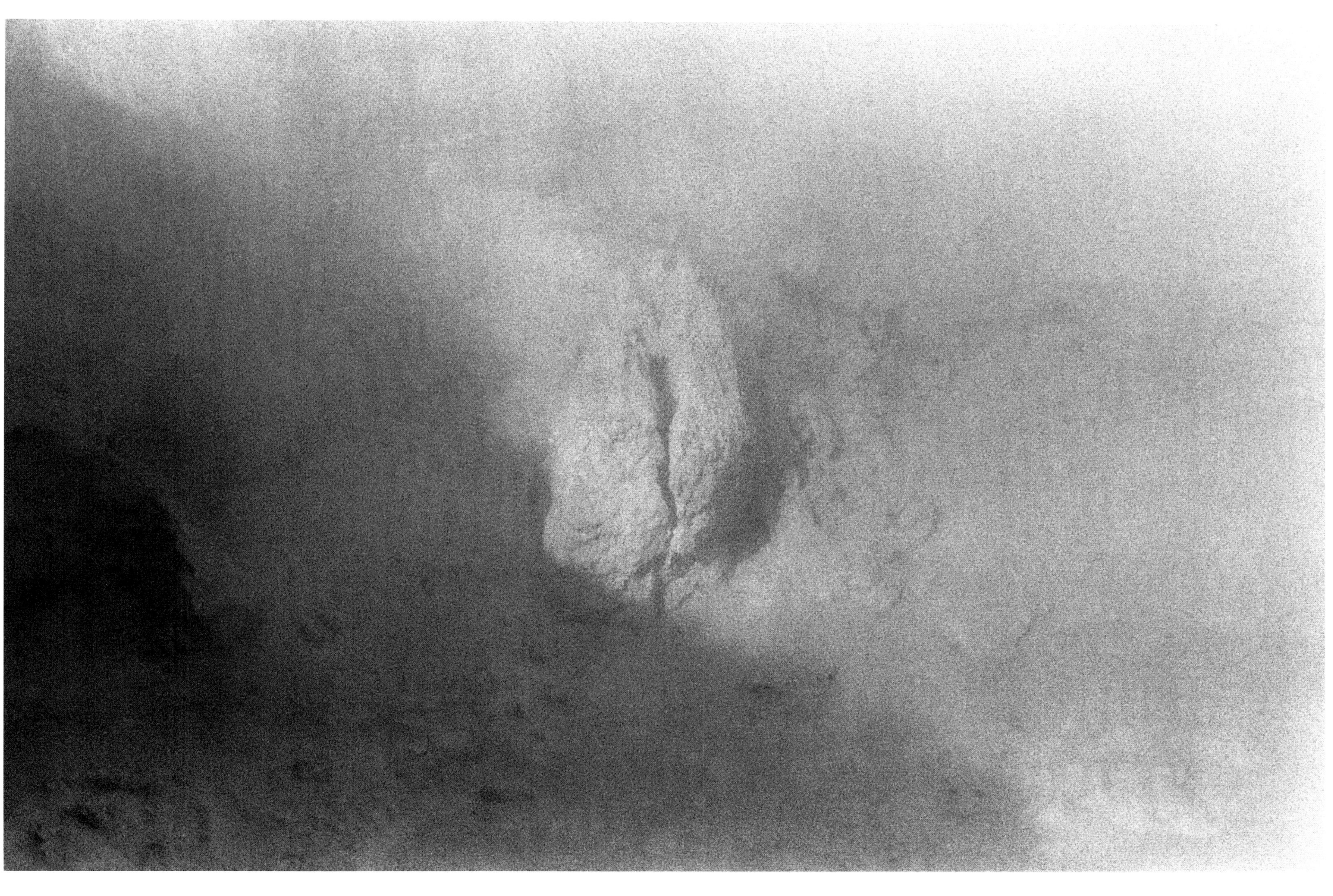

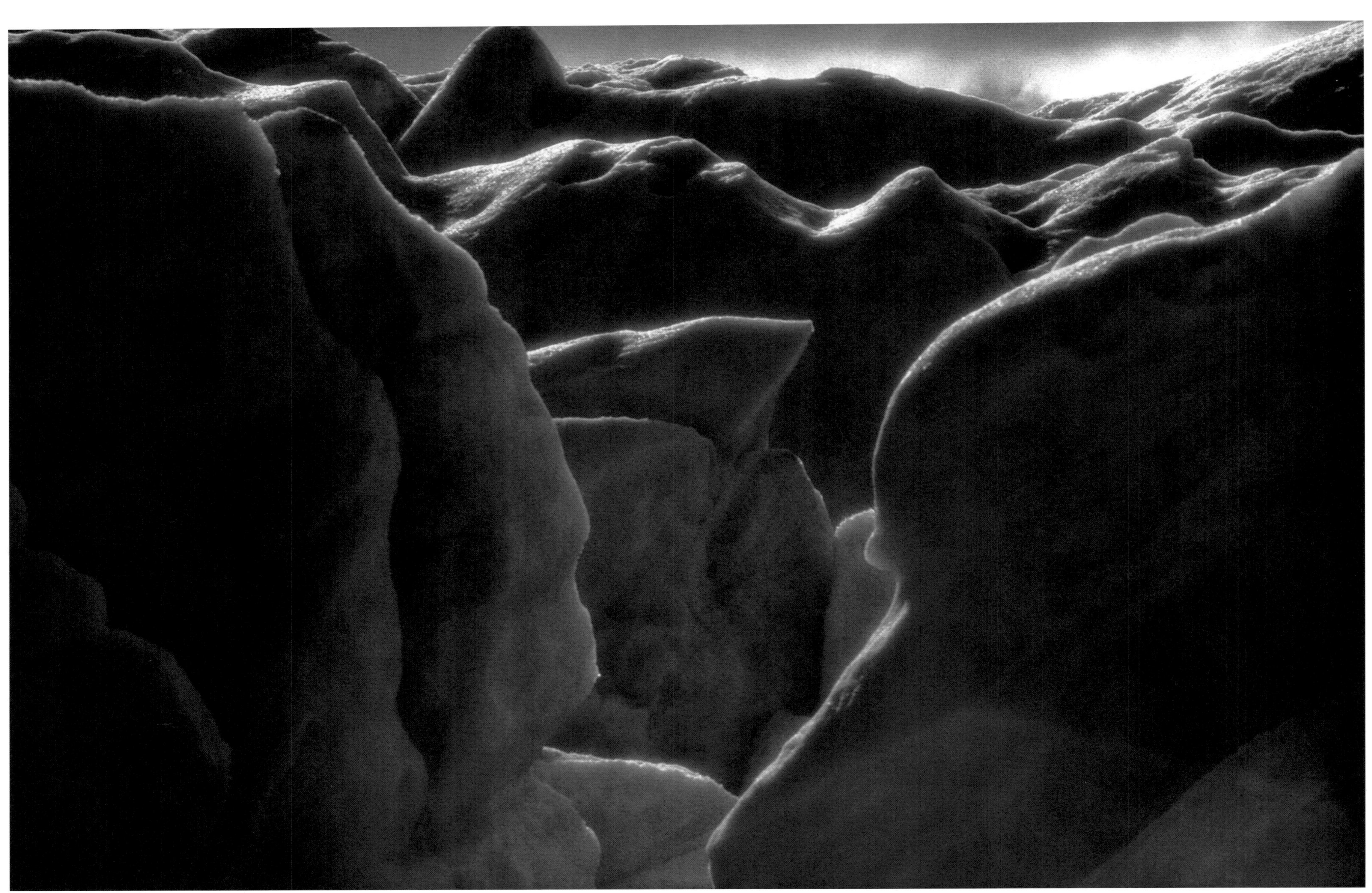

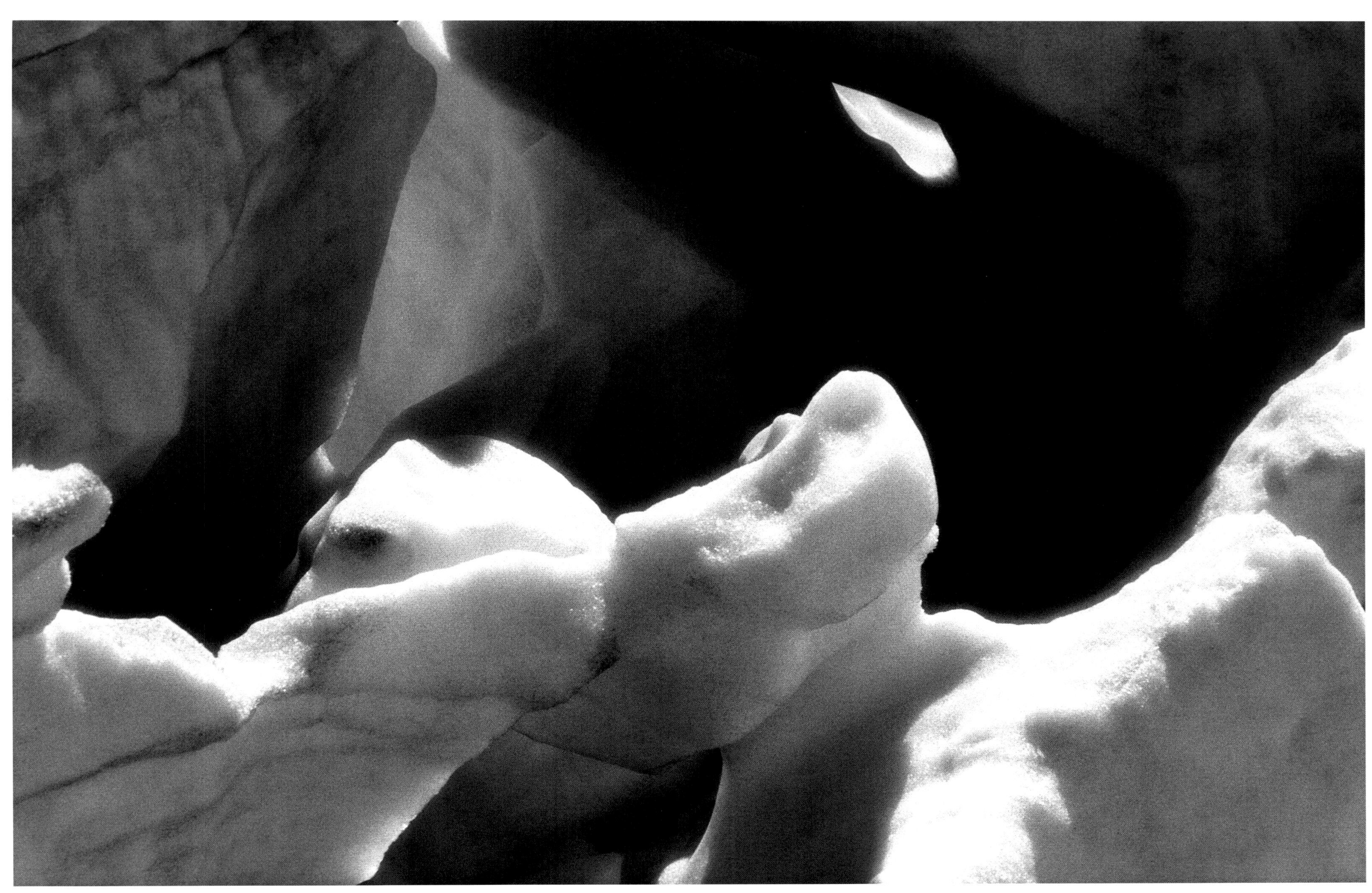

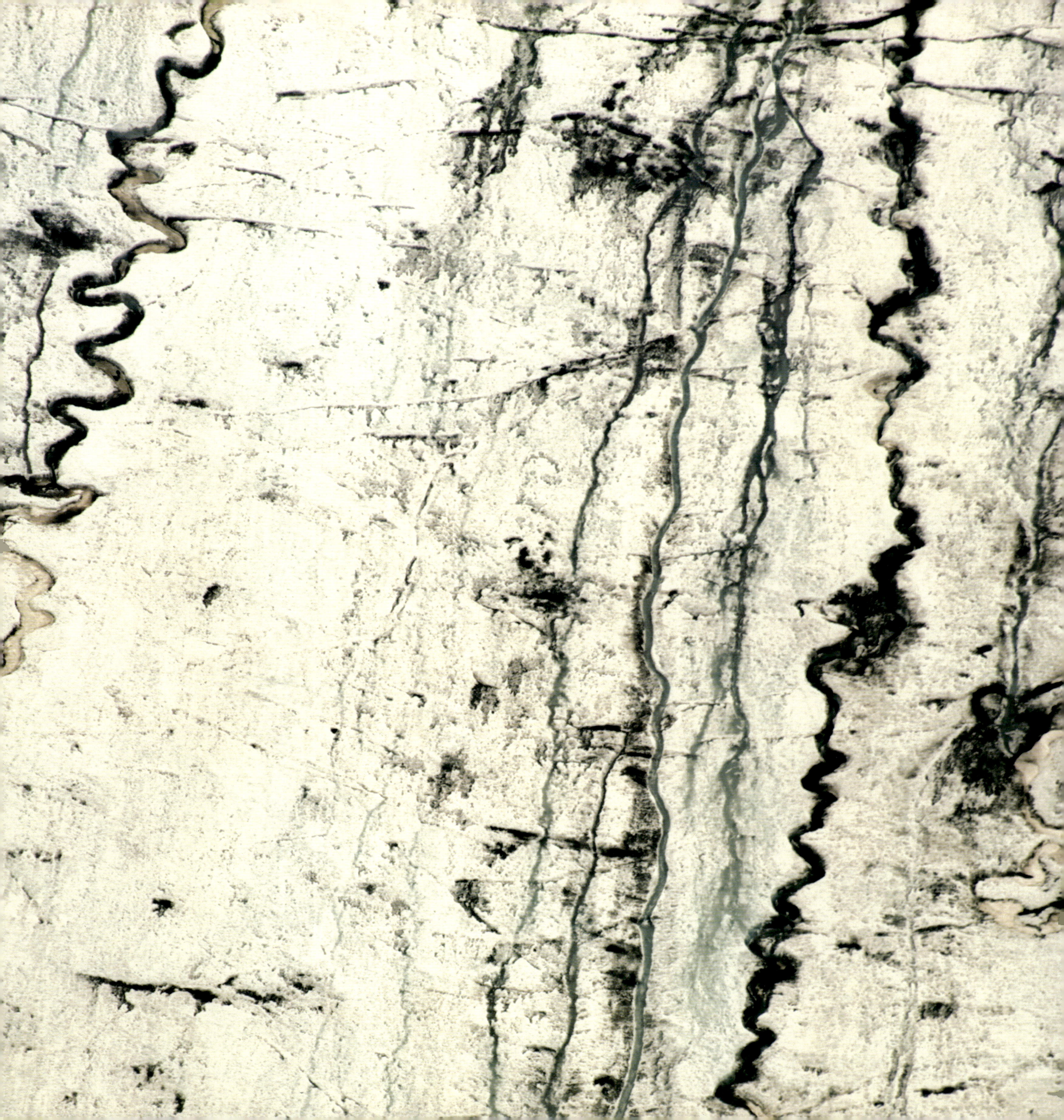

On a return trip to Iceland in 2008, Tuft found that the relative lack of fresh snowfall in recent years was insufficient to cover up deposits of volcanic ash, evident in the title of "Fire and Ice" as well as the actual image. The pictures once again present us with fractal miniatures that resonate with the larger landscape. The threads of ash on frozen water in "Fire and Ice" recapitulate as a fractal the edges of glaciers and the coastline at increasing scales. The "Saga" image reads as a map of the terrain as well as a synecdoche of it. In both infrared and ultraviolet works, the world we recognize in optical light is still there, but that small part of the spectrum has been enlarged and heightened.

Although Tuft tends to title her black-and-white infrared works as numbered images in named sequences, most photographs in her color ultraviolet series receive titles. As with the Greenland photos, so with the Icelandic Sagas, in this latter case titles reflect Norse and Icelandic myths. Her decision to evoke archetypal motifs deliberately points the viewer away from the traditional scientific uses of ultraviolet photography, principally by astrophysicists, and toward a more intuitive understanding of the universe. This, too, is a heightening of the subject matter, a way of enlarging the intellectual spectrum in addition to the aesthetic one.

icelandic sagas

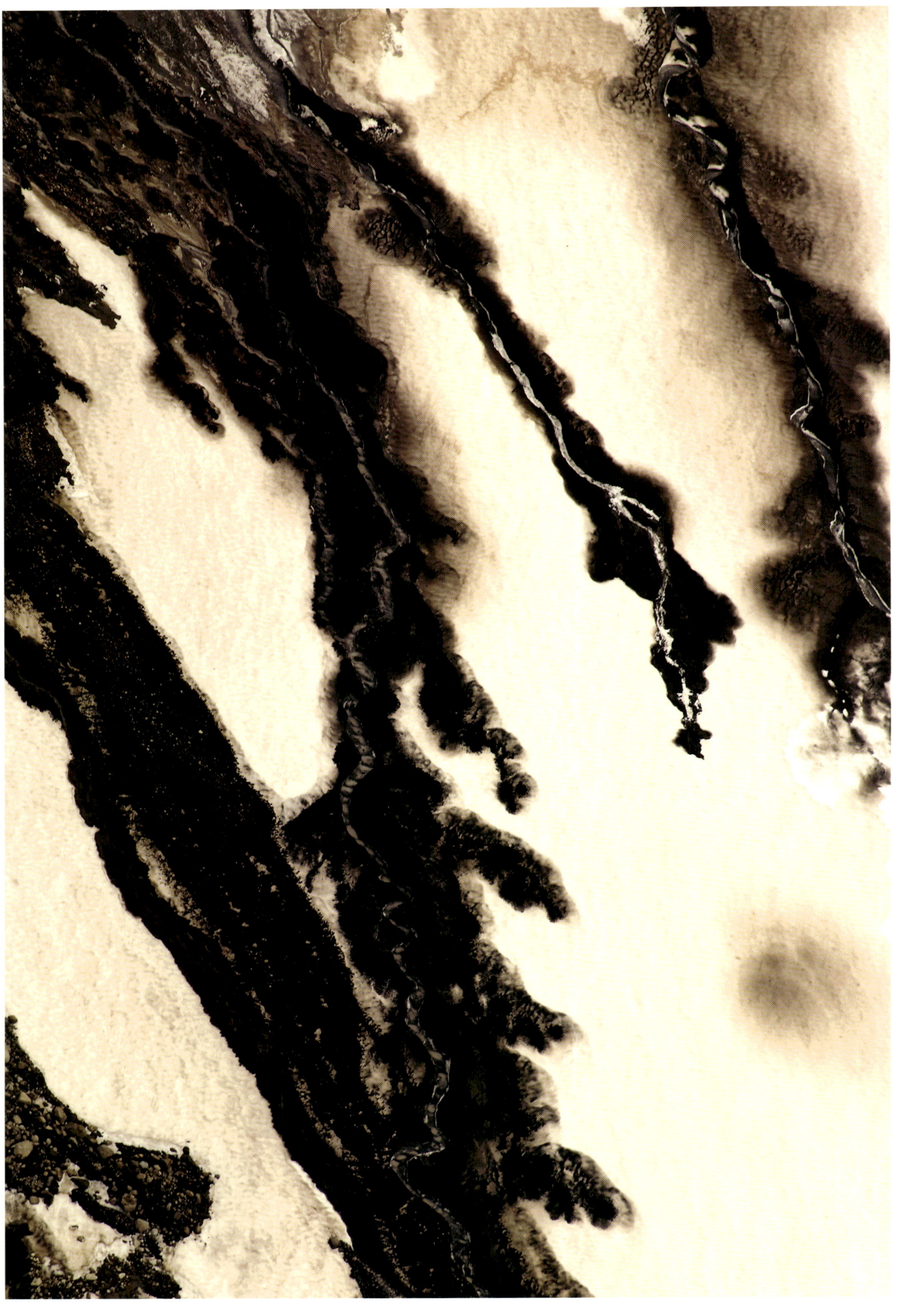

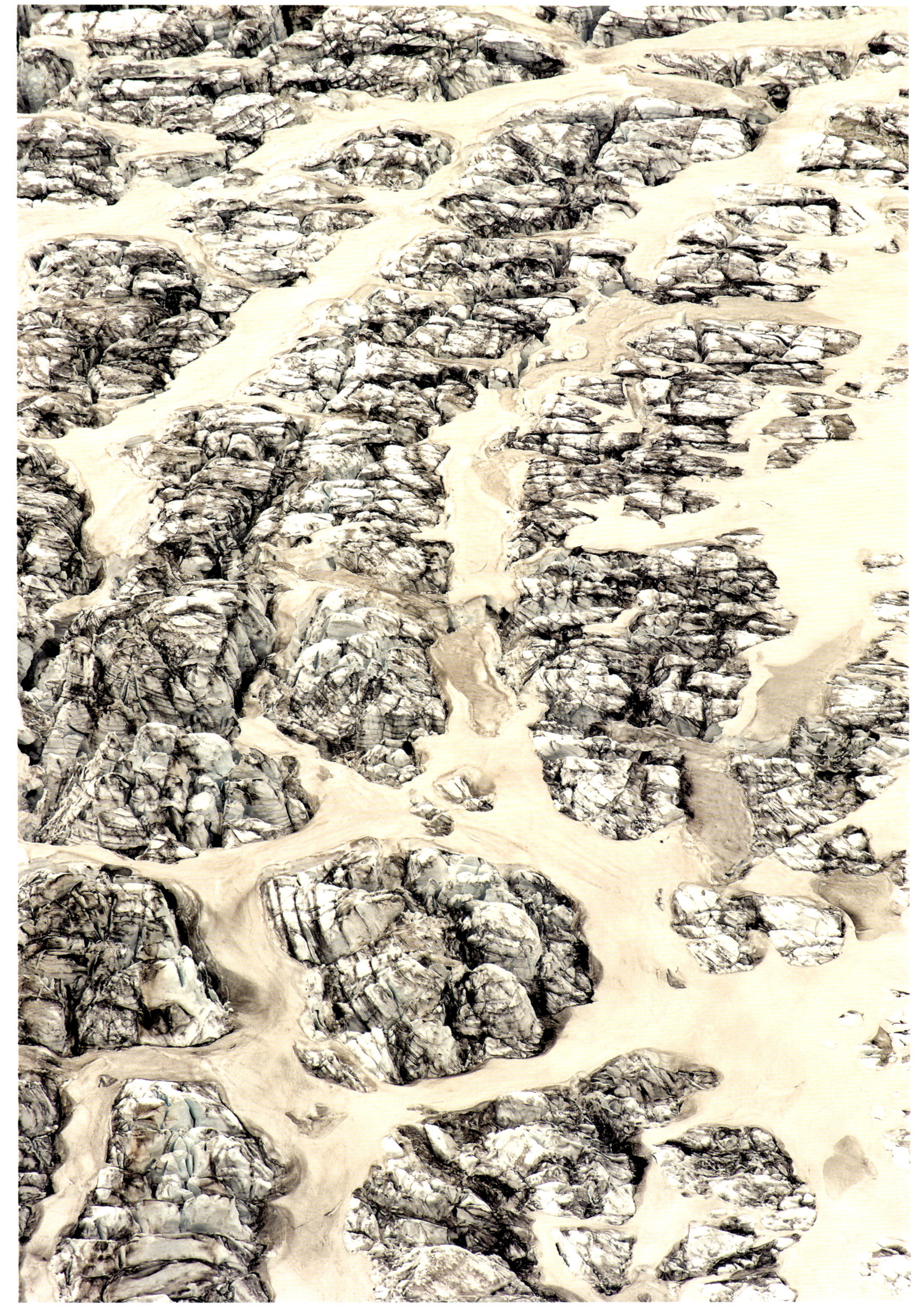

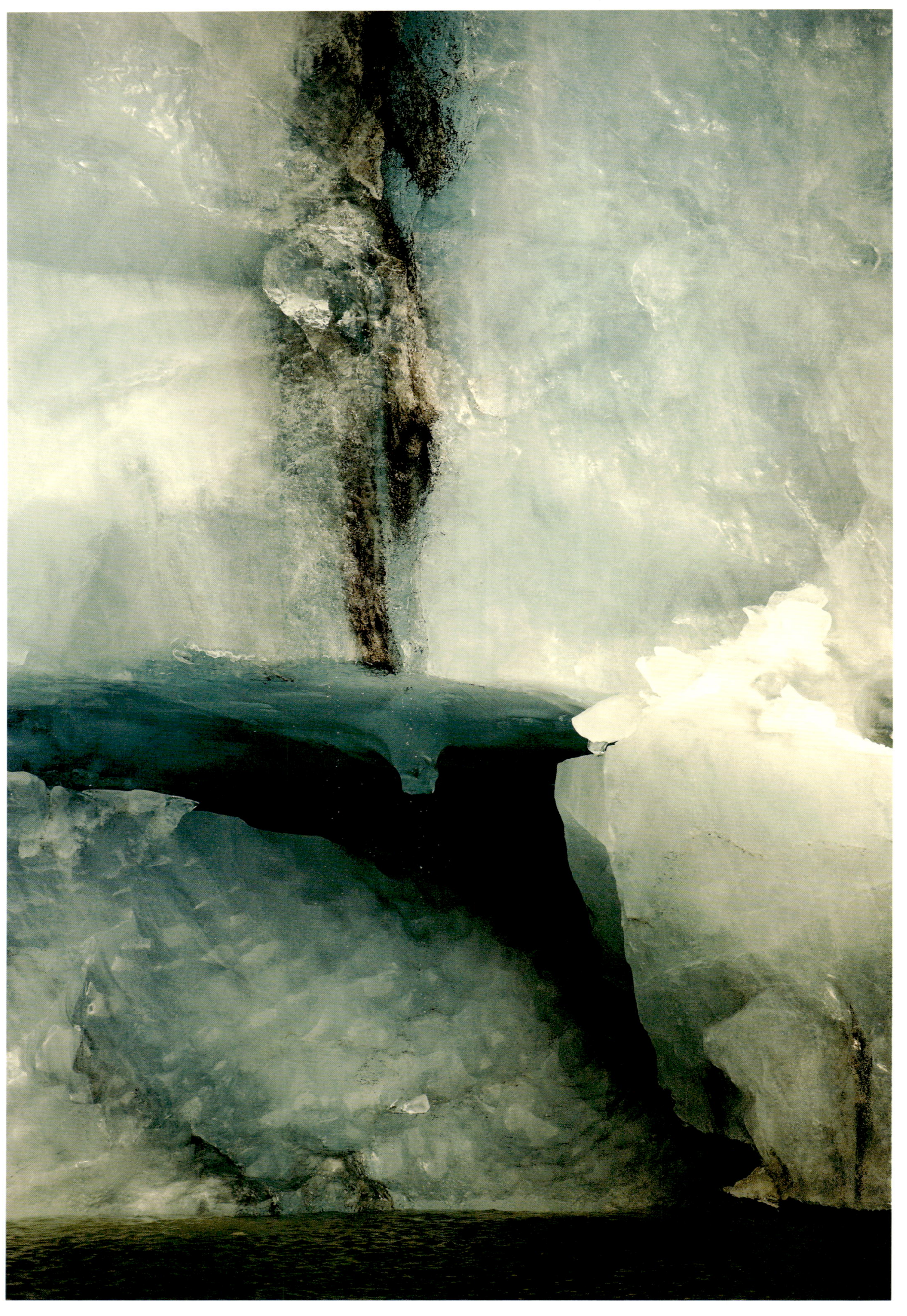

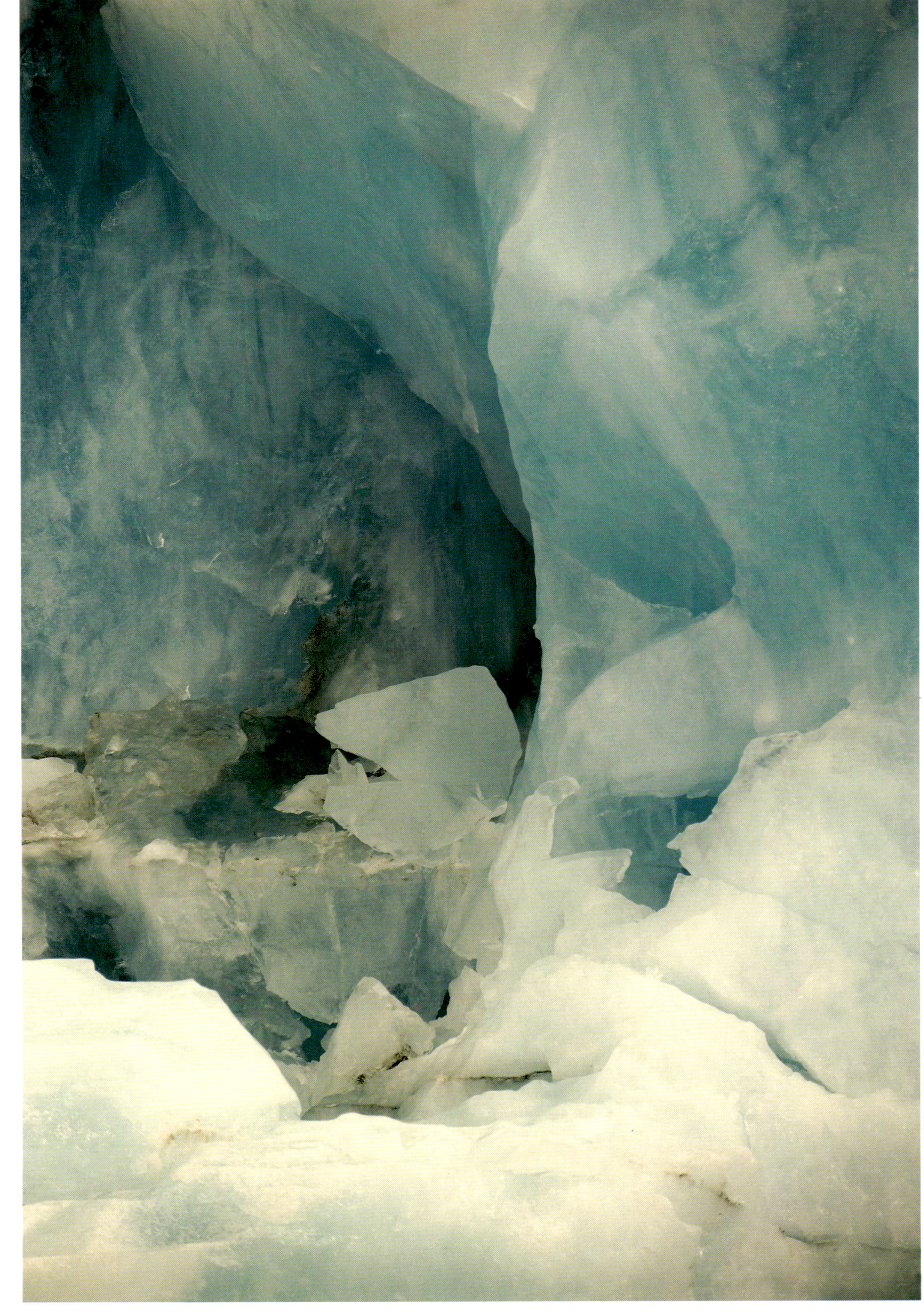

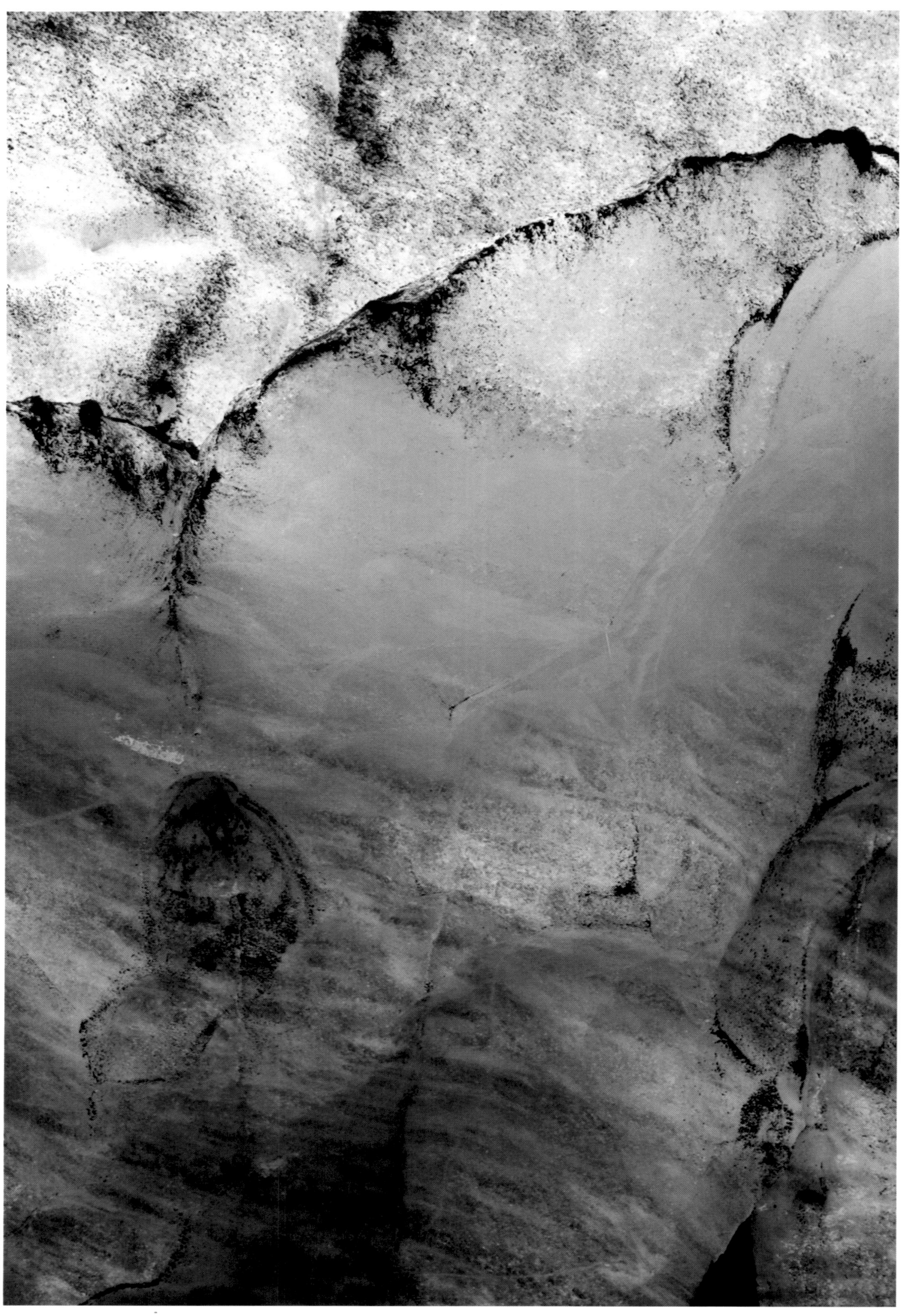

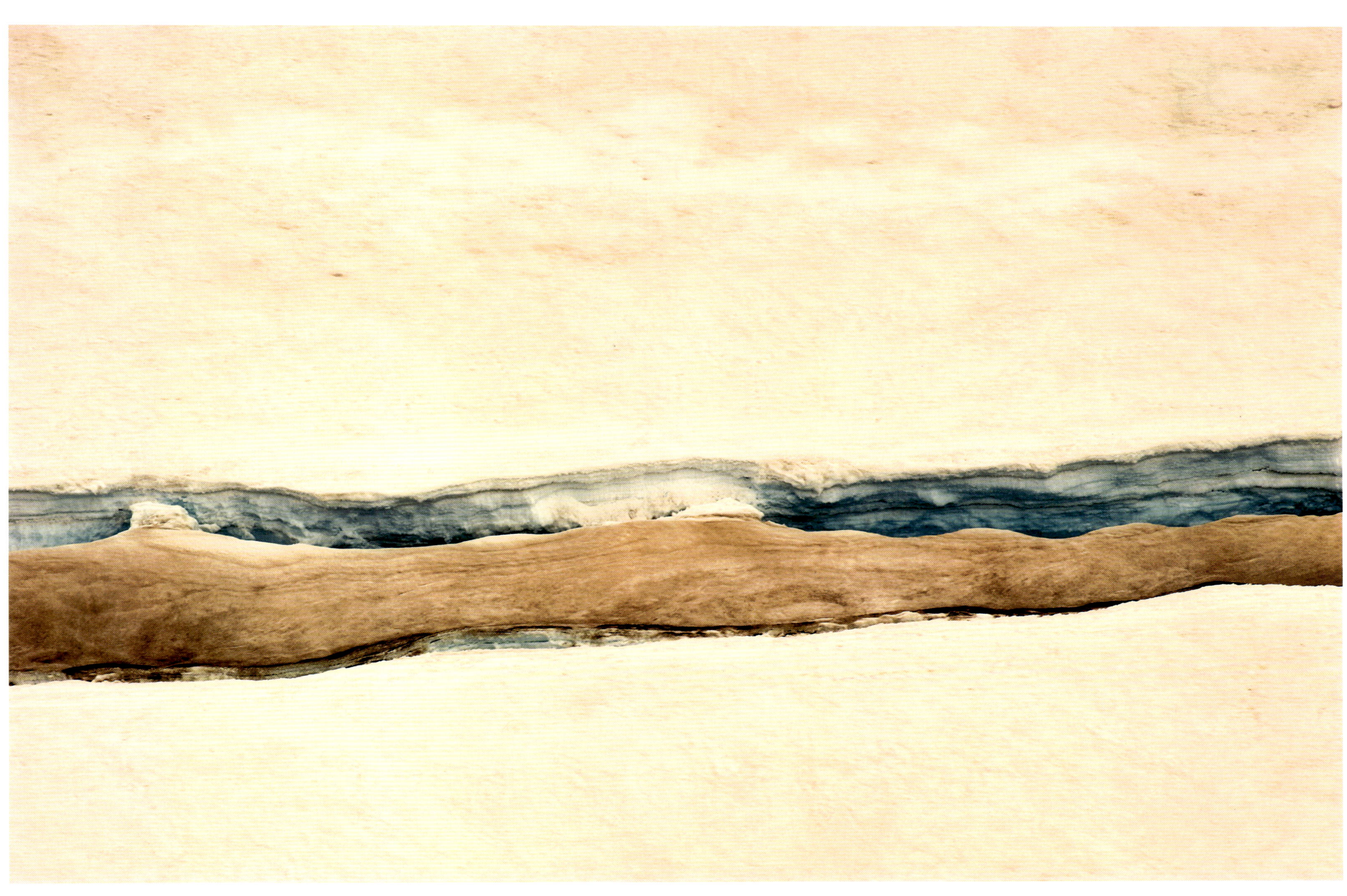

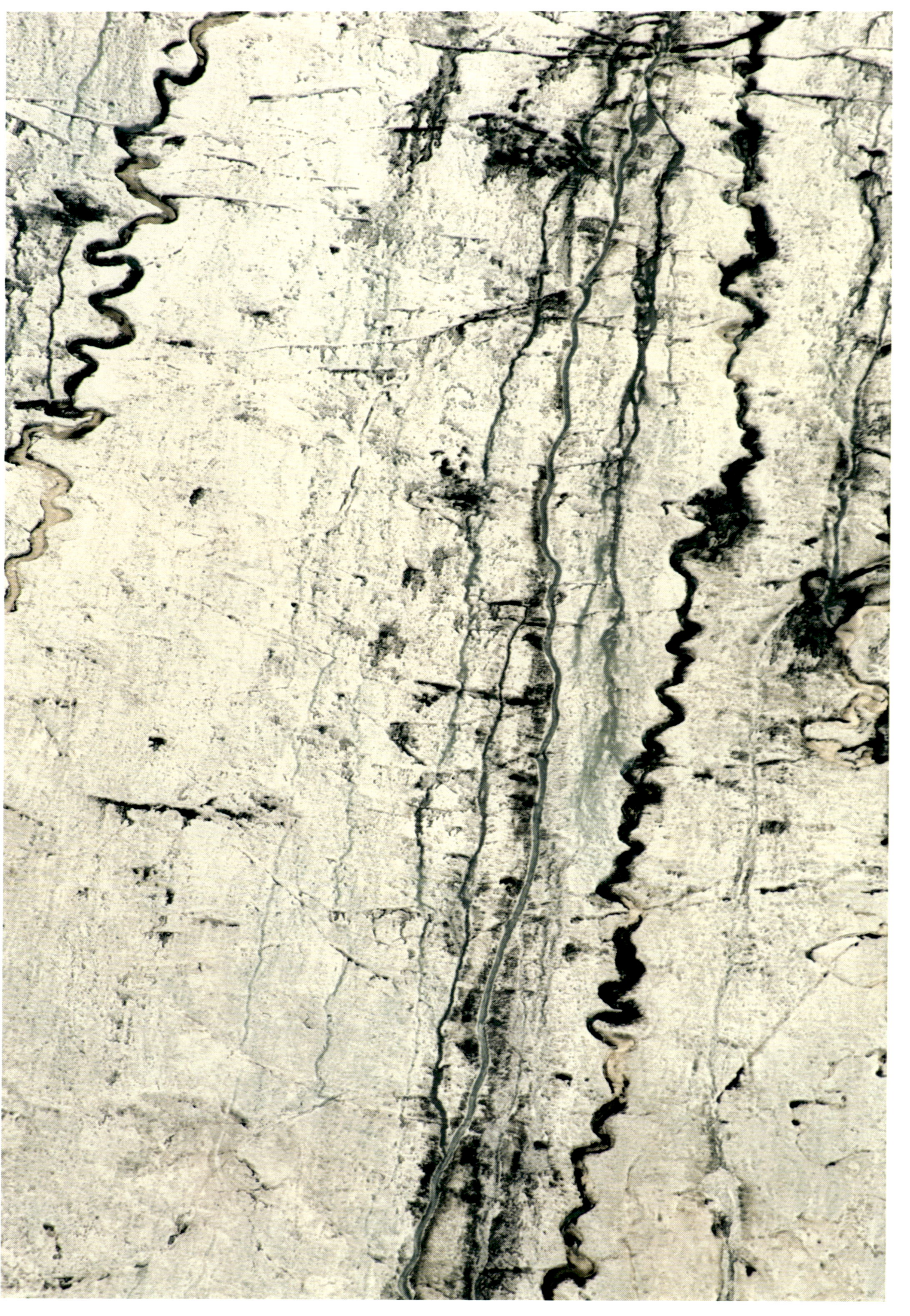

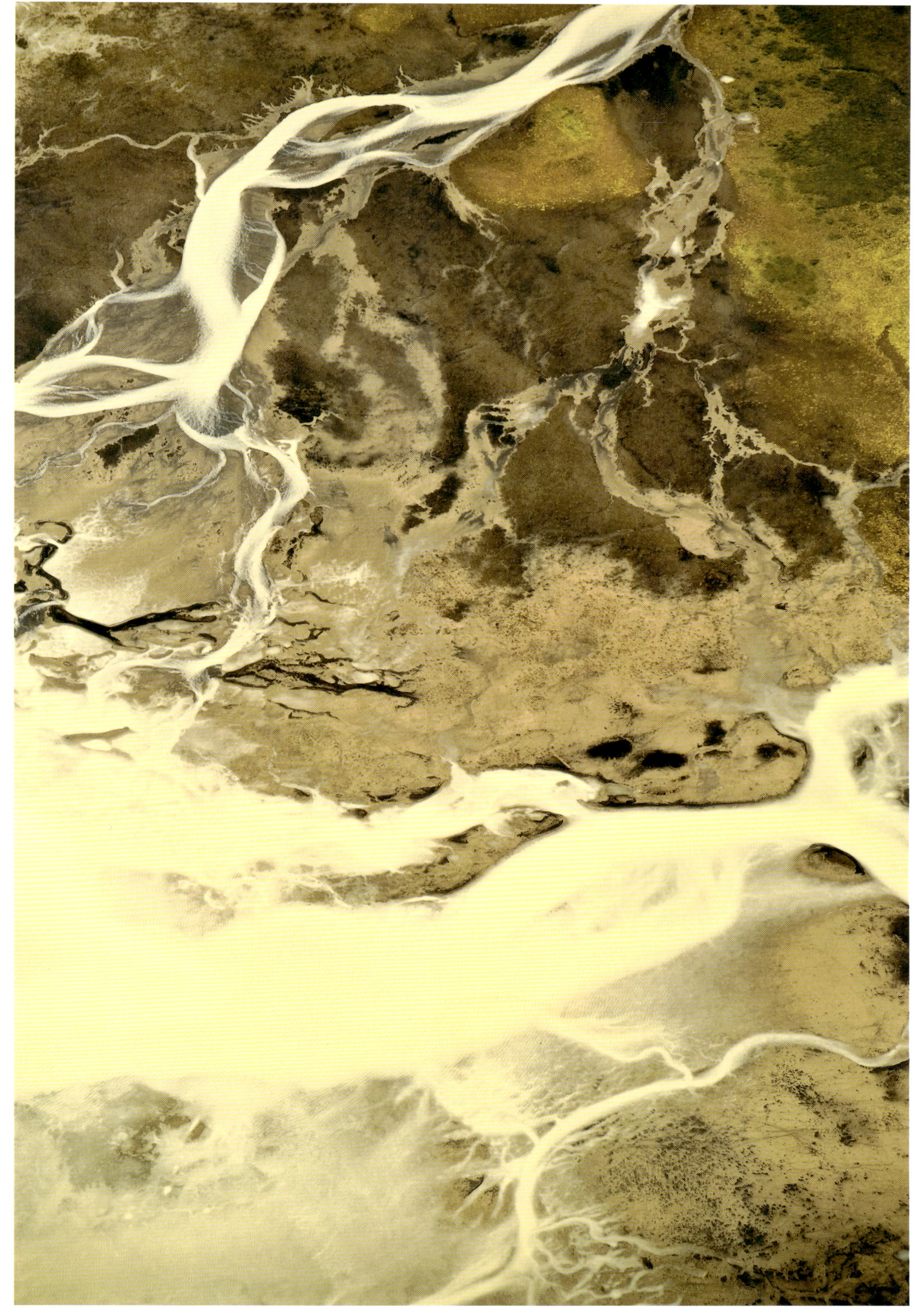

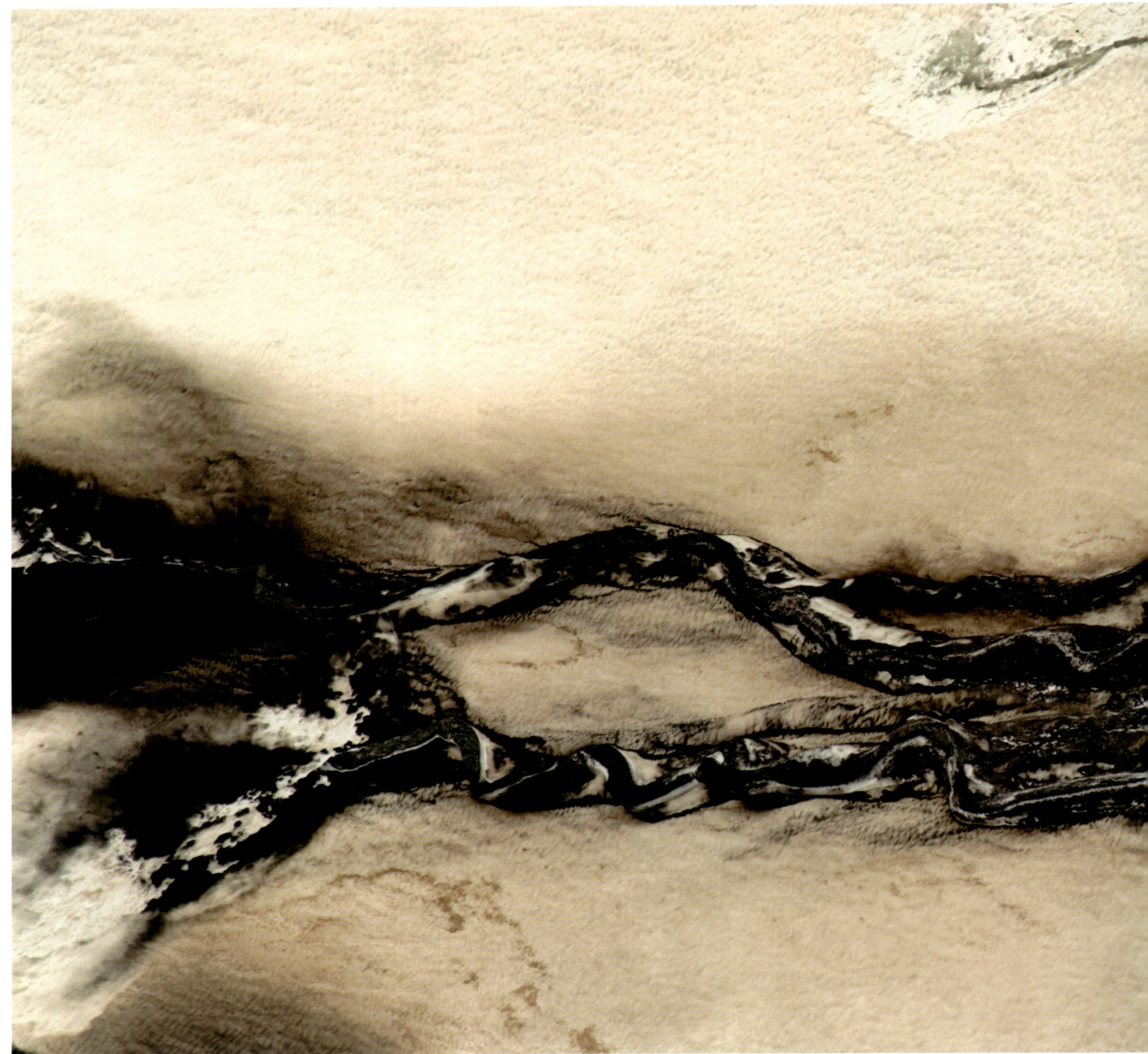

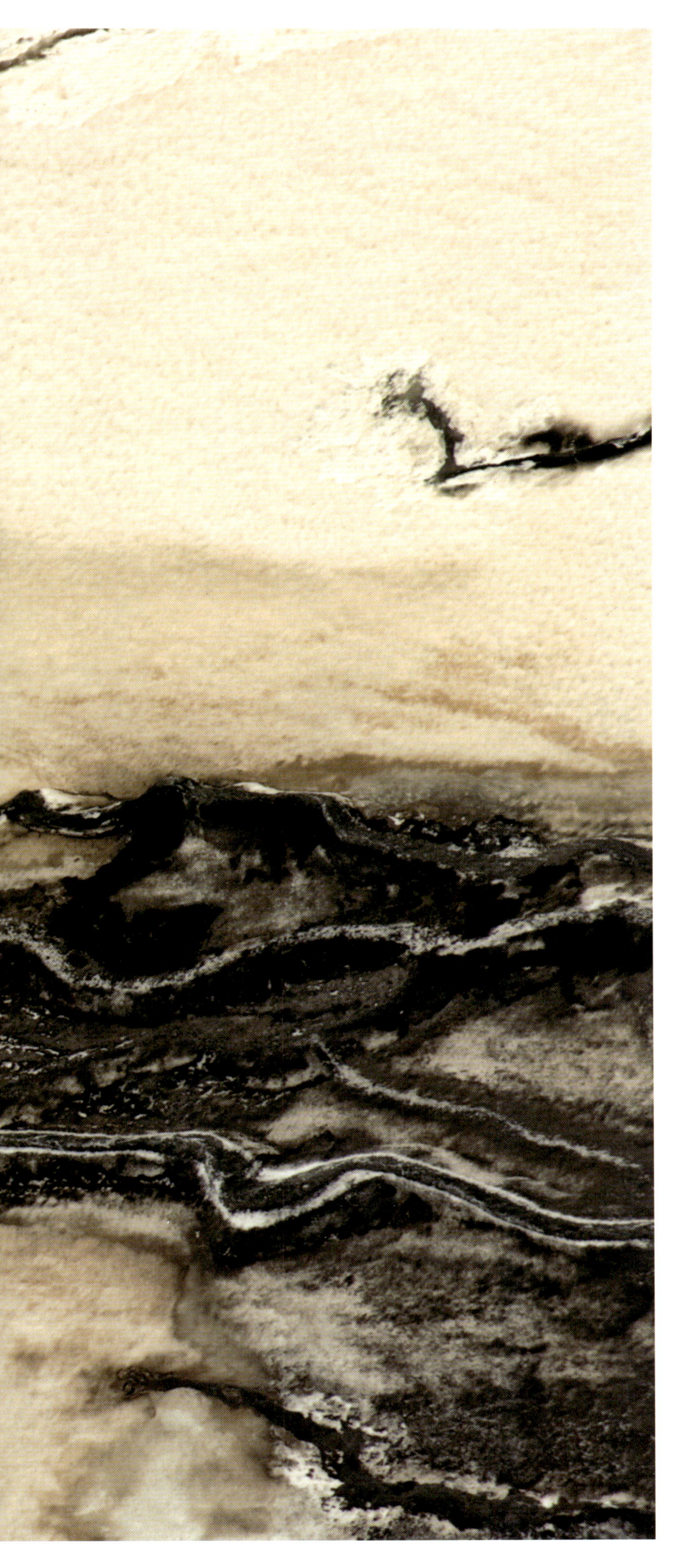

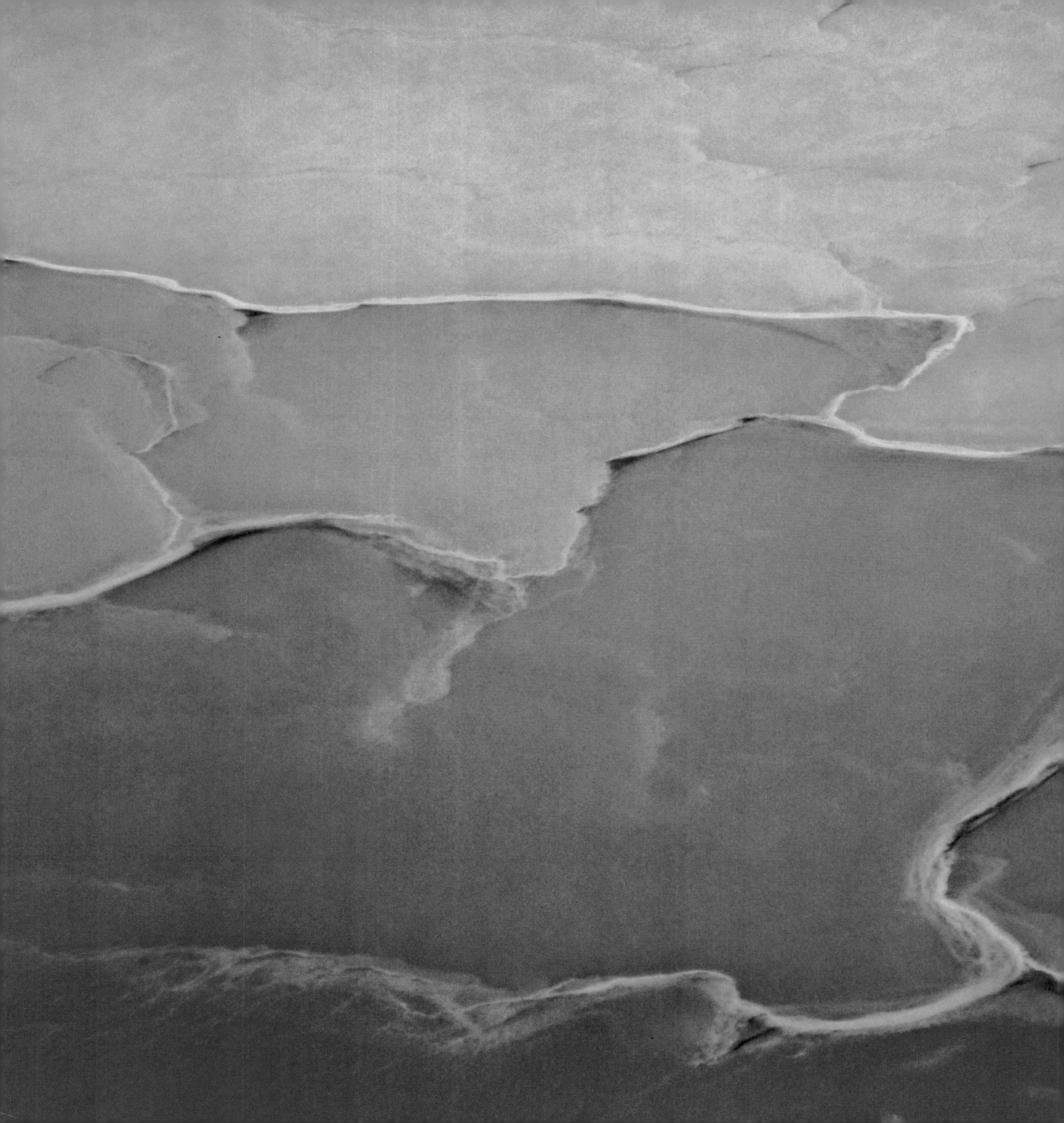

Tuft first began photographing in the ultraviolet range in 2005, while using a digital camera during a helicopter flight over "Spiral Jetty." Upon her return to New York, she couldn't believe the intensity of the colors revealed. It took her awhile to figure out that both the camera and the environment were responsible. Not only can digital cameras surprise us with the saturation of color they present in images, but the lake environment captures a tremendous amount of UV. Bright unclouded days and dry atmospheric conditions, both hallmarks of the high elevation of the Great Basin desert, are rich in ultraviolet. The Great Salt Lake also contains Halobacteria, which thrive under harsh UV by developing a protective crust of salt opaque to the radiation. That crust gives the lake waters their distinctive reddish hues; the covering also reflects ultraviolet and thus heightens the surreality of "Red Sea," as true to the awe felt on the lake shore as a photograph can present.

salt lake reconsidered

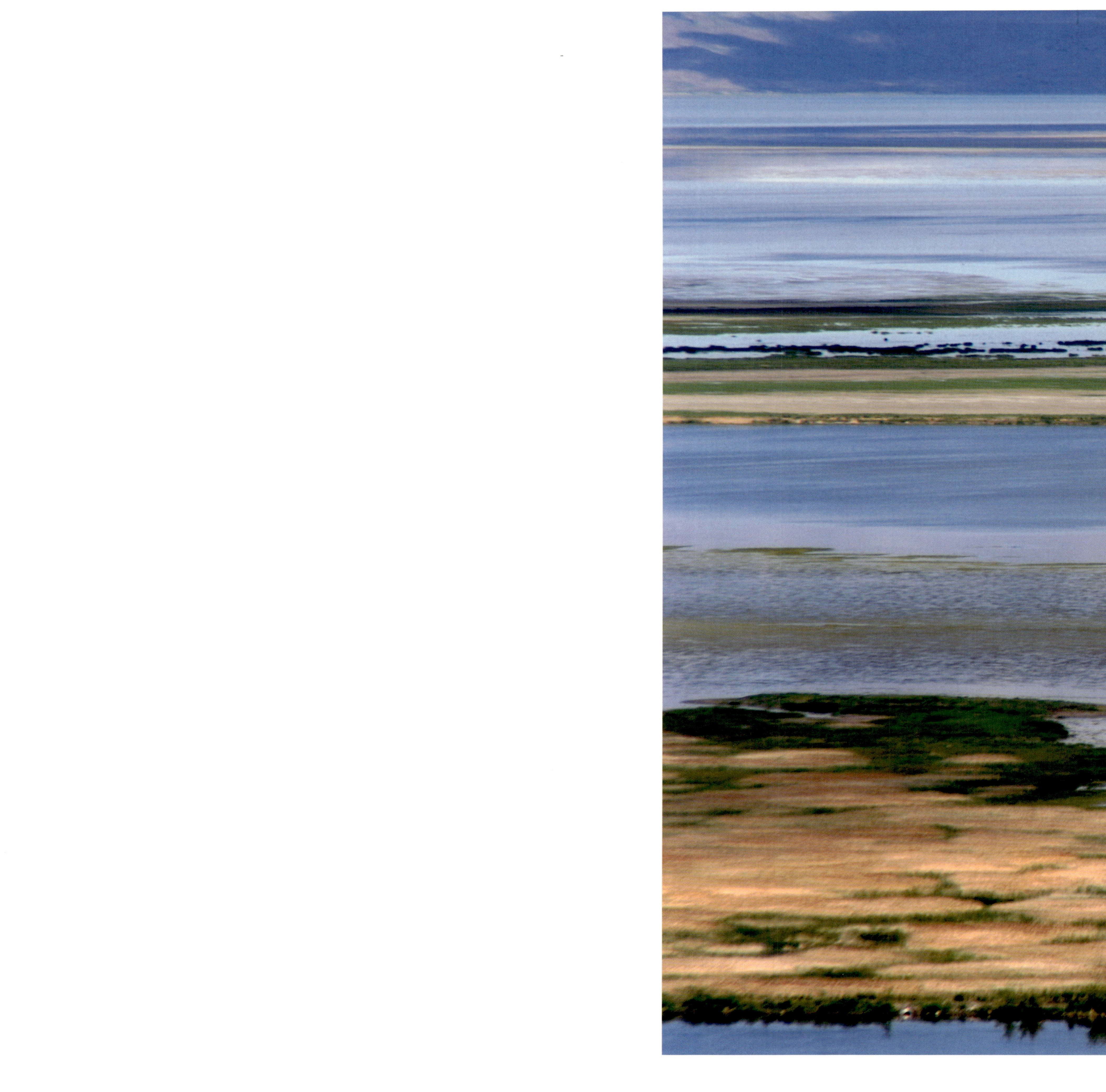

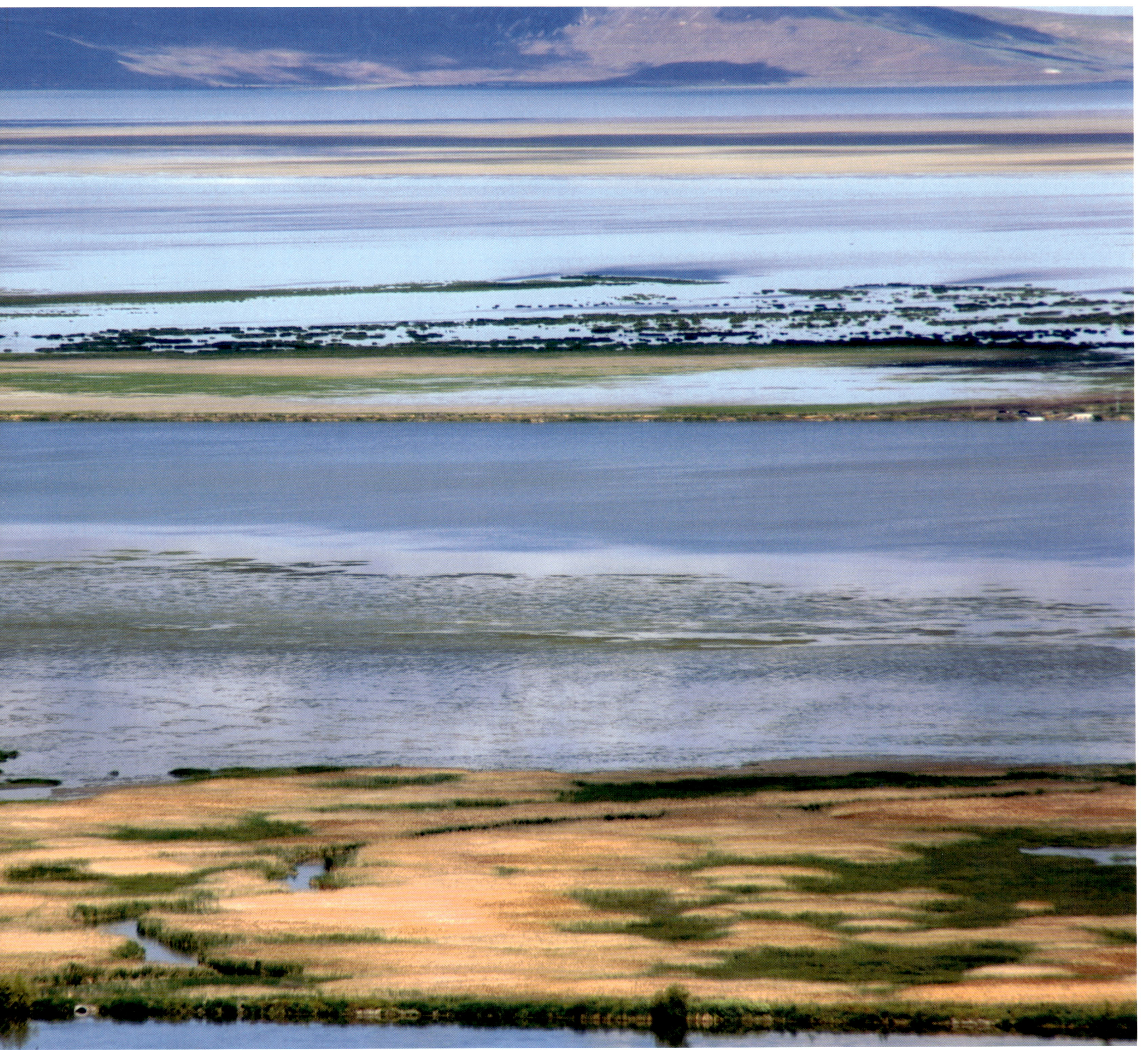

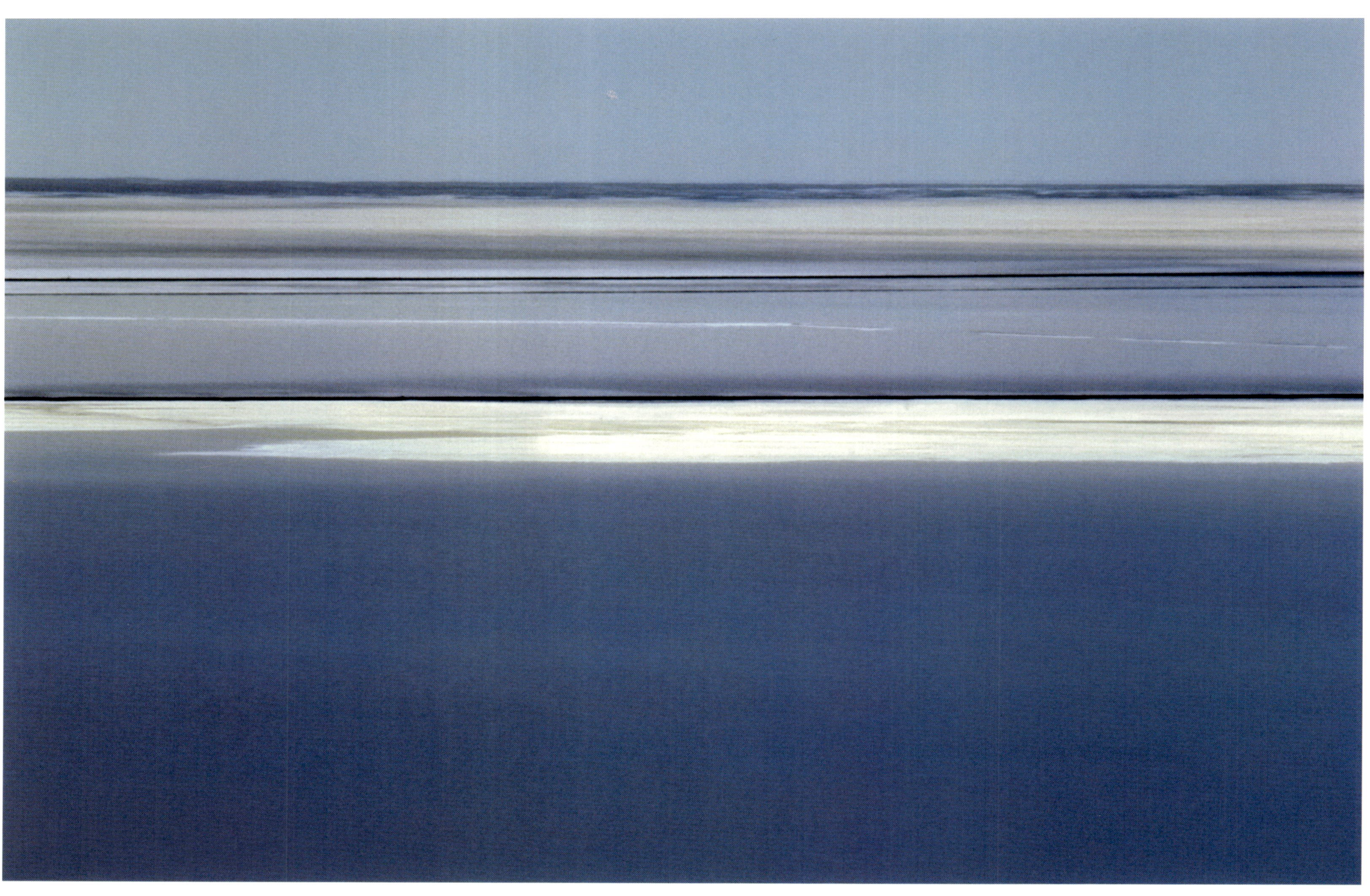

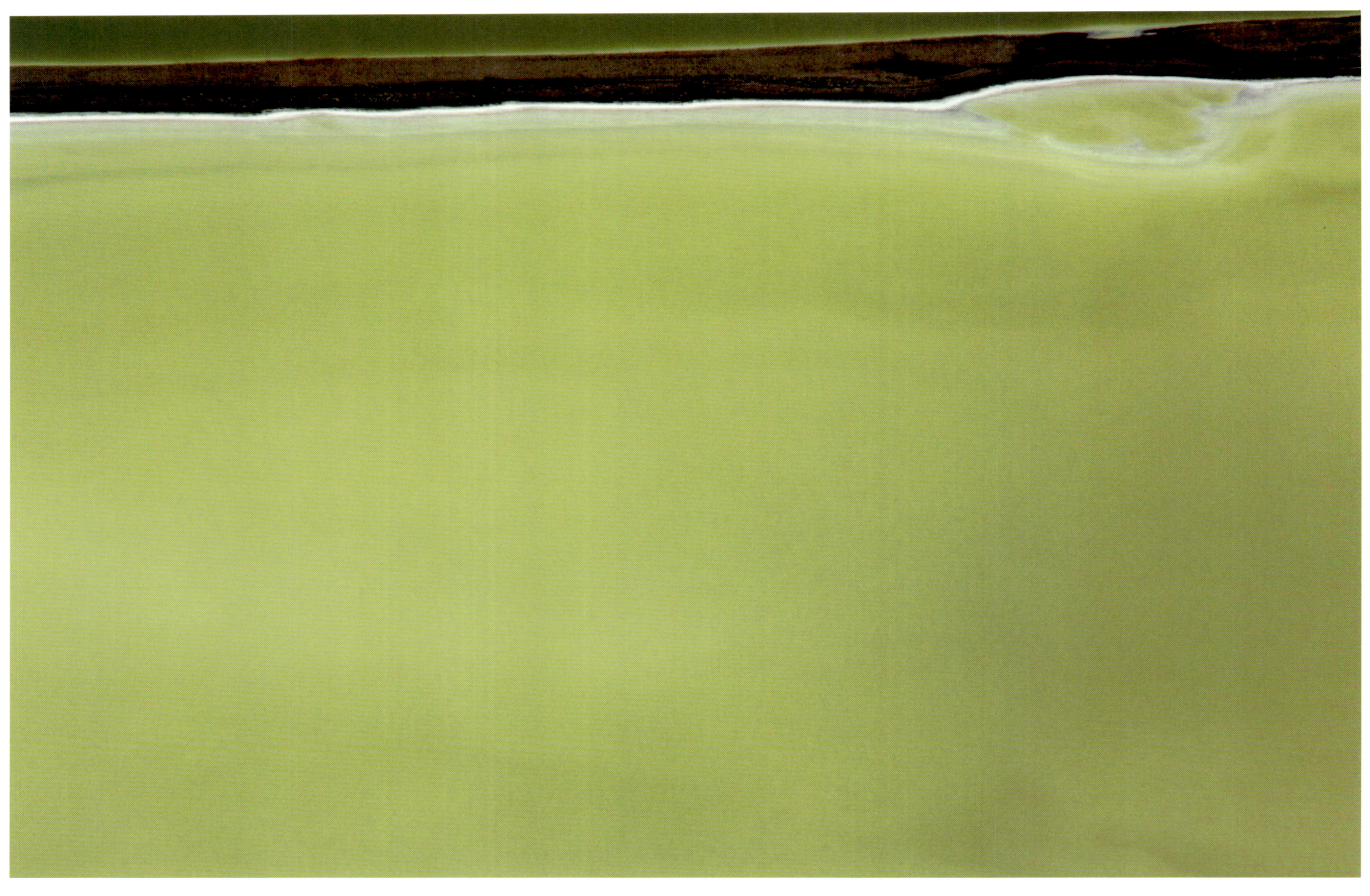

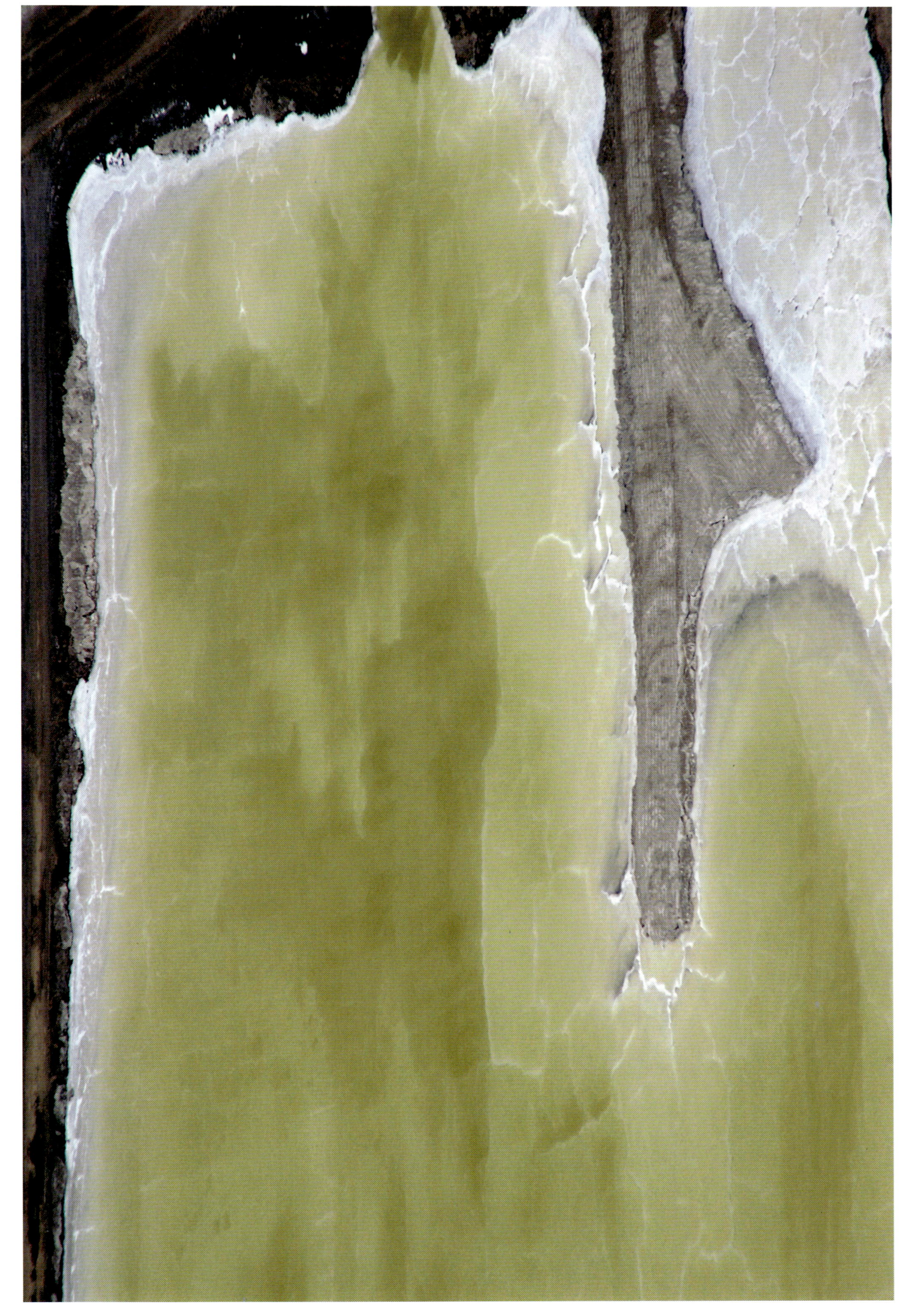

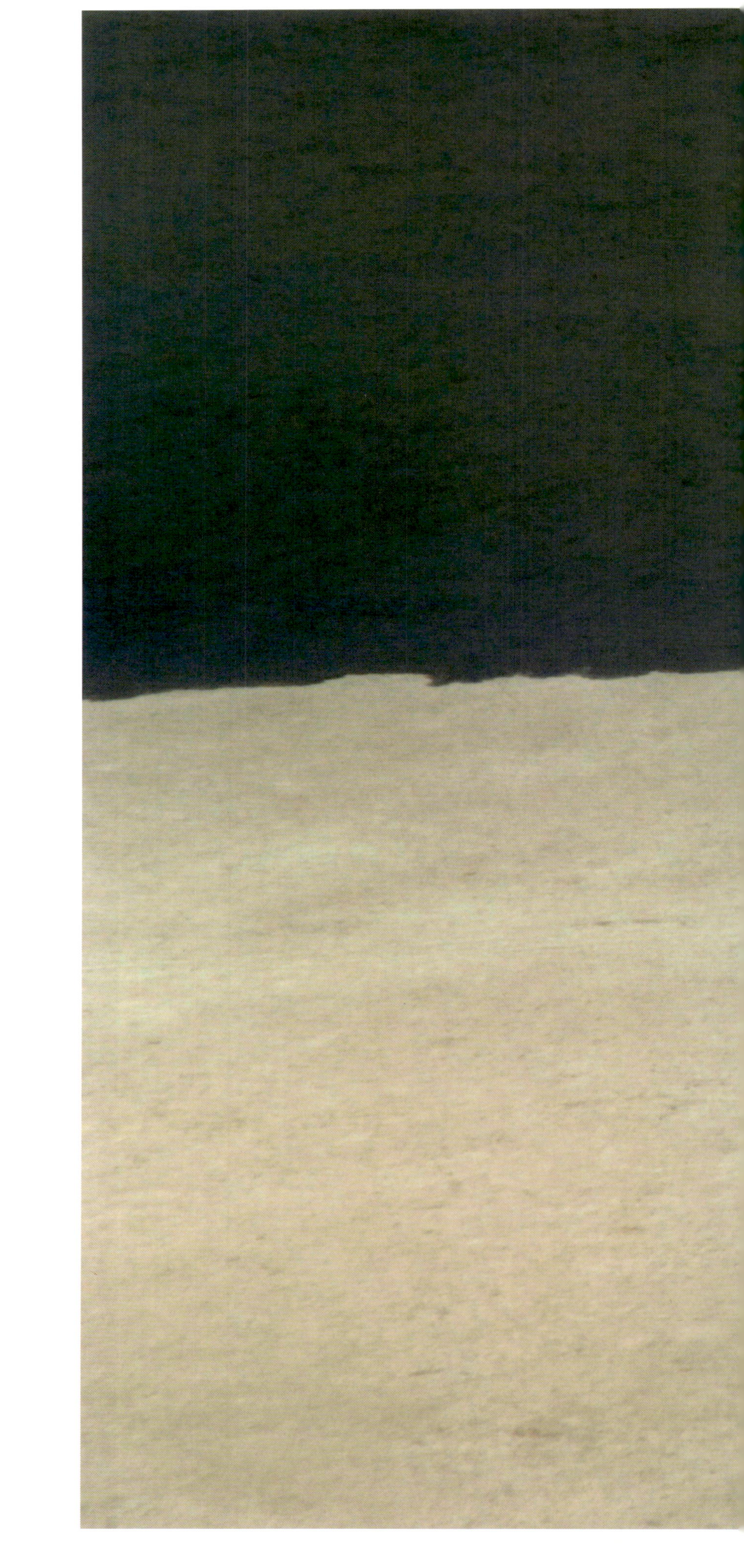

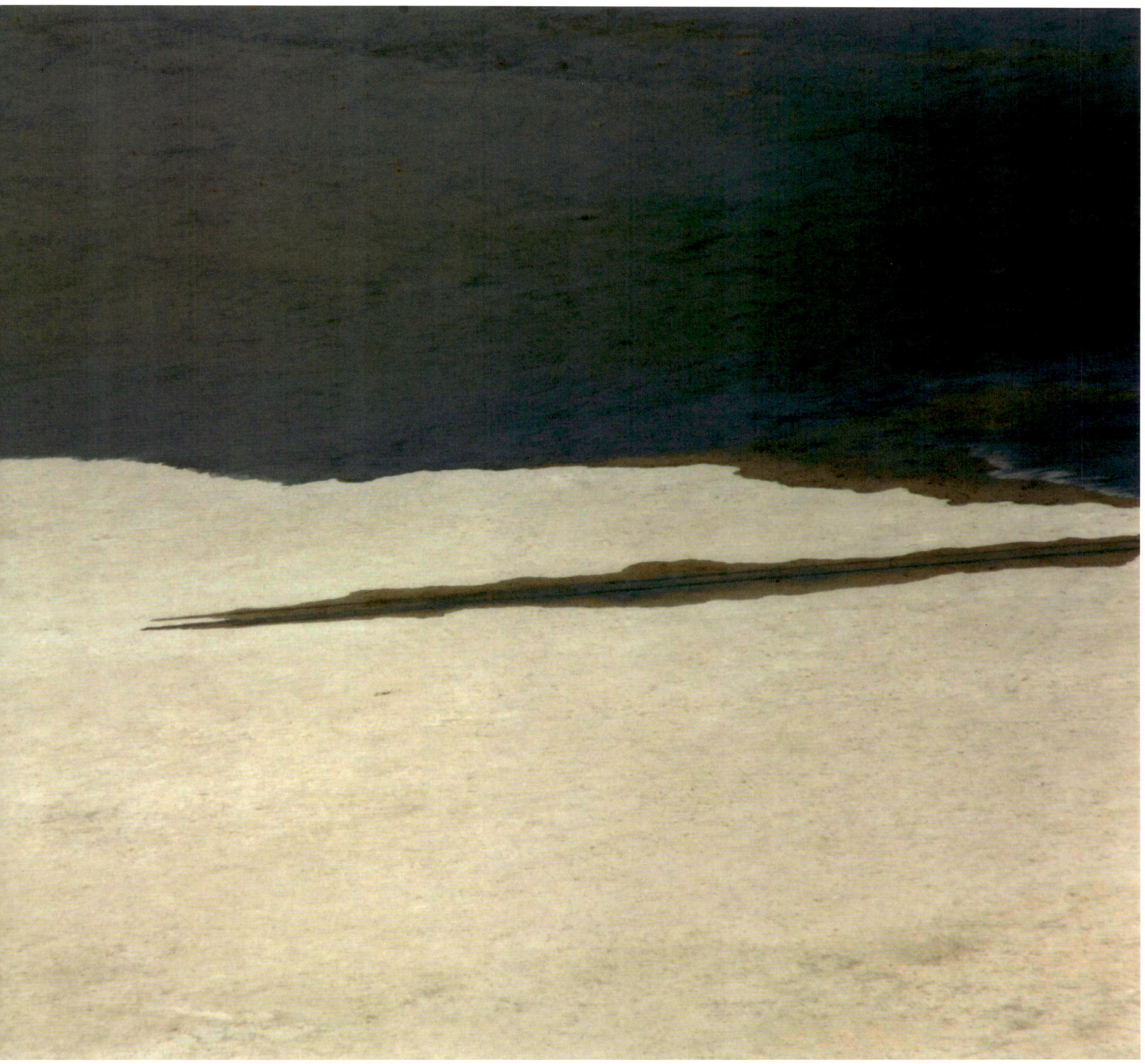

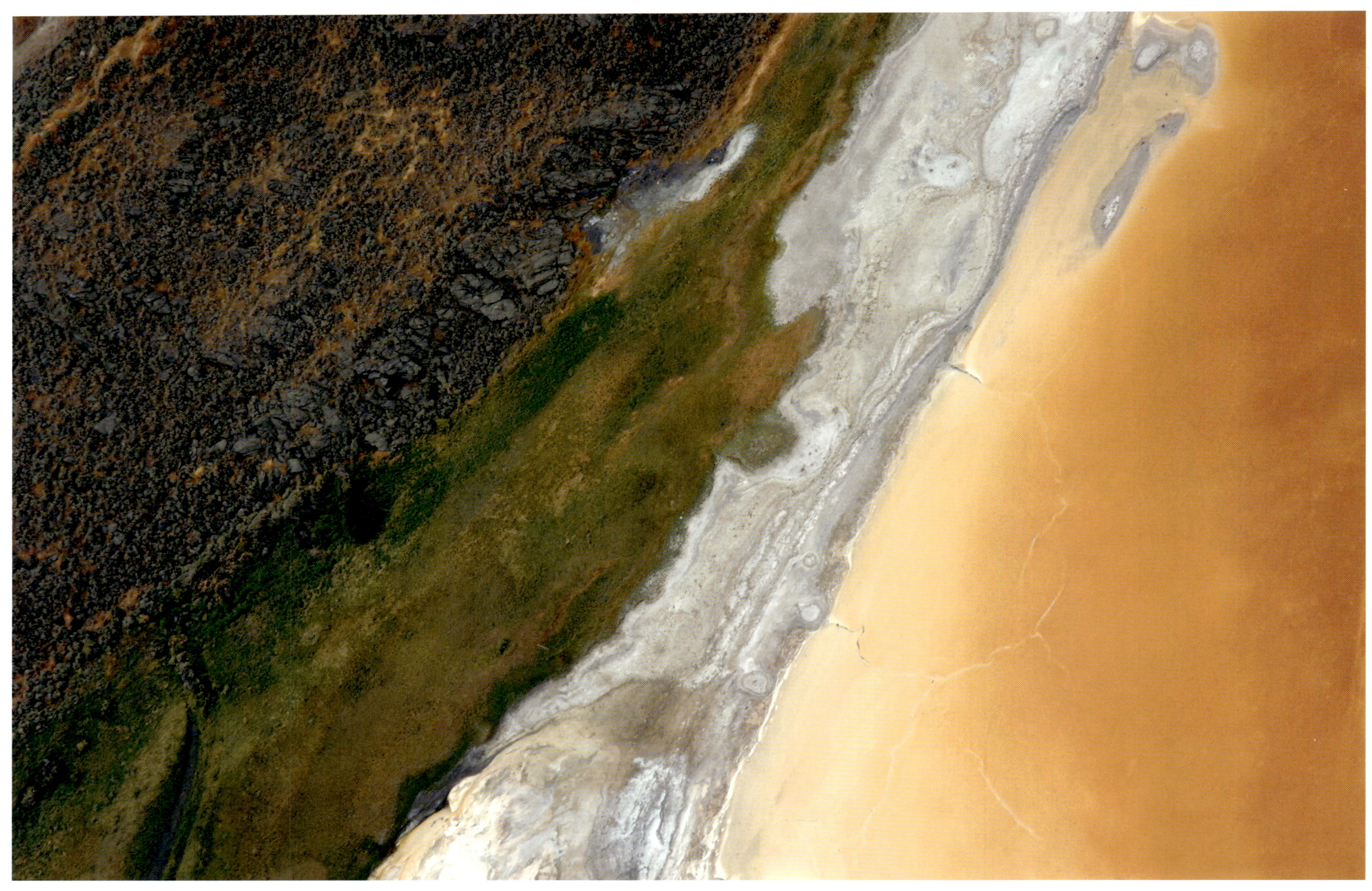

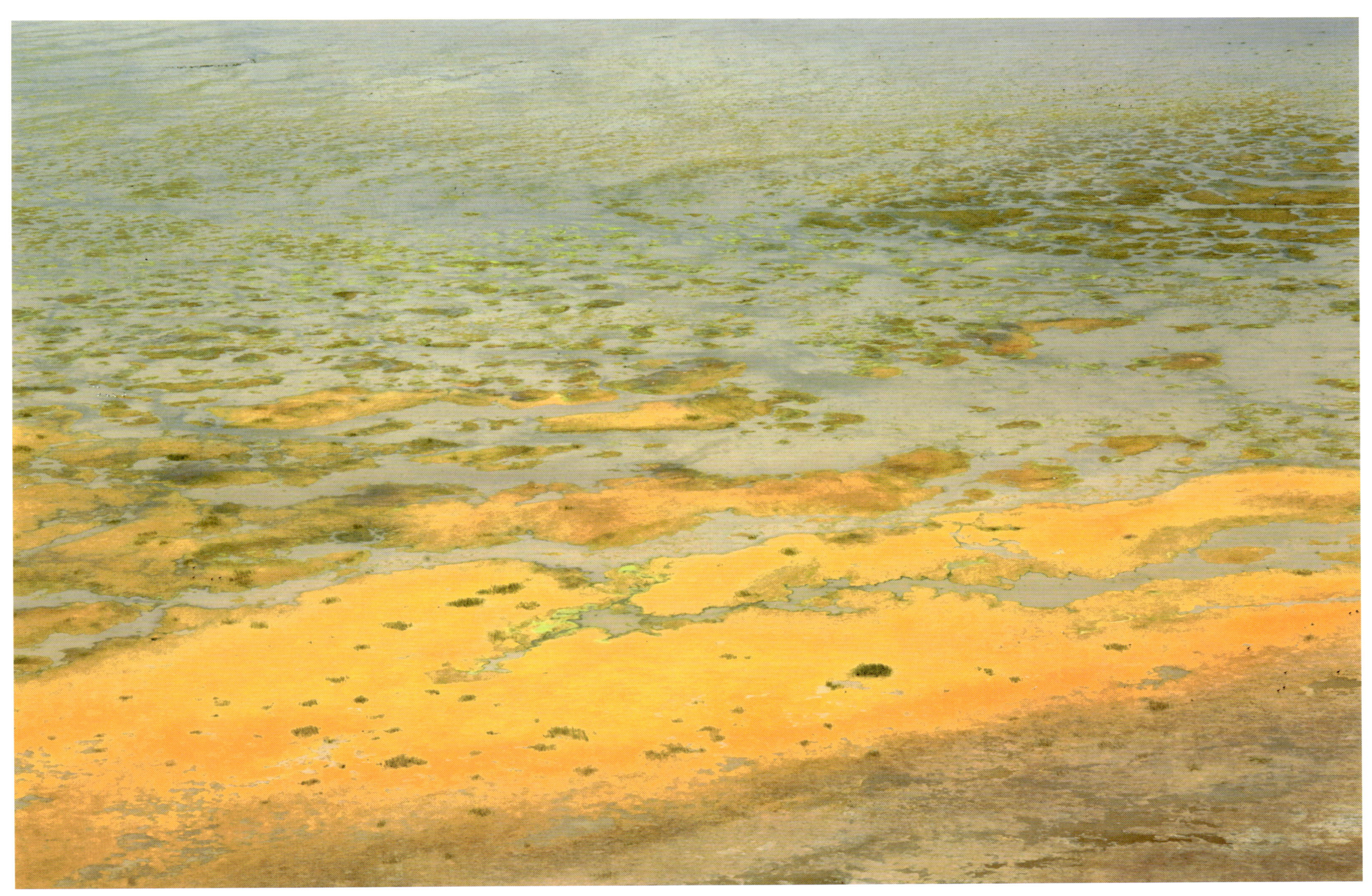

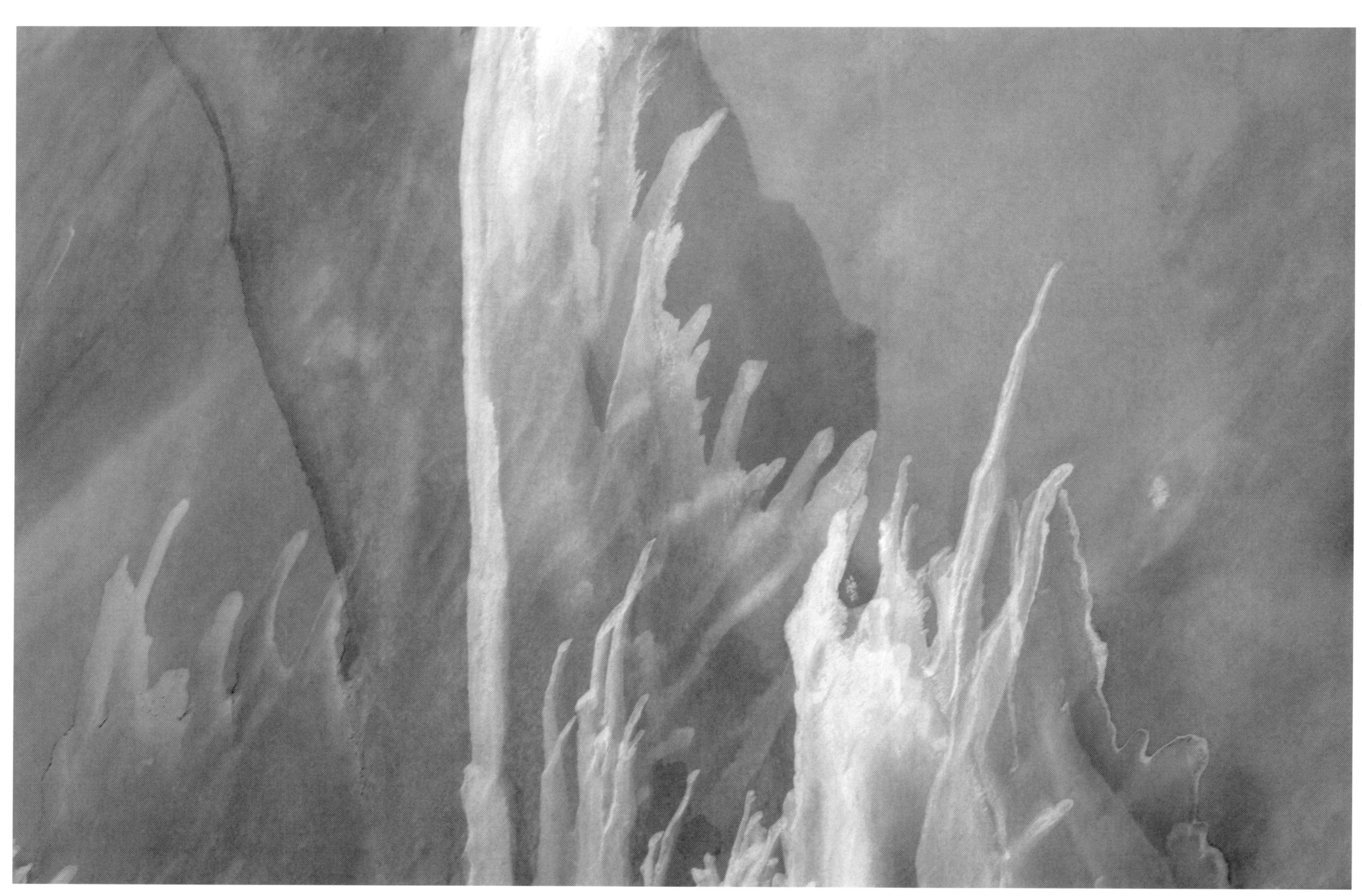

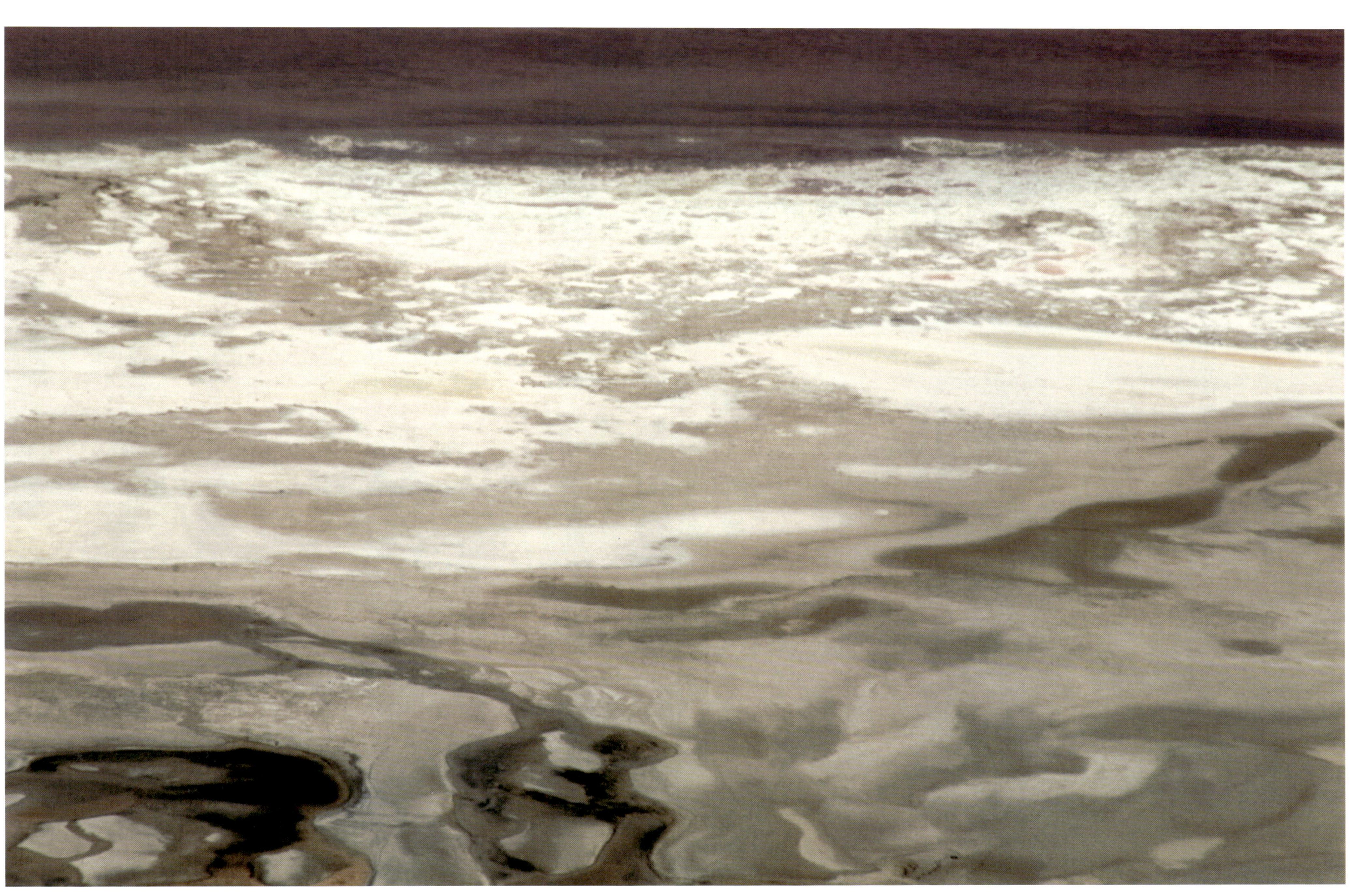

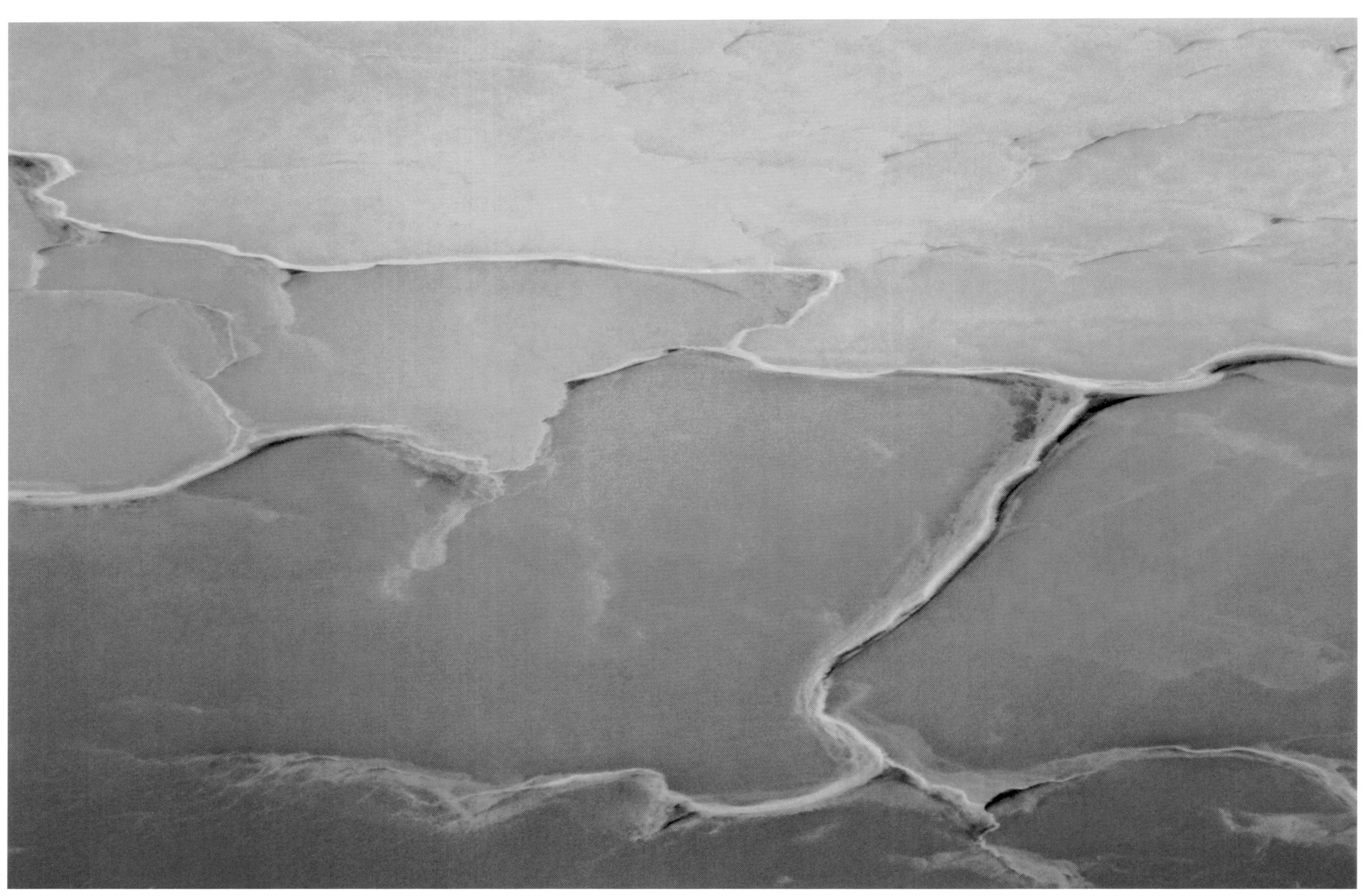

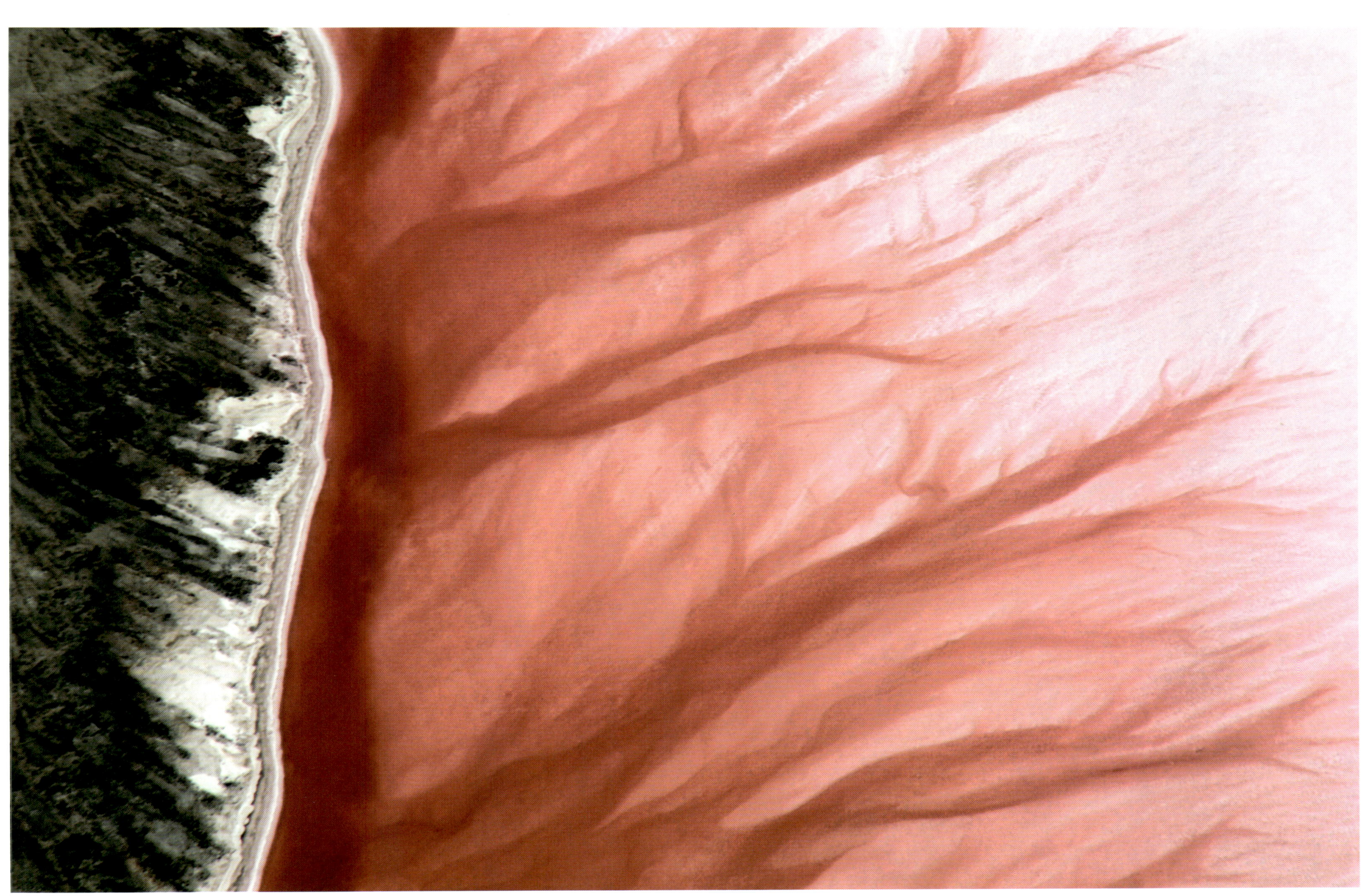

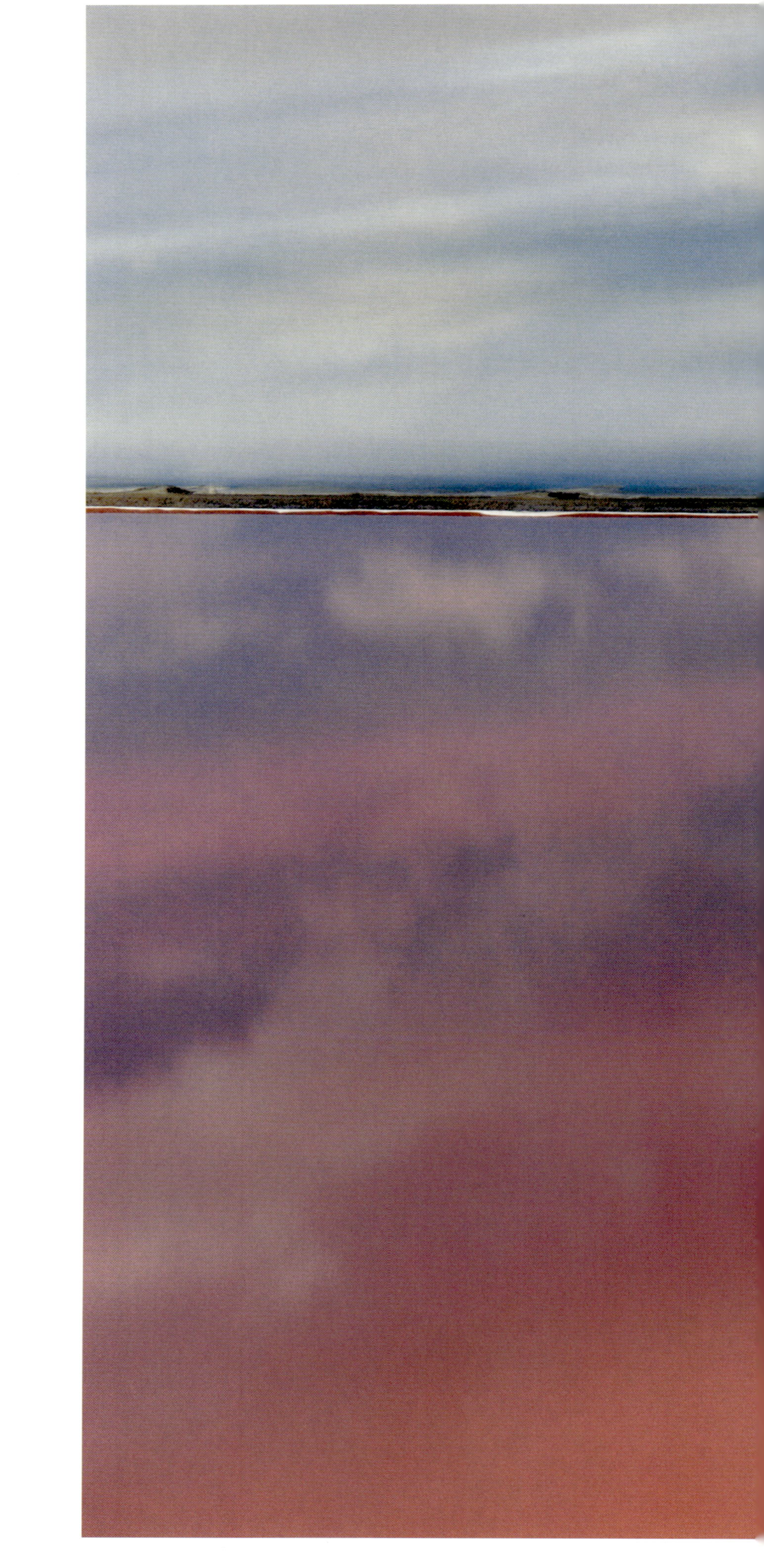

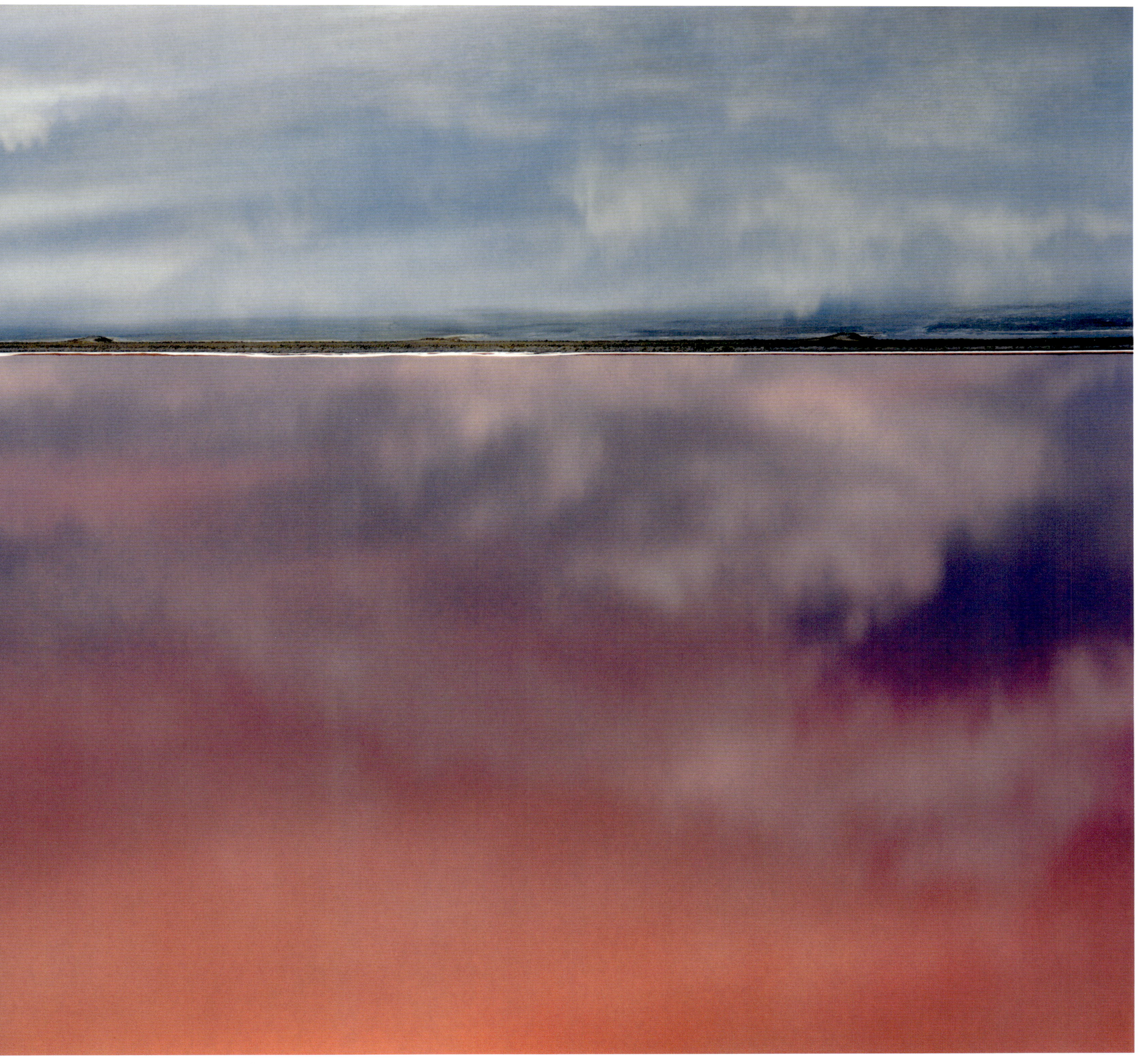

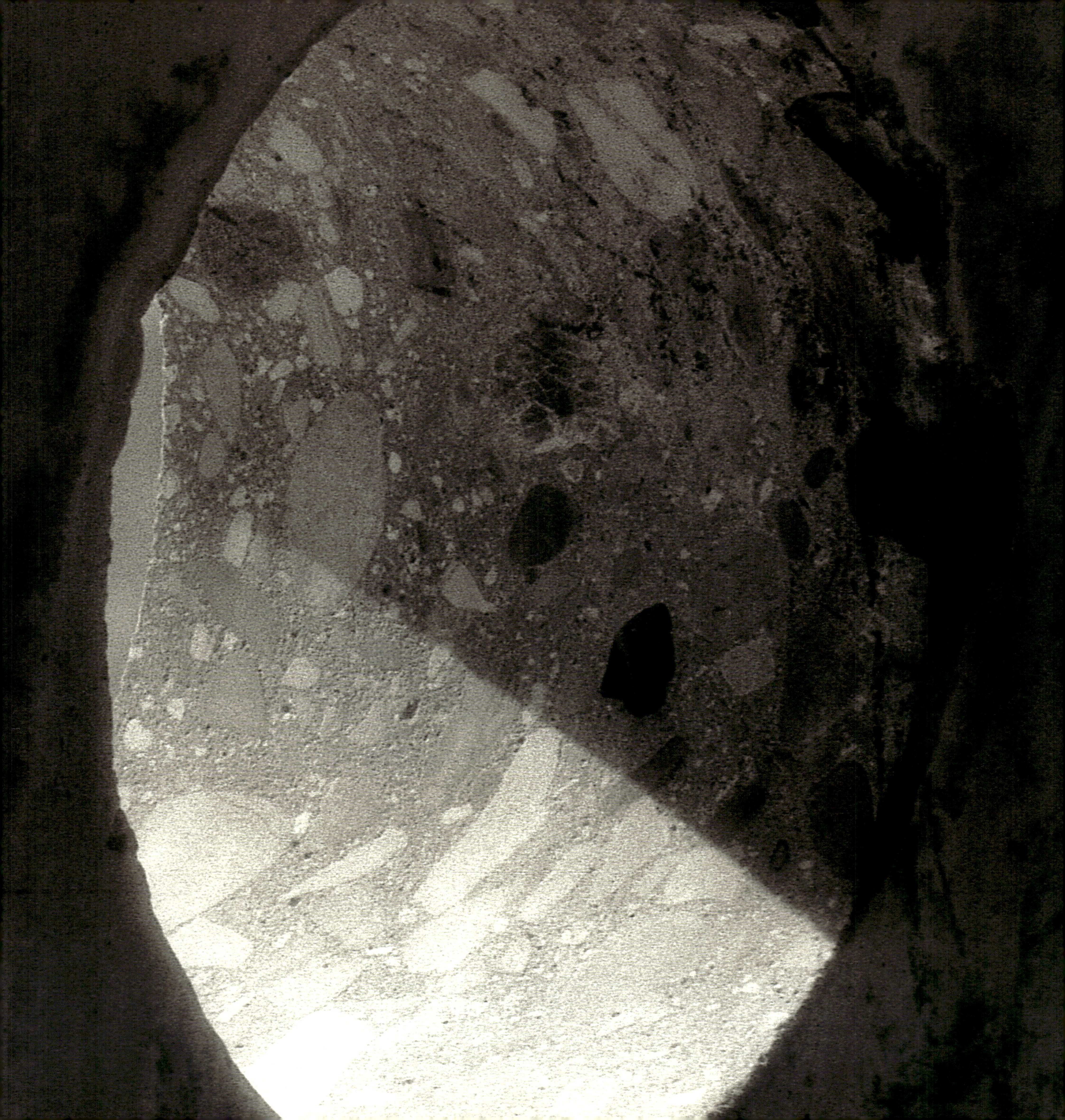

Extreme environments with intense light are among the places where the ends of the spectrum are more easily apprehended. The deserts of the American Southwest, in particular the highest of those, the Great Basin of Nevada and Utah, have attracted photographers working in infrared. But imaging earthworks in that light is perhaps unique to Tuft, and her pictures of Nancy Holt's "Sun Tunnels," constructed in 1976, reveal aspects of the sculpture that we don't normally notice. The four large concrete tubes are splayed open in a wide X and oriented to the sunrises and sunsets of the winter and summer solstices. Holes of varying size are aligned with stars of varying magnitude in constellations above the horizon at those times of the year. In person the sculpture is large yet modest, even stark, but in the photos, given the increased contrast of the infrared film, the apertures large and small become rich with surface details, the now-visible matrix of the concrete like its own universe of signs and symbols. Tuft's photographs are among the most striking images made of this earthwork.

"Spiral Jetty," by Robert Smithson, Holt's deceased husband, is located across the Great Salt Lake from "Sun Tunnels" and is another iconic earthwork: a 1500-foot-long spiral bulldozed out into the brine. The dark basaltic rocks were encrusted with salt after years of immersion and subsequent resurfacing during the current drought. Tuft's photos—many of them again close-ups, this time of salt instead of ice—often provide no clue to scale. The rivulets of wet salt amongst the rocks could be glaciers winding between mountain peaks, showing us why the work attracts the lingering attention of visitors. While it is usually the large-scale gesture at "Spiral Jetty" that we first perceive, when walking on the rocks we're drawn increasingly to the complexities and subtleties of the intimate scale. We walk with our heads down to examine these miniature valleys, versus walking with our heads up to gaze up at the horizon.

sun tunnels

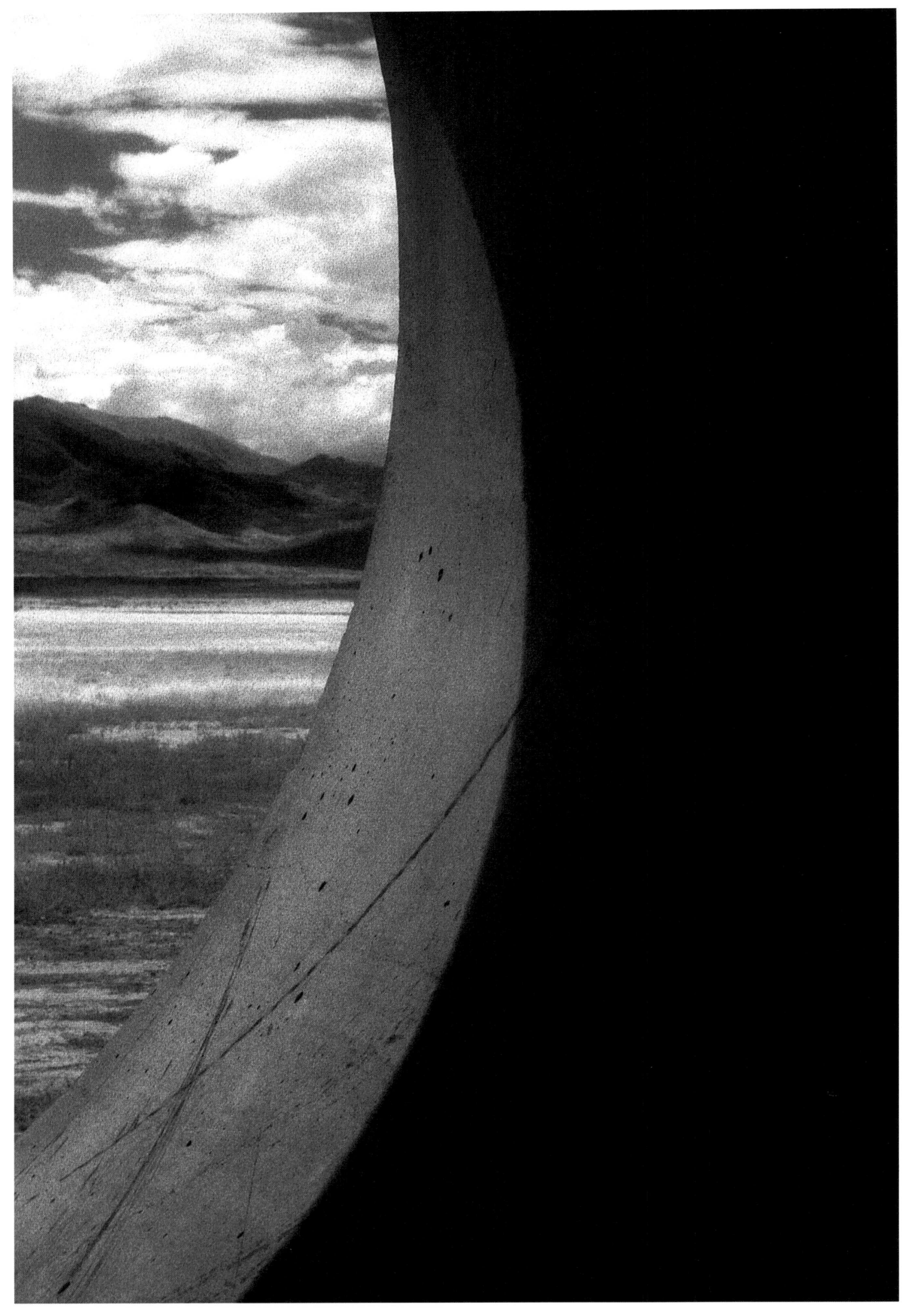

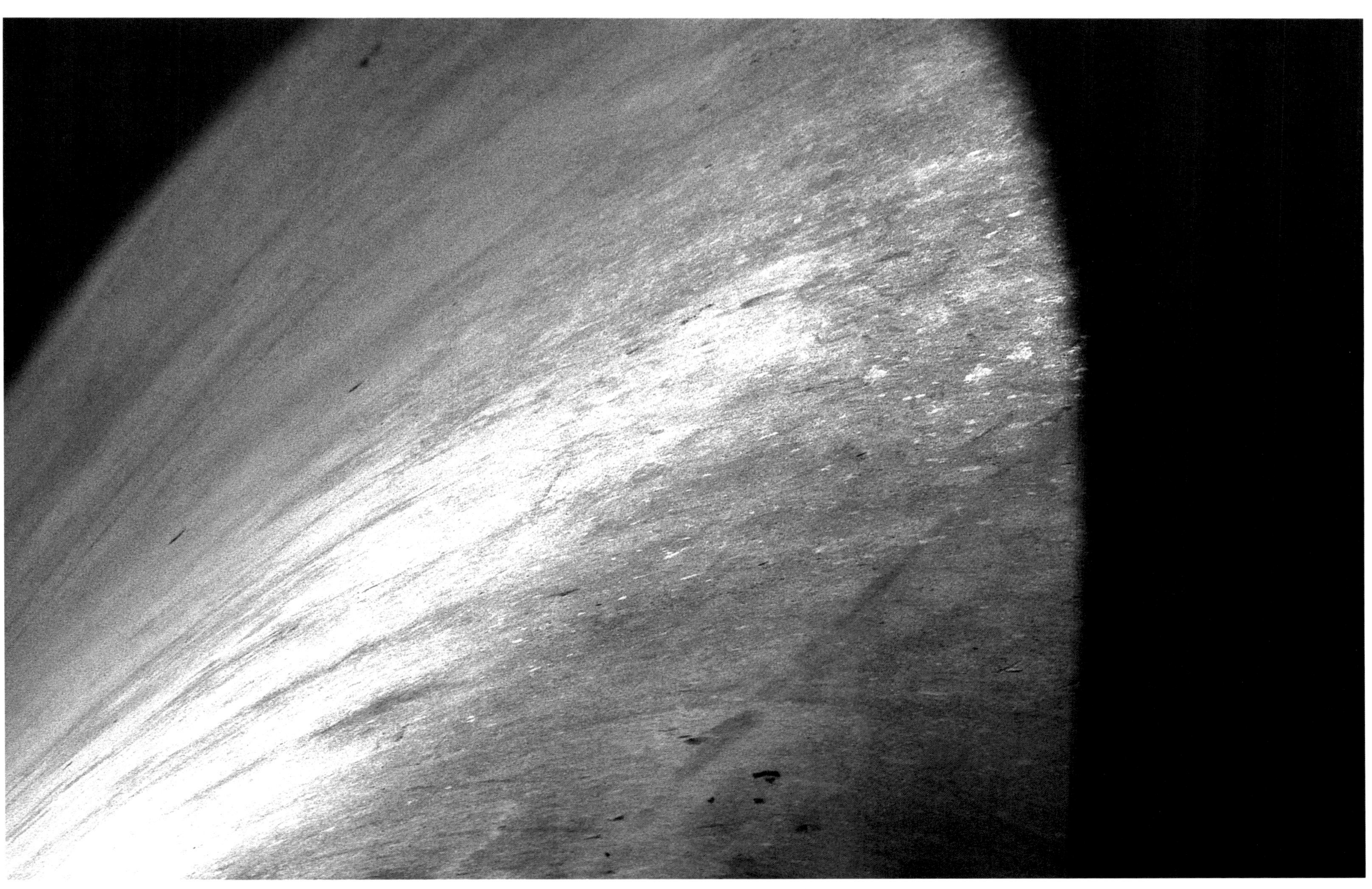

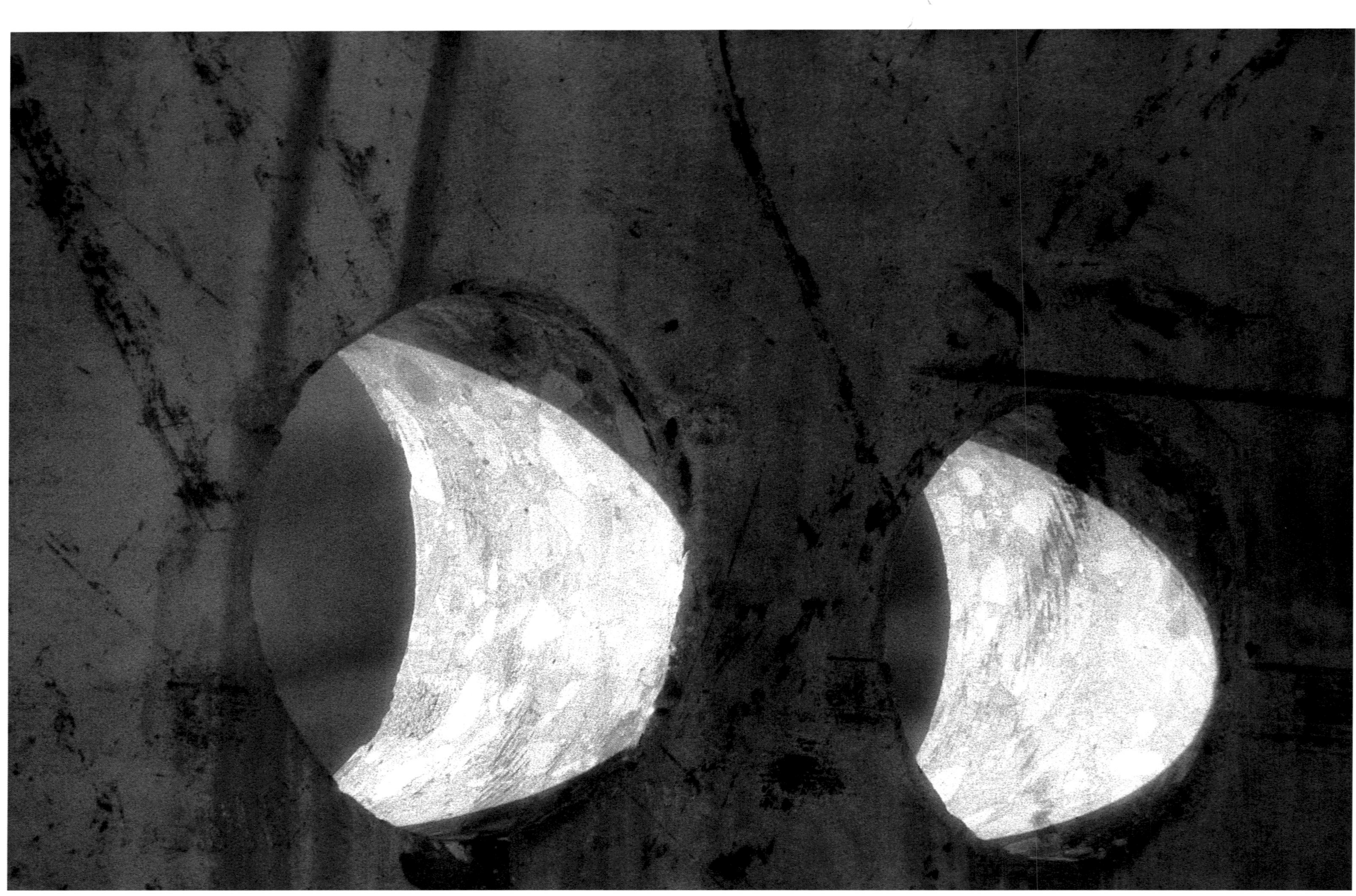

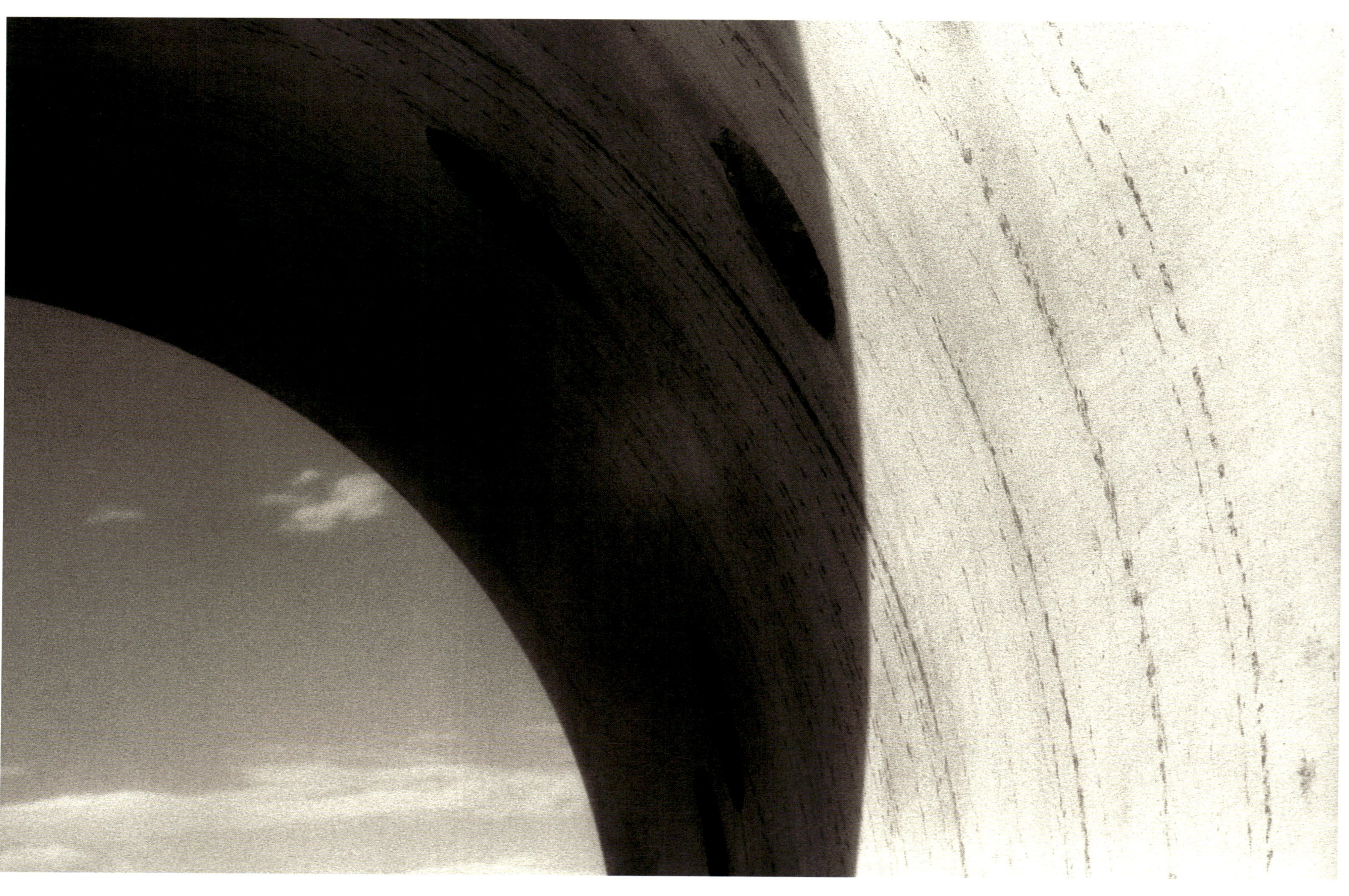

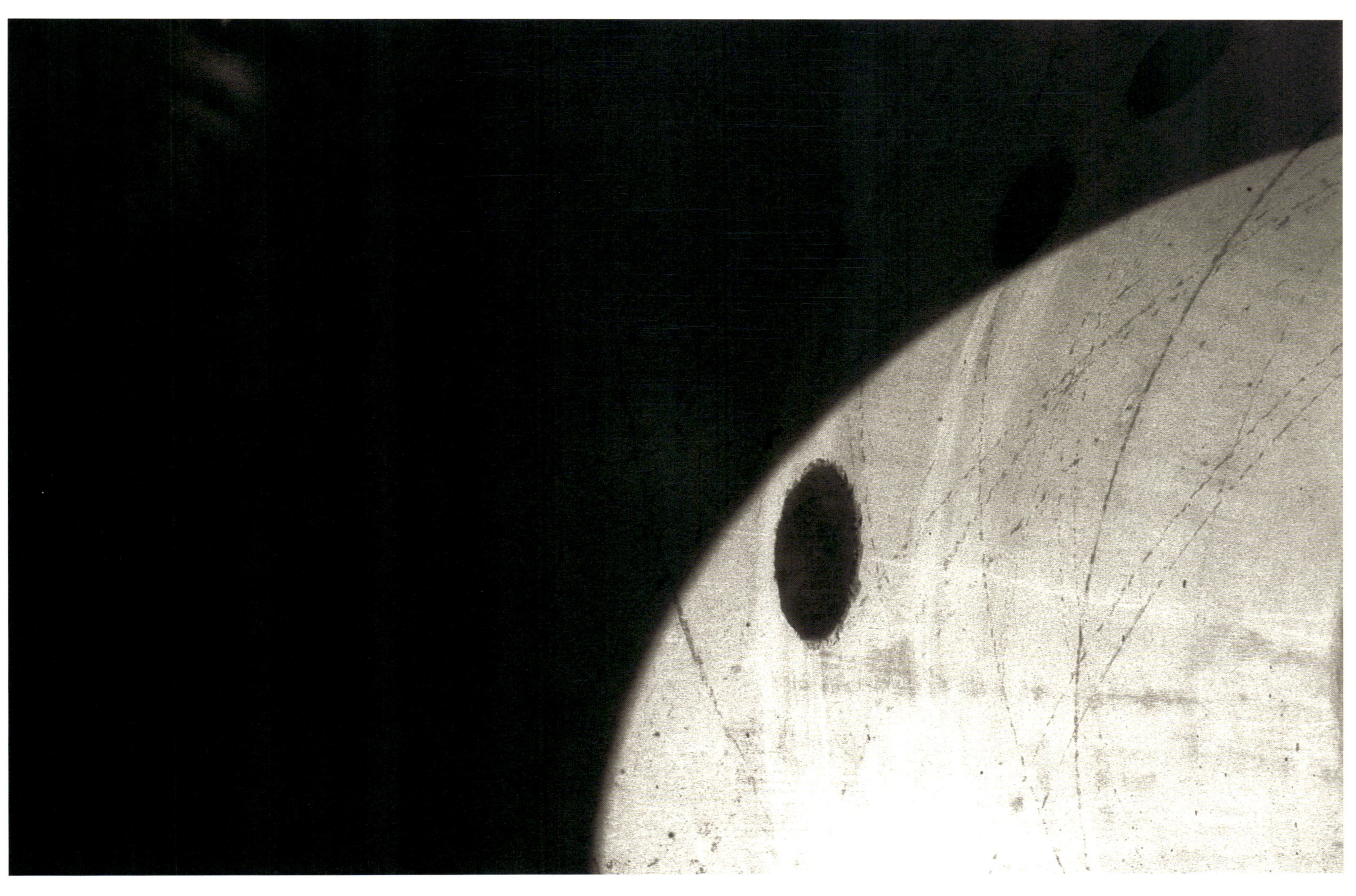

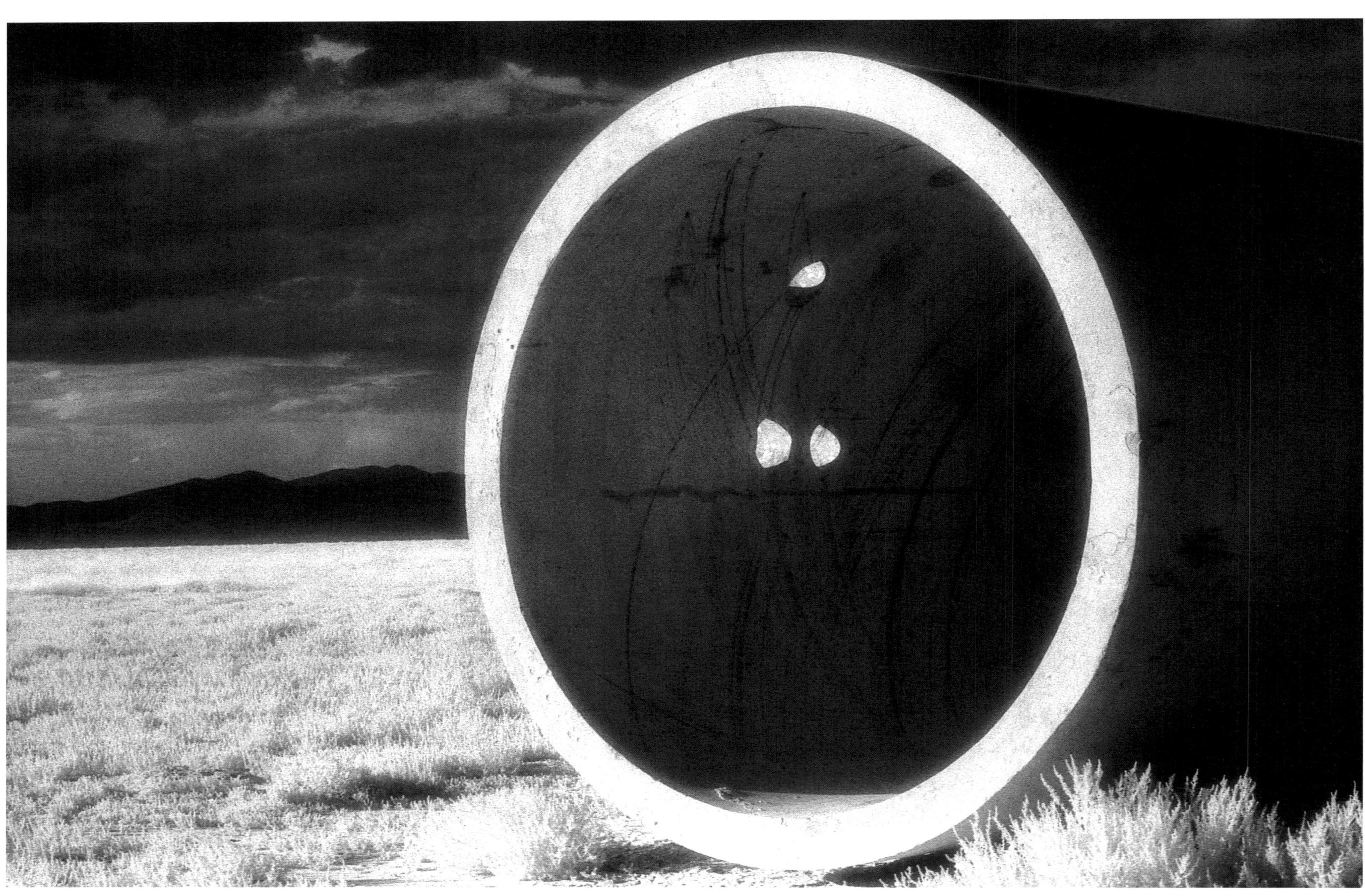

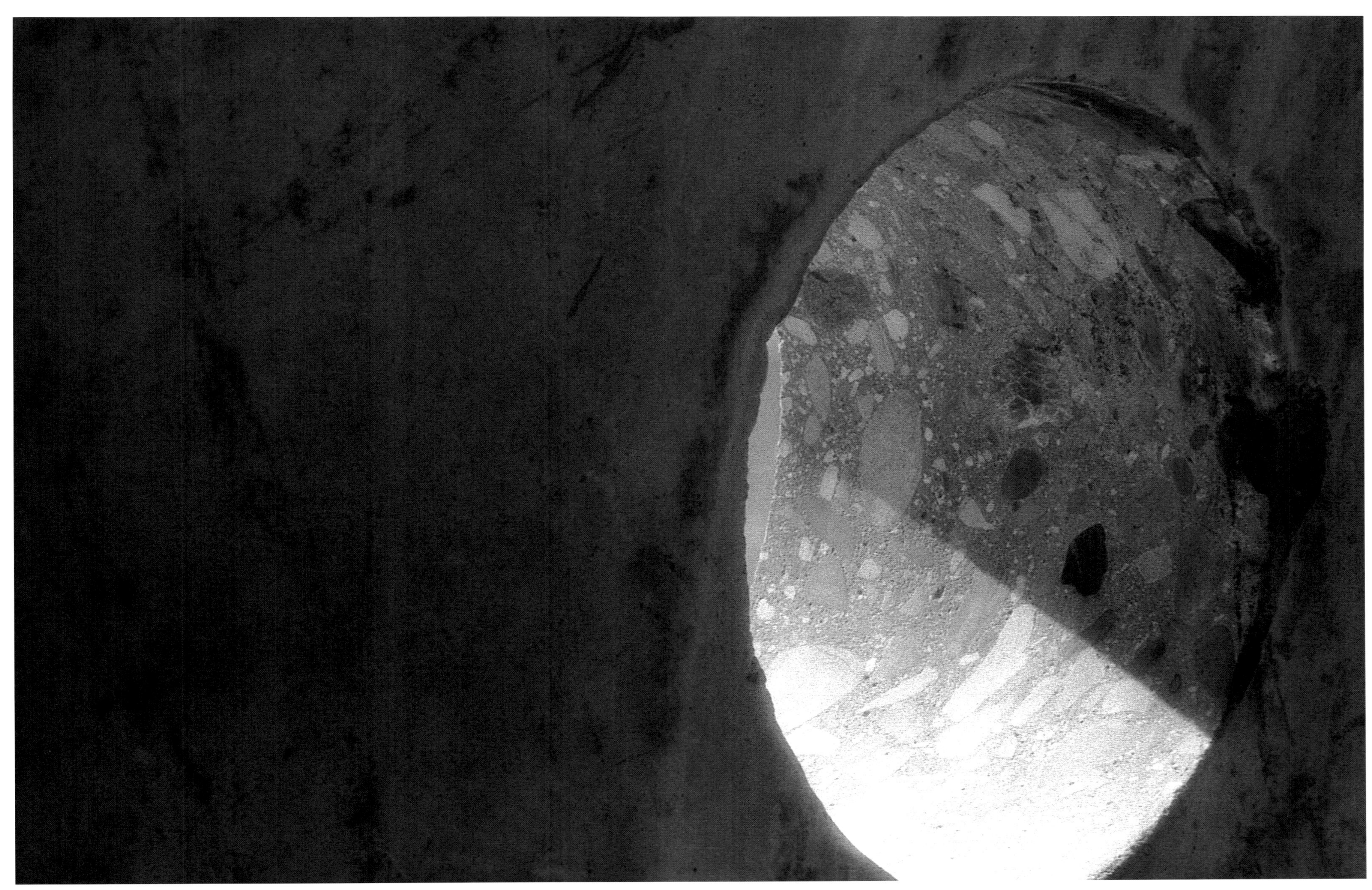

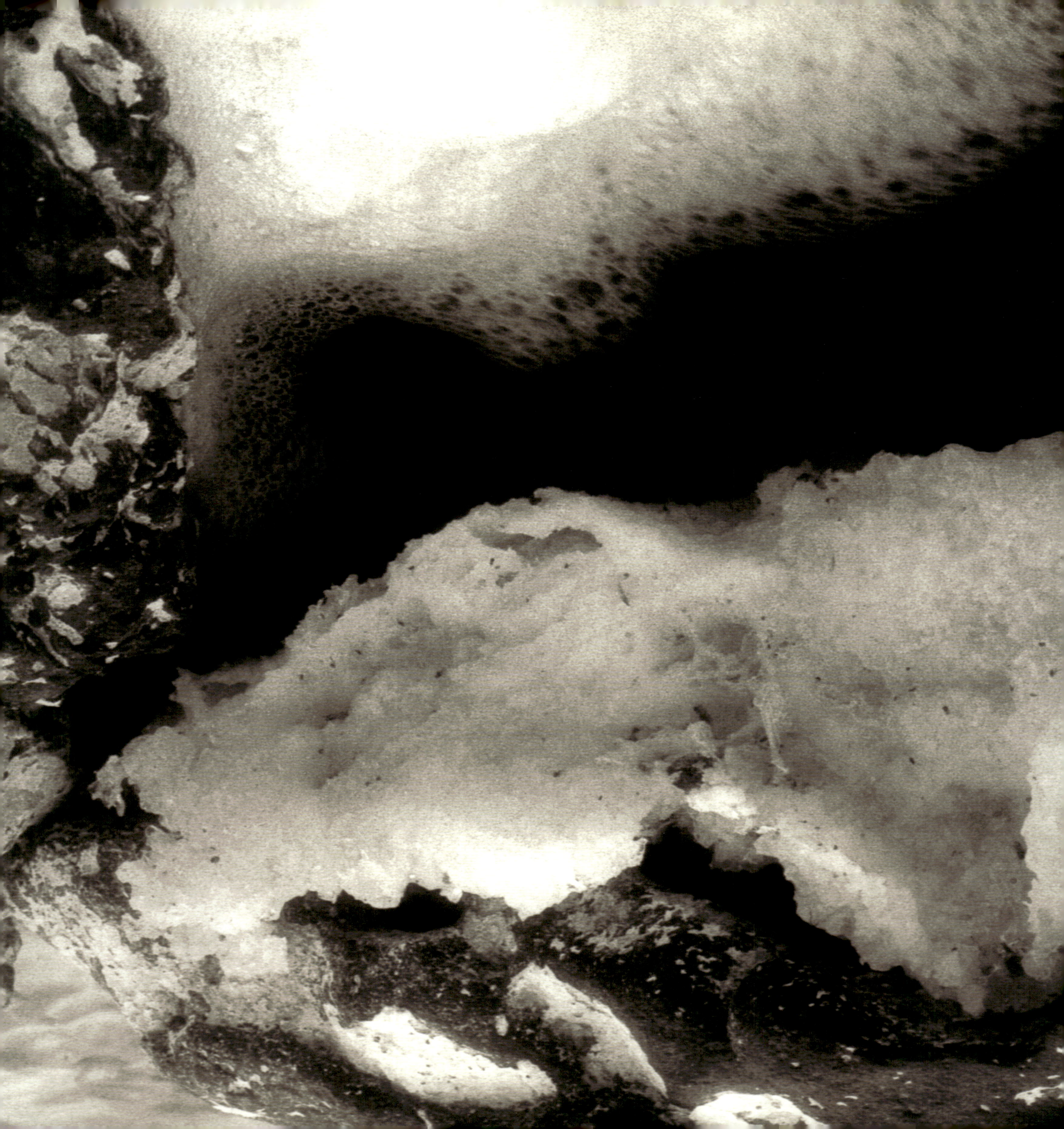

Photographers have gone to the ends of the Earth ever since the invention of photographic technology; artists traveled up the Nile to reach a geographical and historical terminus within six months of Daguerre's announcement in 1839. As the world has become ever more altered by humans, an increasing number of artists have taken to our harshest environments, places where the evidence of our presence is minimized, in order to test the limits of what we can see. Iceland and Greenland are typical, as are Namibia and the Antarctic, both destinations in which Tuft would like to work in the future.

Likewise, artists now increasingly venture to and incorporate the leading edge of technology—another new territory to explore. Sadly, just as an increasing number of artists have recently shown interest in the outer ends of the spectrum, infrared film has been discontinued, forcing Tuft to buy up what existing stock she can find on eBay. Digital camera manufacturers are responding to the need, however, releasing models that can photograph more effectively in both IR and UV. Although the cameras are designed primarily with medical, scientific, and law enforcement needs in mind, artists, including Tuft, will be experimenting with them.

Going to extreme places—the edge of geography and the known world—and deploying technology to pass over the borders of the visible are methods old and new used by people to define the world. Tuft says that she believes "nature has more to say to us than we can understand . . . so many cultures around the world worship the landscape. Rocks are revered in Japan, trees in Iceland, rivers in India—many cultures find spiritual elements in landscape to worship. Perhaps if we use a light that we cannot see, it will explain their inner essence." Her concerns as an artist turn out to be those of the scientist and the worshiper—to discover if what we see can lead us into what we cannot, and then to ascertain the patterns common to both realms. It is no mystery, then, that she would work in the unseen spectra alongside practitioners of both science and faith. It is, in fact, her interest in science that makes such a foray possible, and her photographs a manifestation of our quest to uncover the living spirit of the universe.

spiral jetty

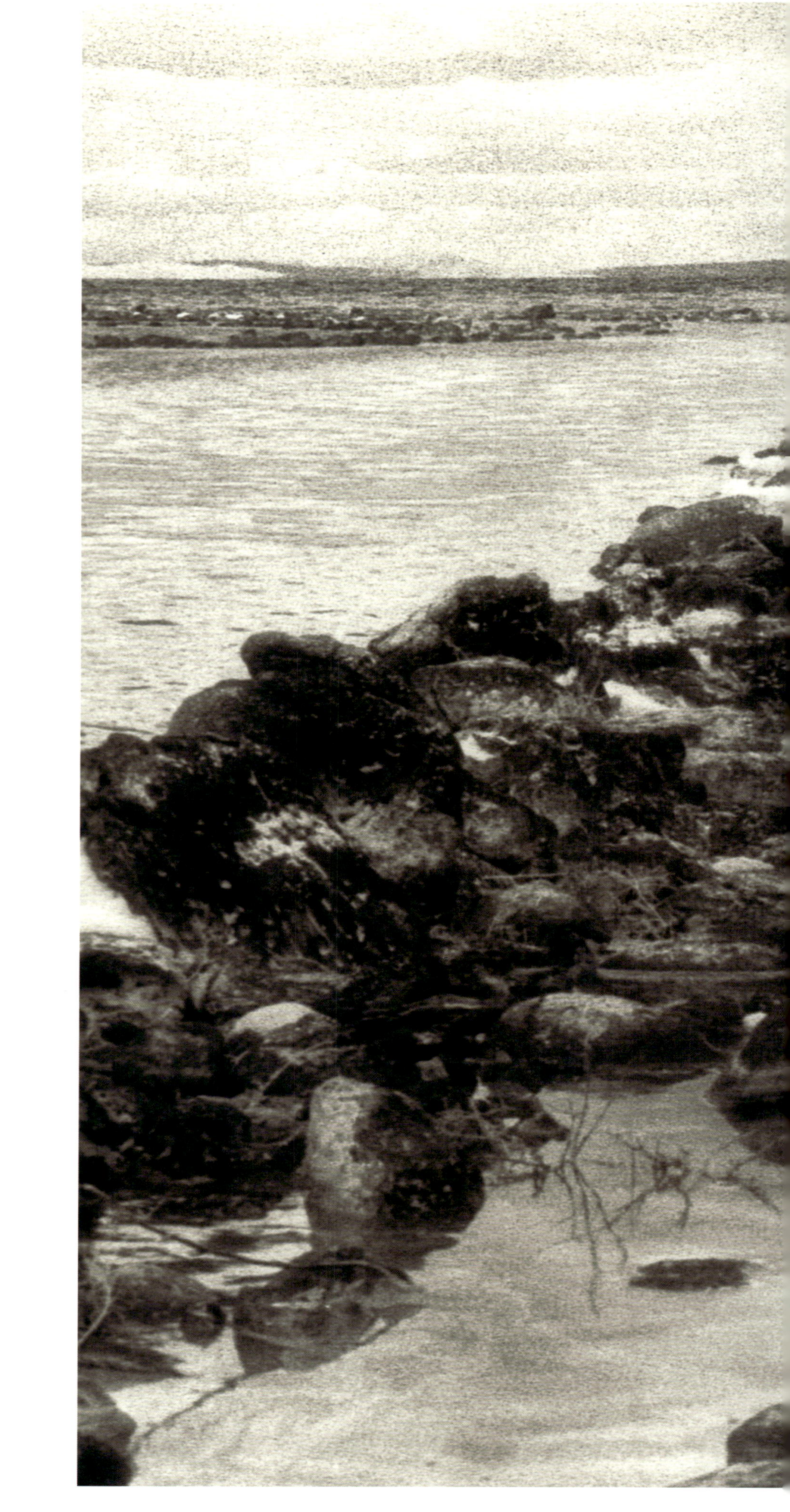

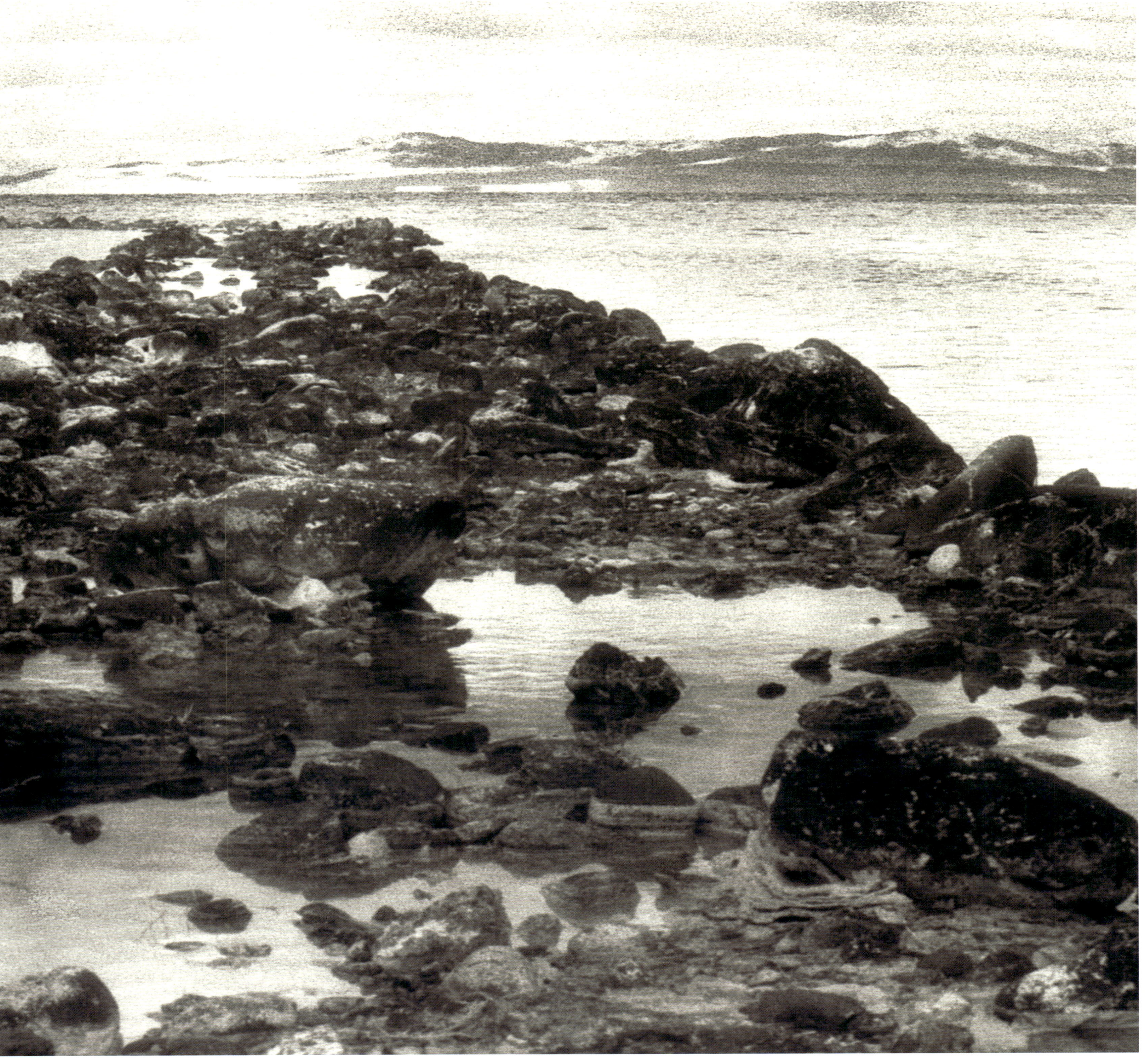

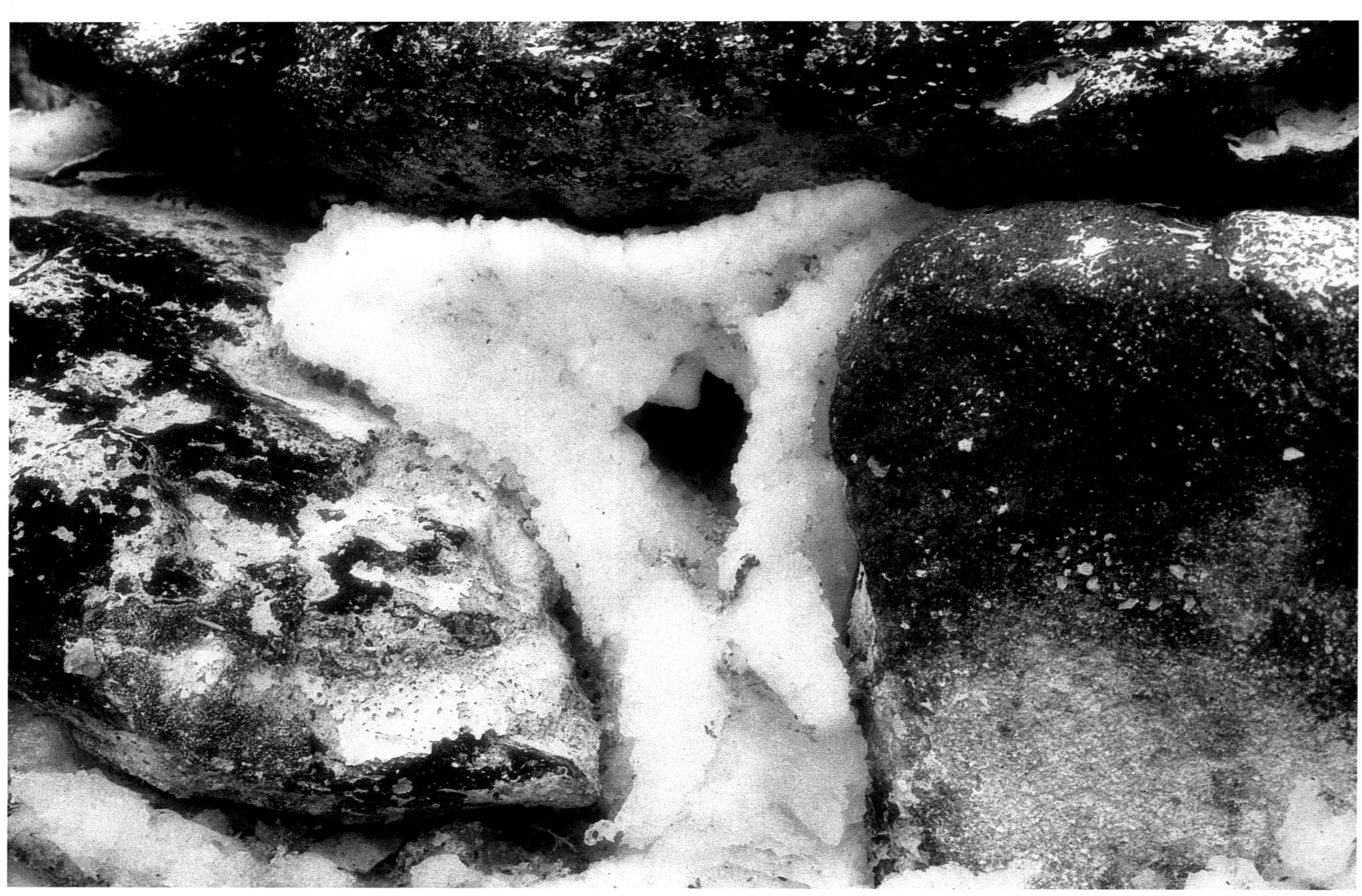

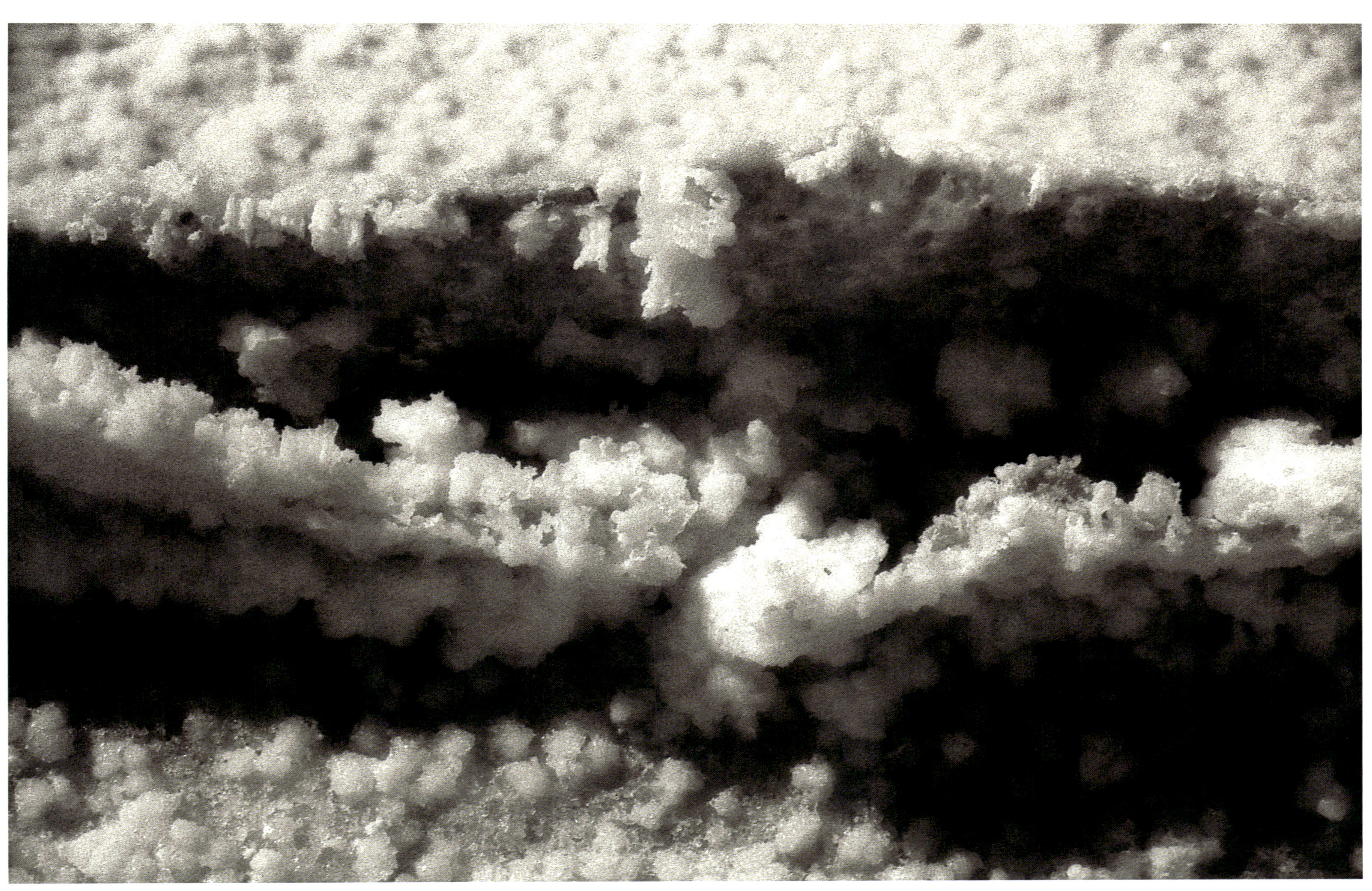

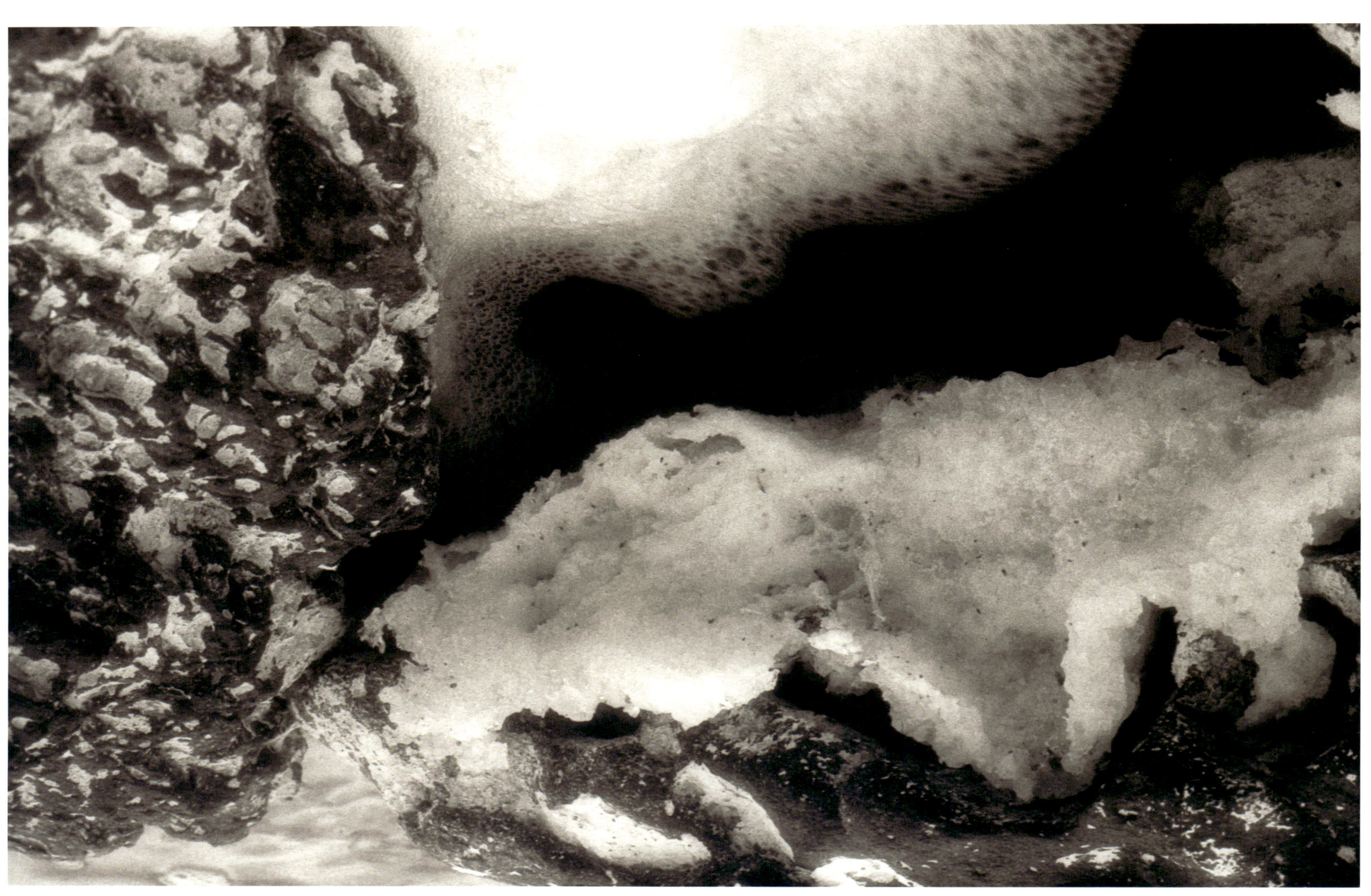

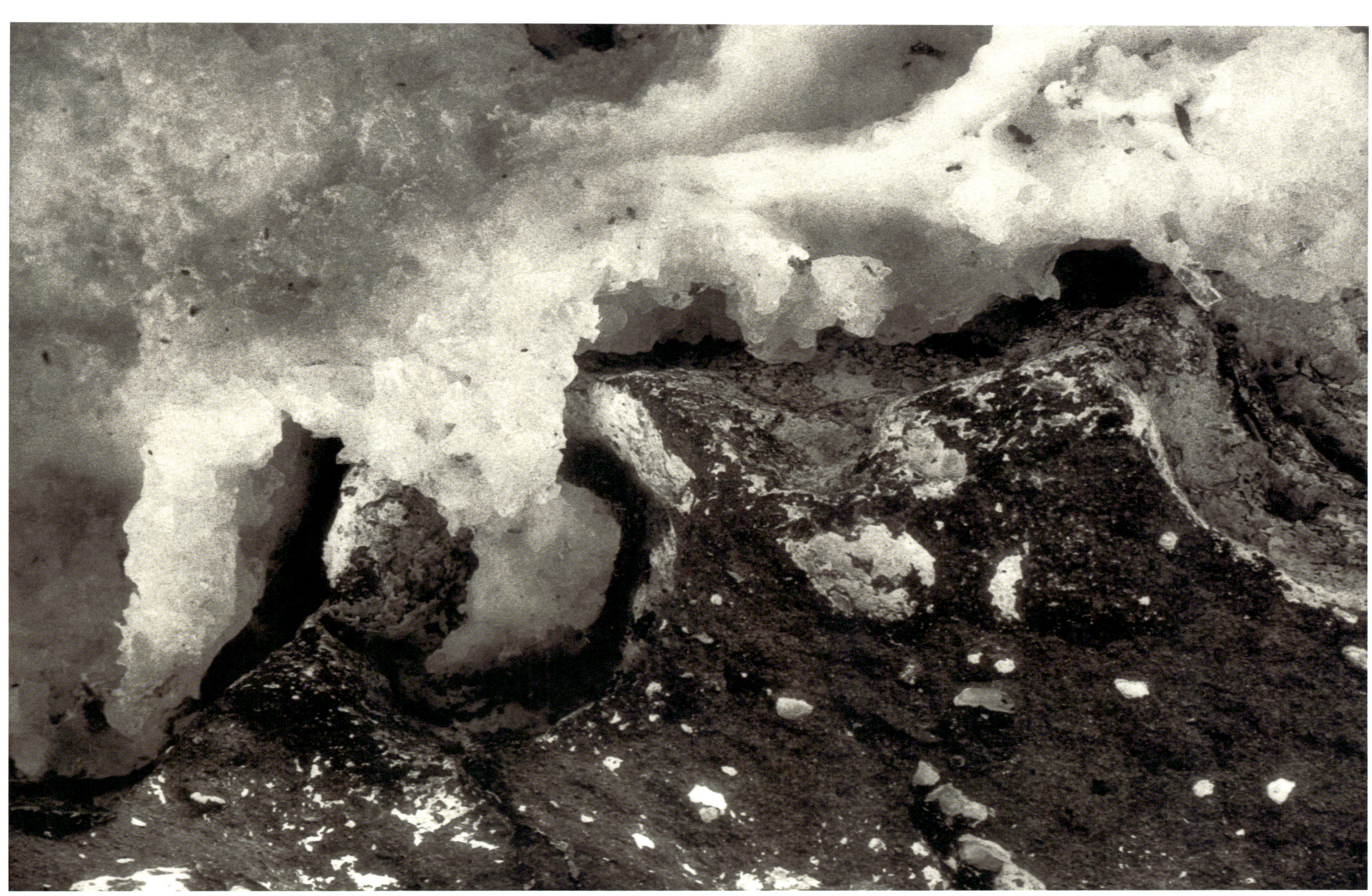

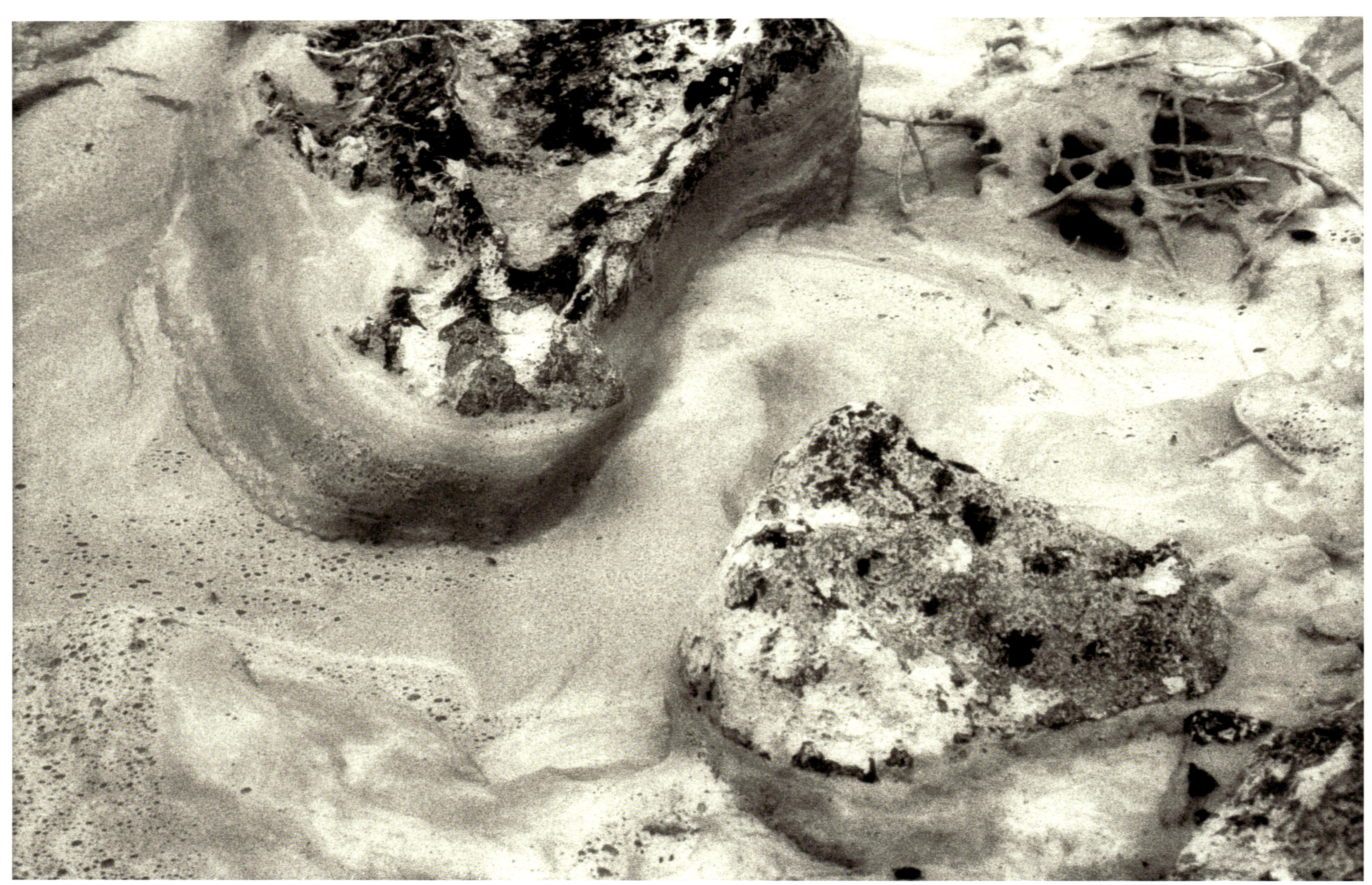

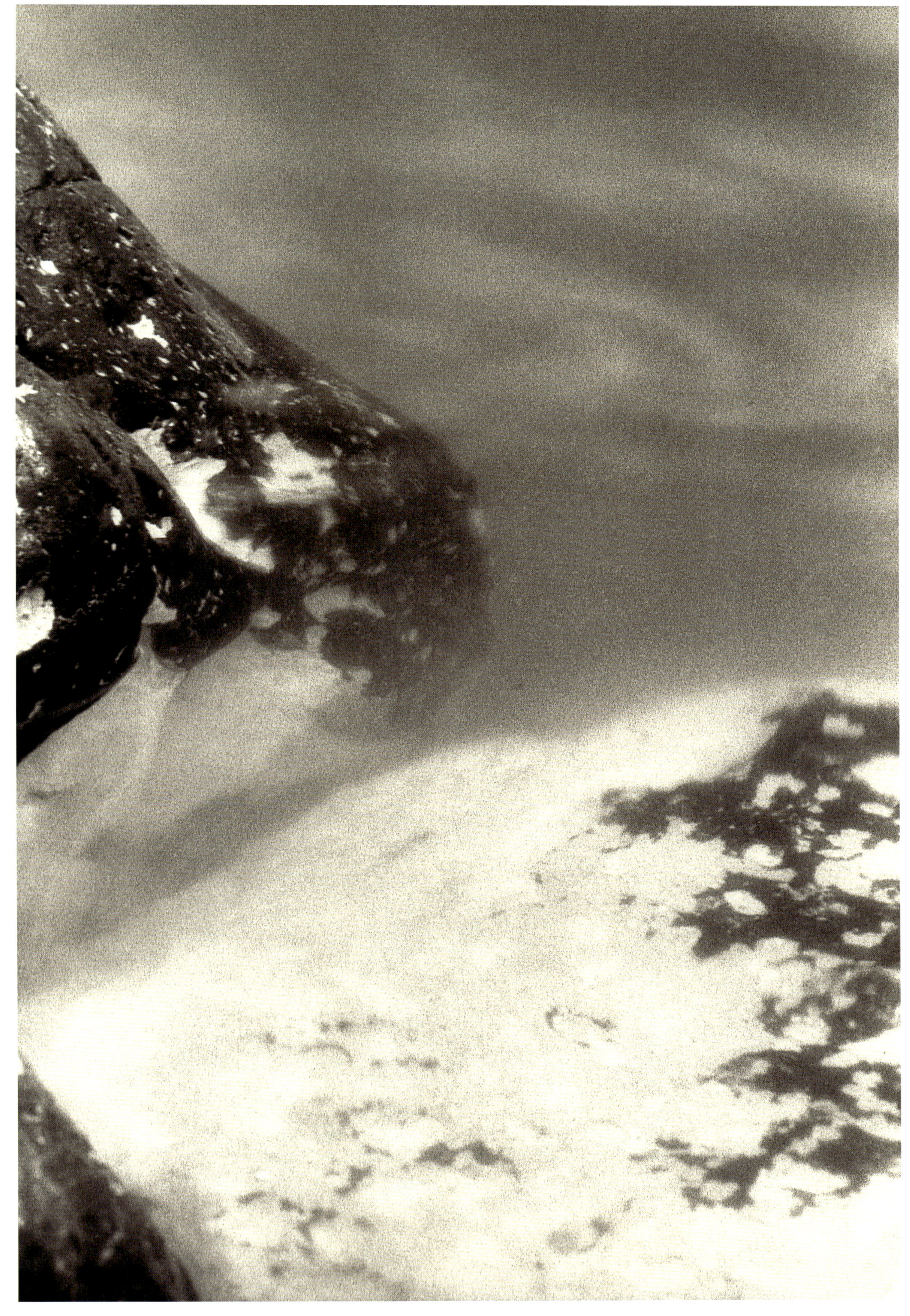

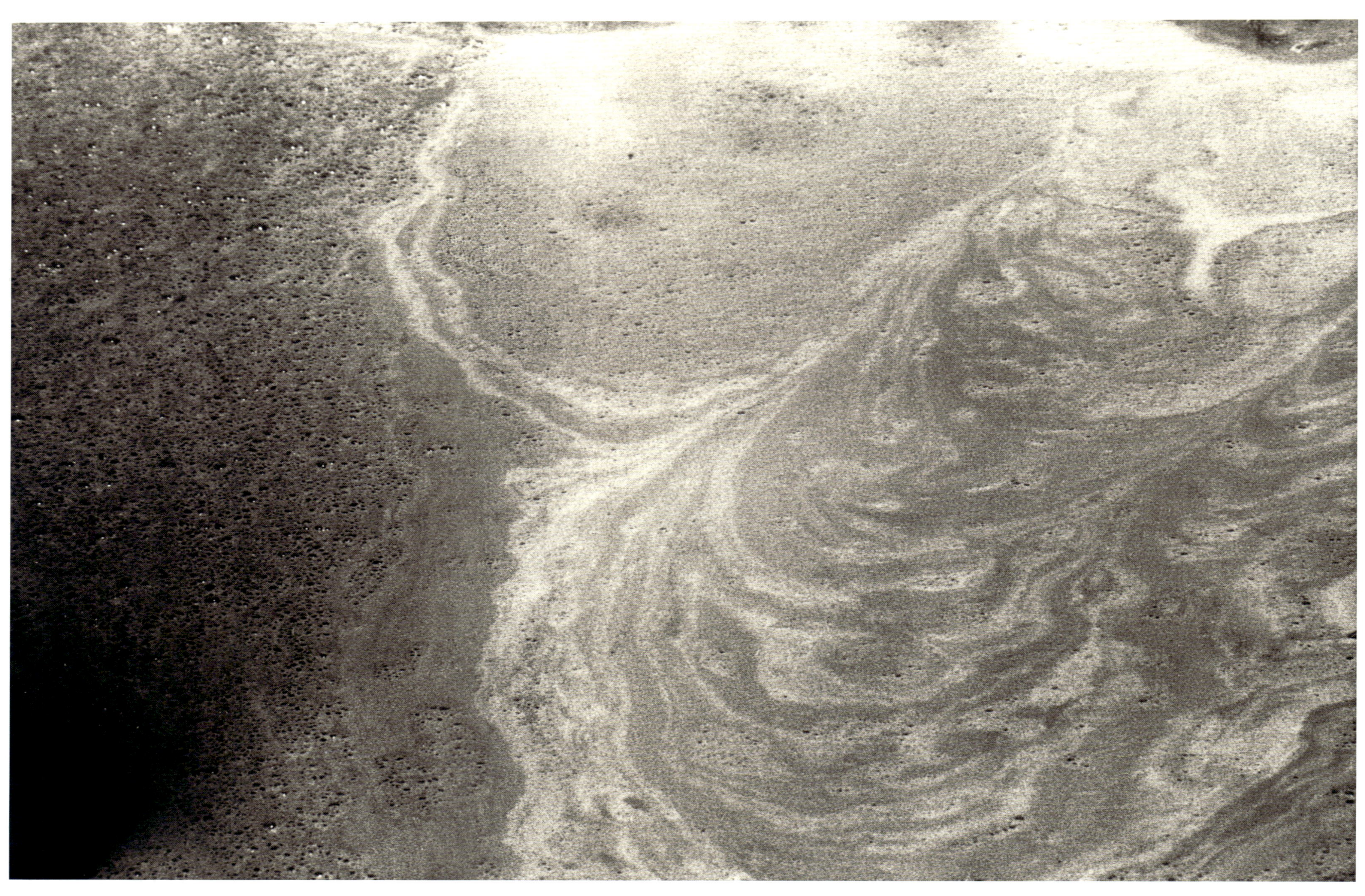

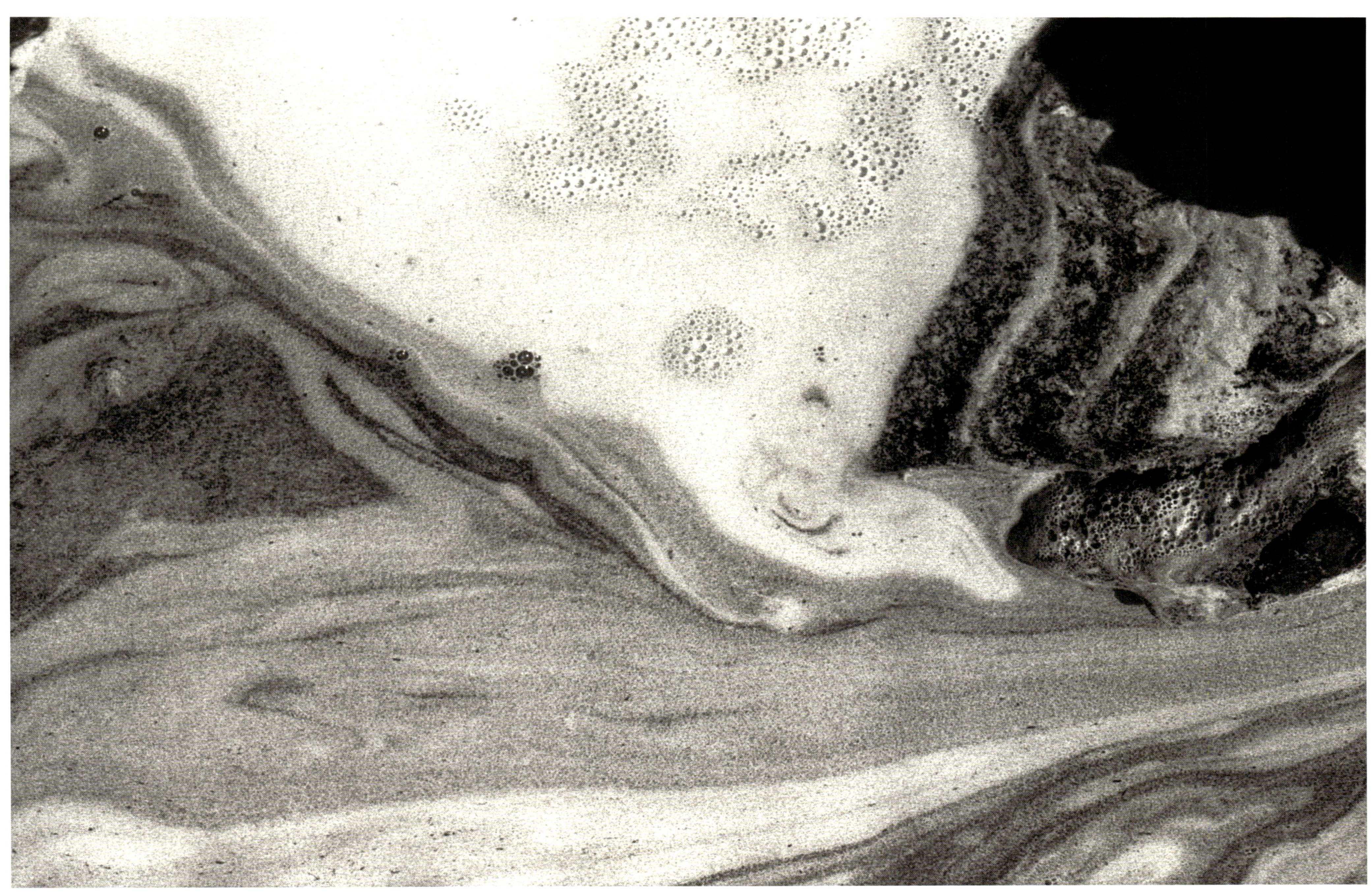

plates

Distillations

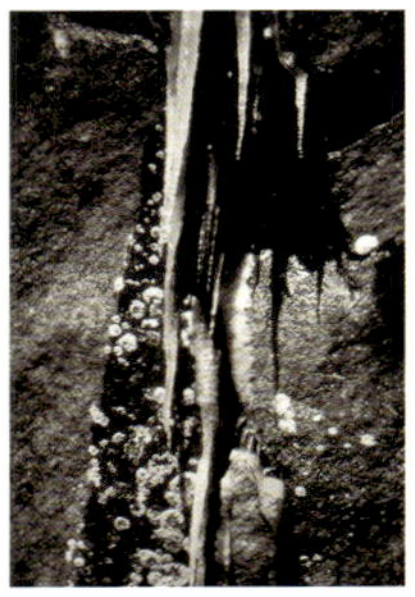

1

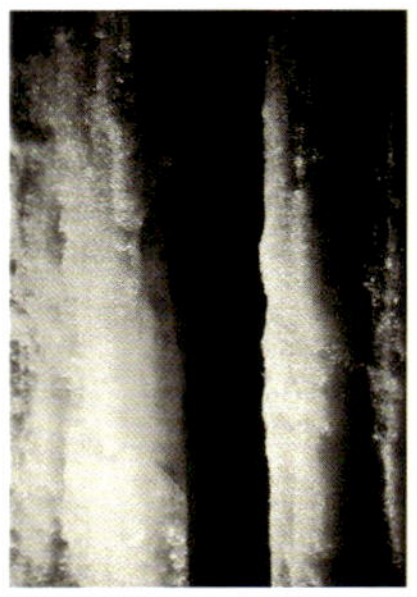

11

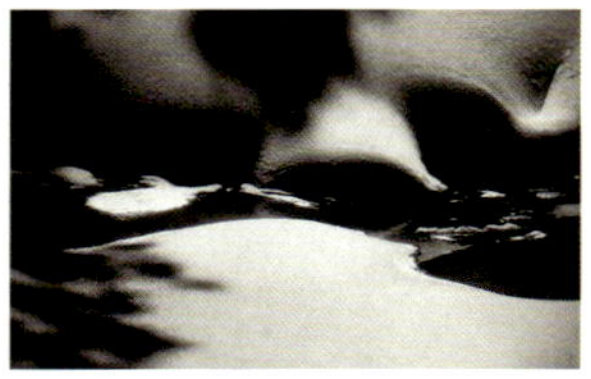

17

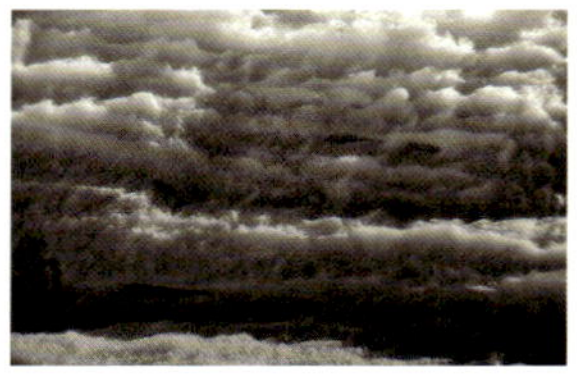

18

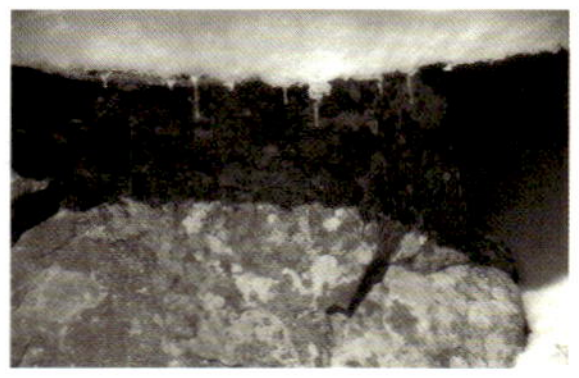

22

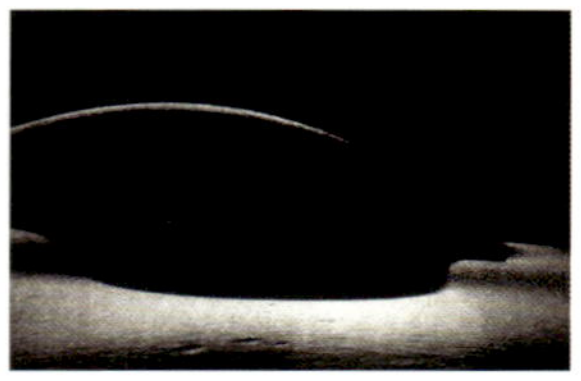

27

Abstractions

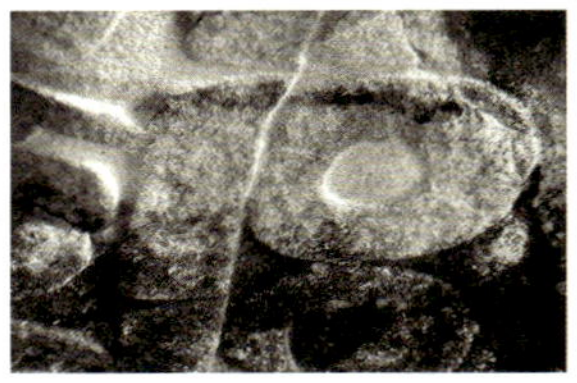

Instability

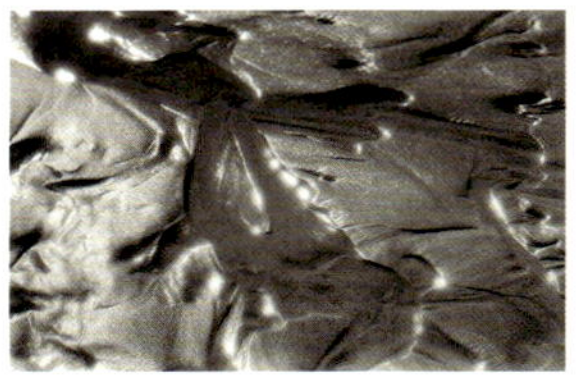

Liquid Emulsion

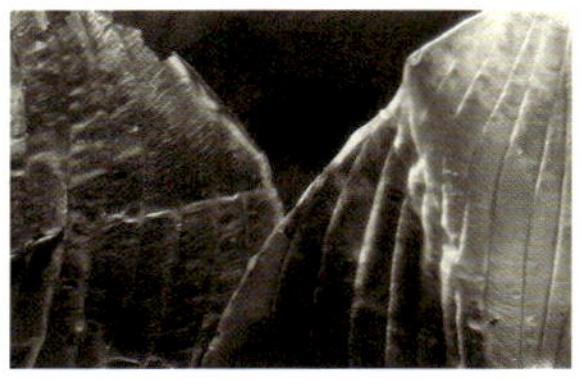

Synthesis

Effervescent 1

Tunisian Fantasy

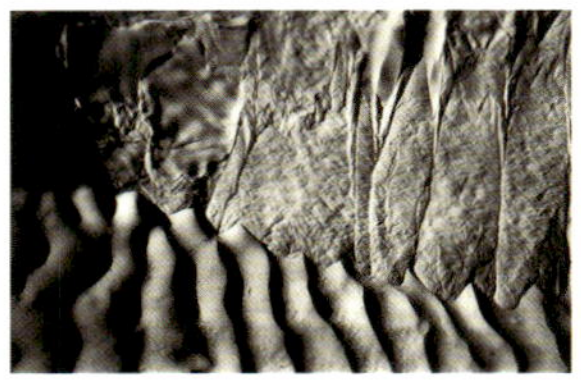

Tunisian 2

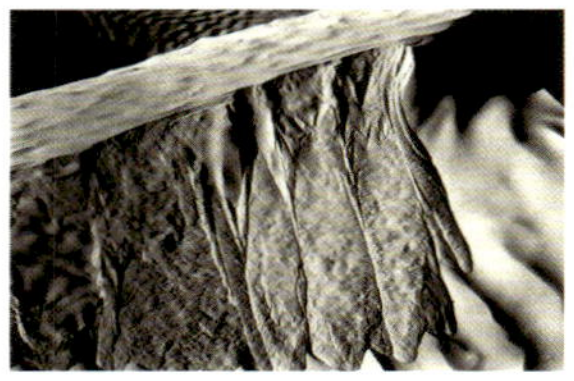

Tunisian 1

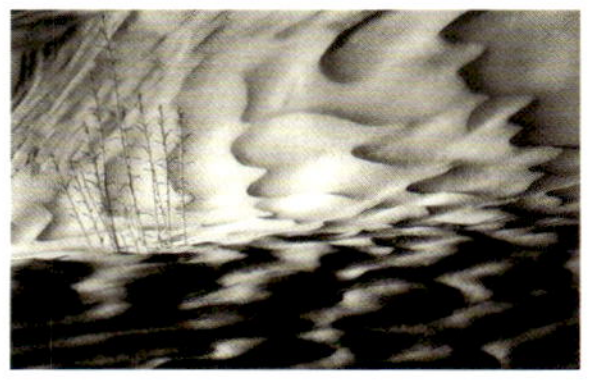

Tunisian 3

Greenland

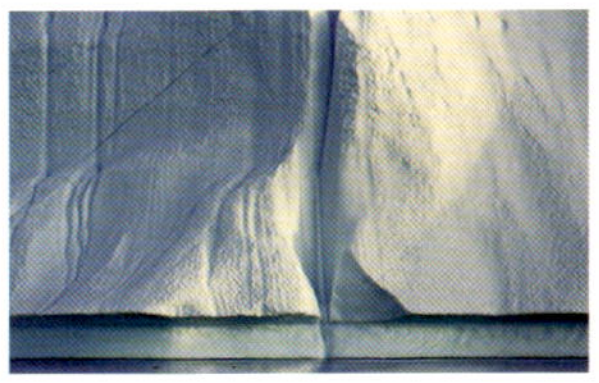

Akna's Embrace

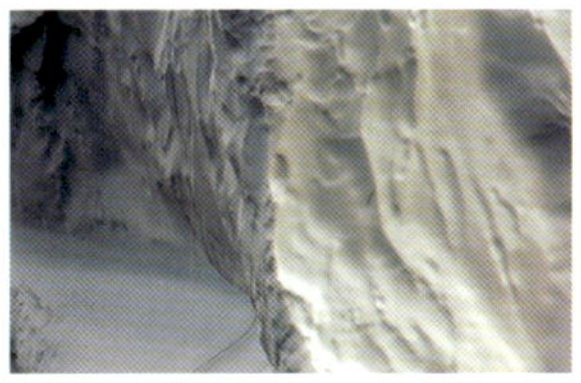

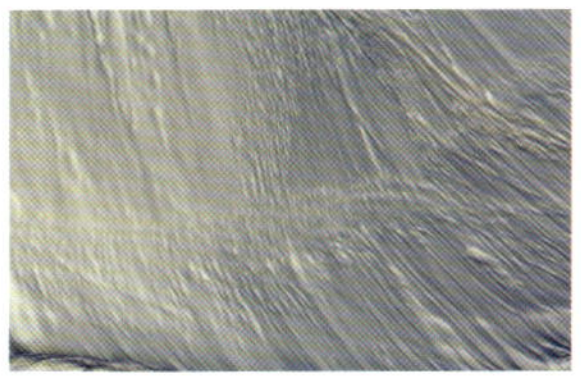

Crest and Trough

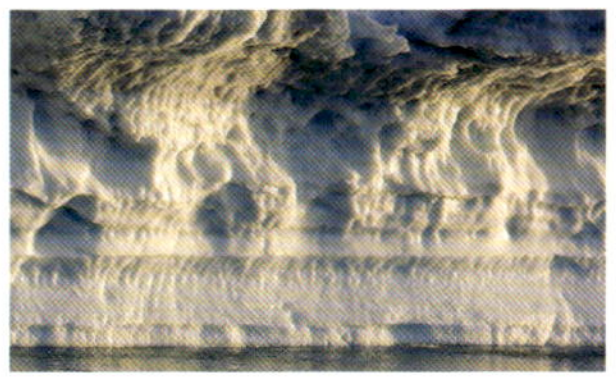

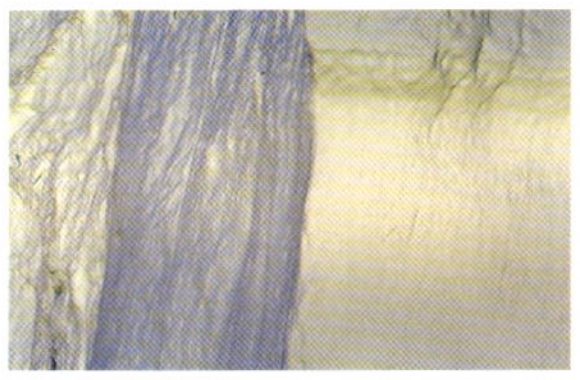

Dendritic Impulse

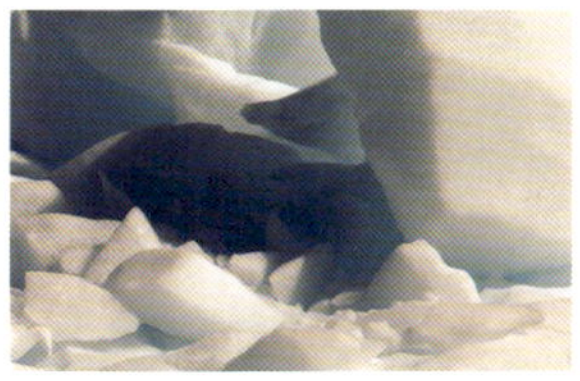

Incarnation

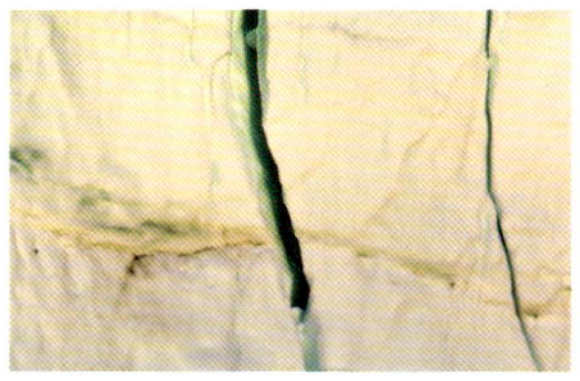

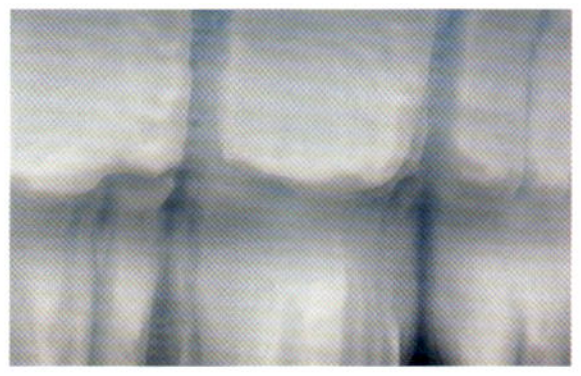

Shadows

Veil

Krya

Overwhelm

Intersections

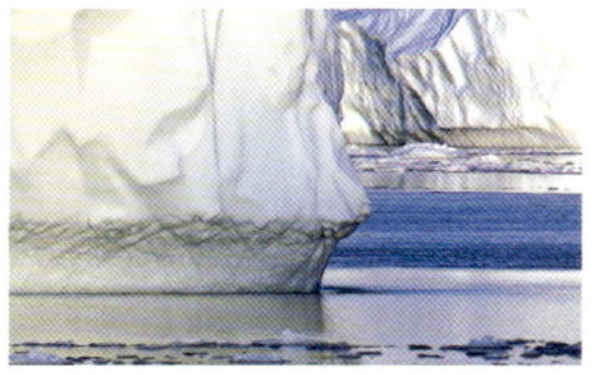

Sedna's Refuge

Icelandic Glaciers

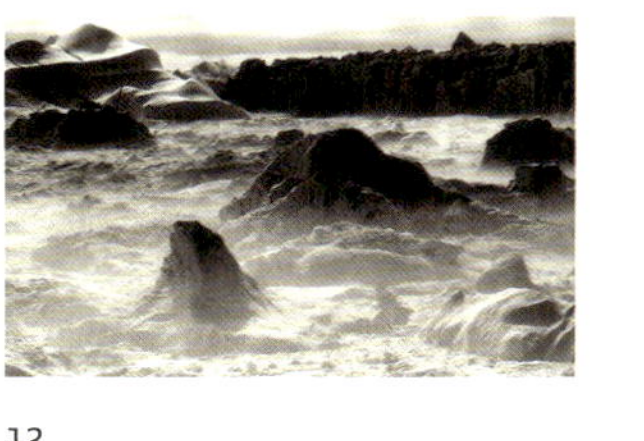

7

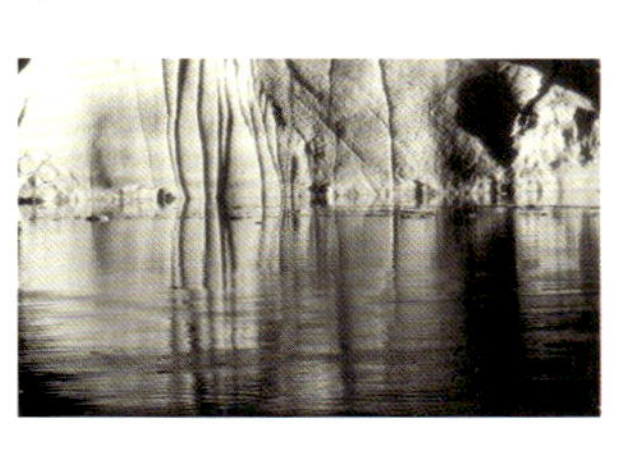

2

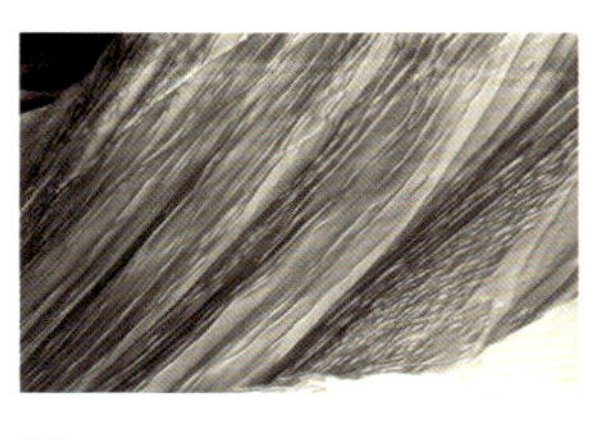

13

15

25

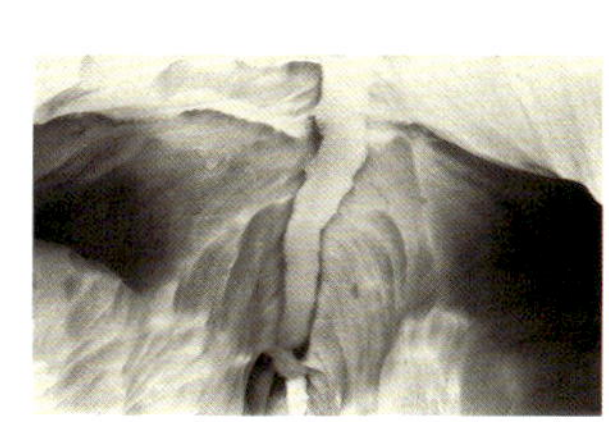

11

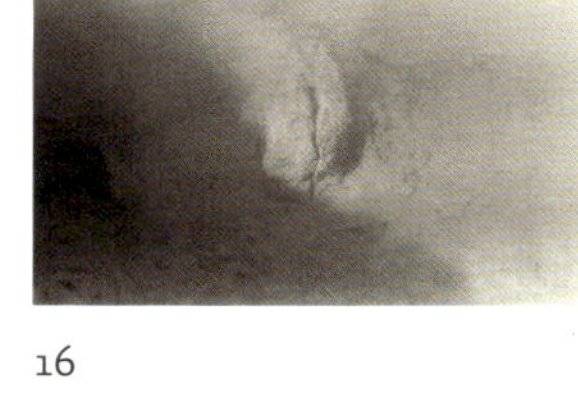

16

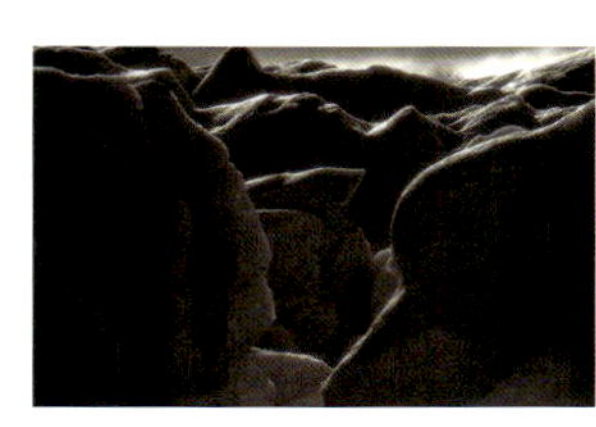

7

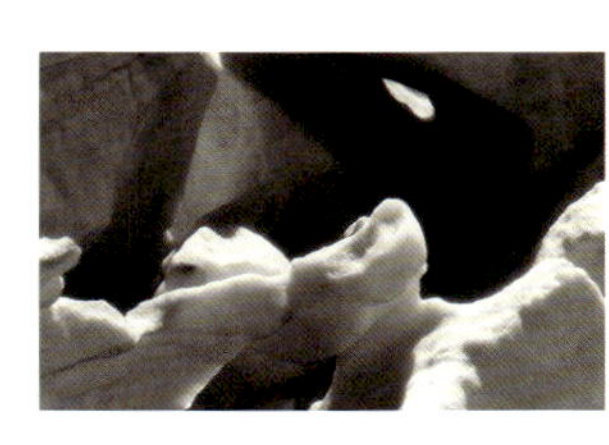

17

Icelandic Sagas

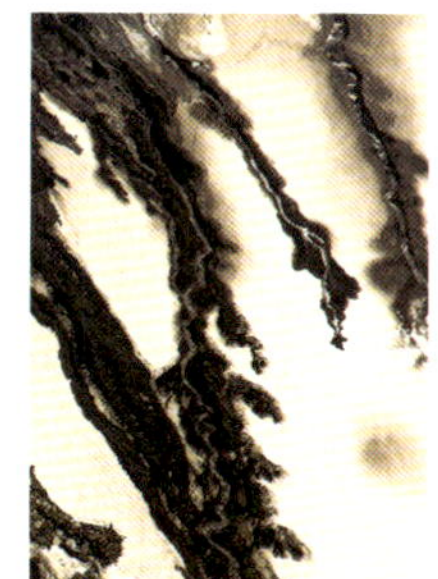

Within a Wood

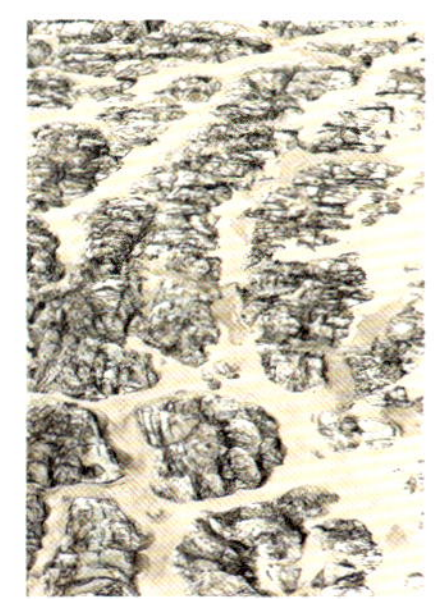

Vanaheim

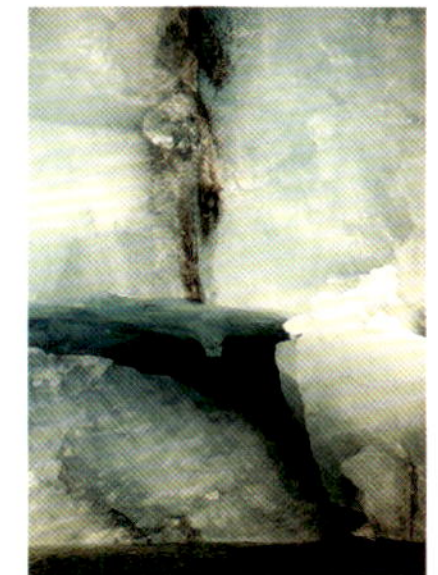

The Third Knock

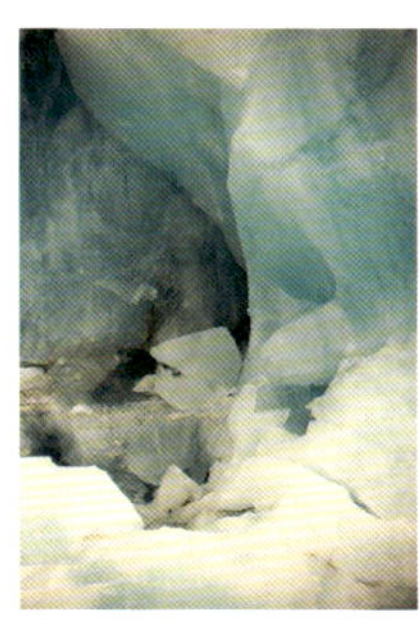

Sea of Aegir

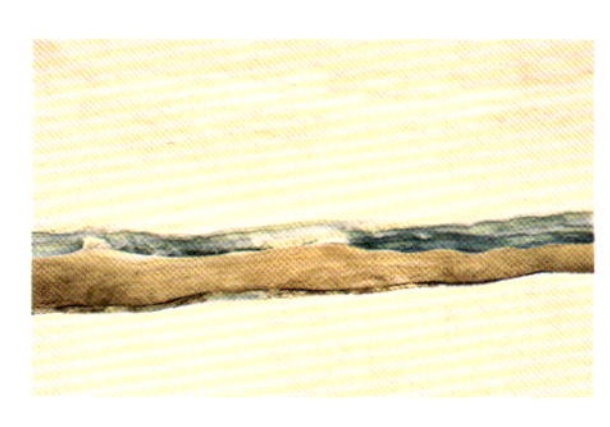

Fire and Ice

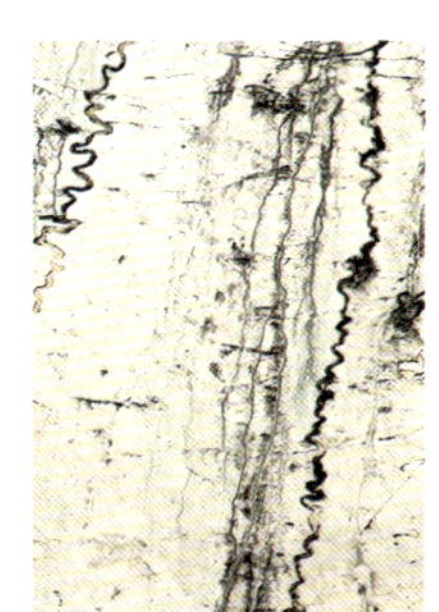

Eyvindor's Crevasse

Saga

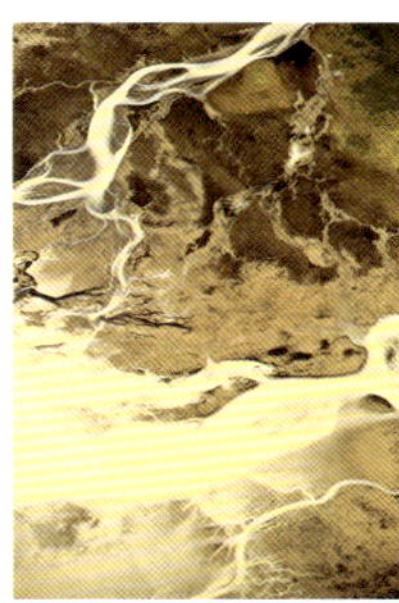

Bragi's Poem

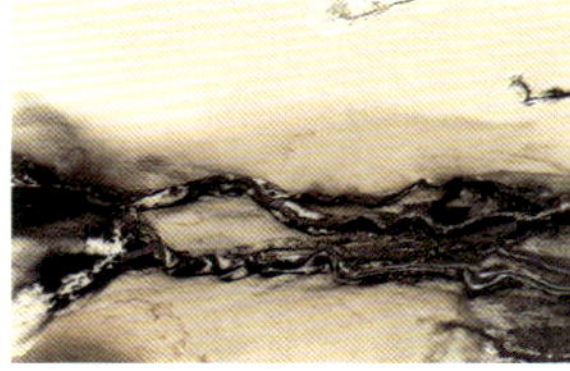

Surtur's Battle

Salt Lake Reconsidered

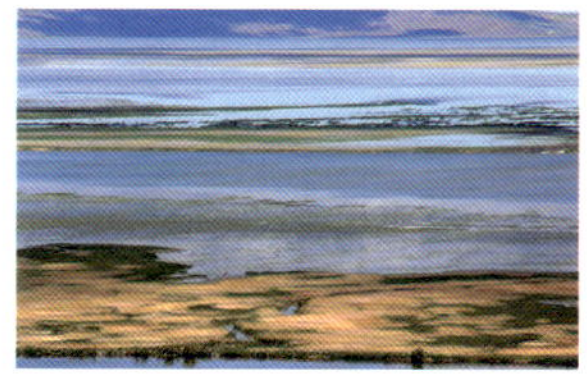

Salt Lake 1

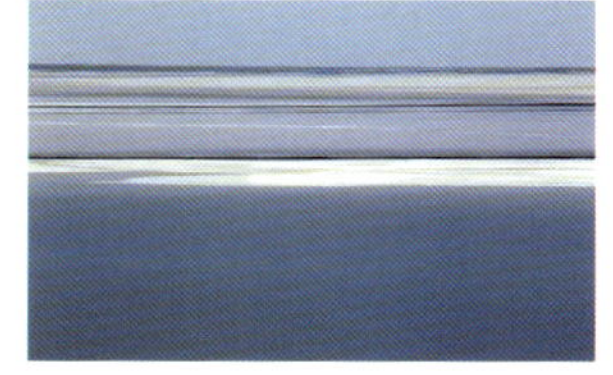

Unbounded Time

Beyond My Ken

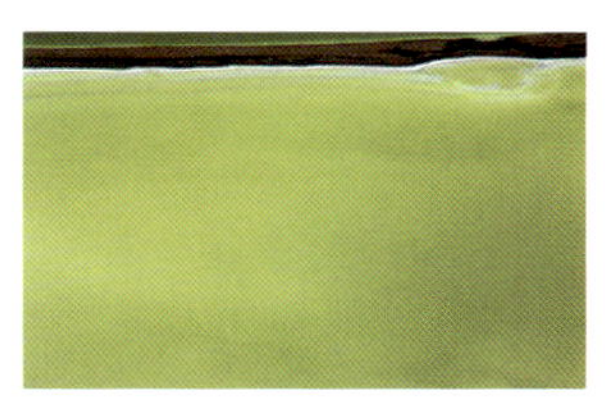

Purlieus

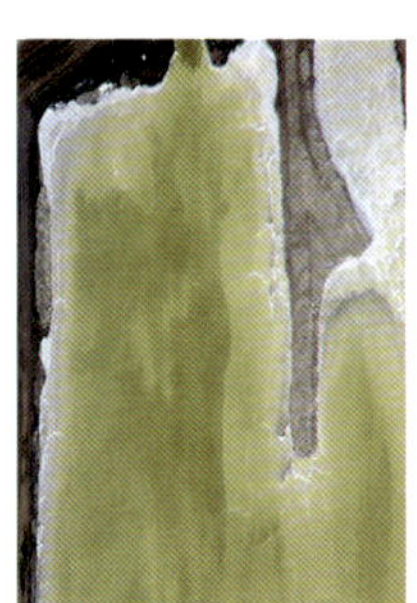

Chalcedony

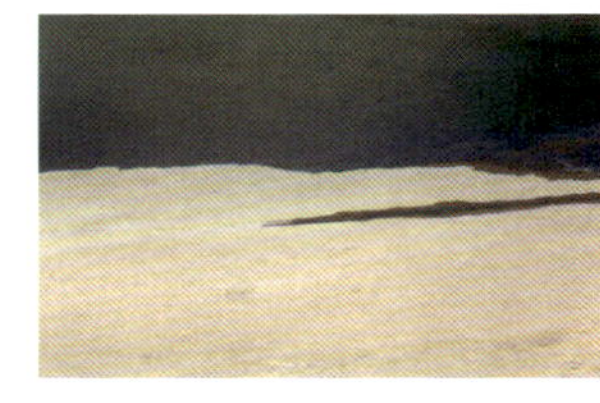

Since

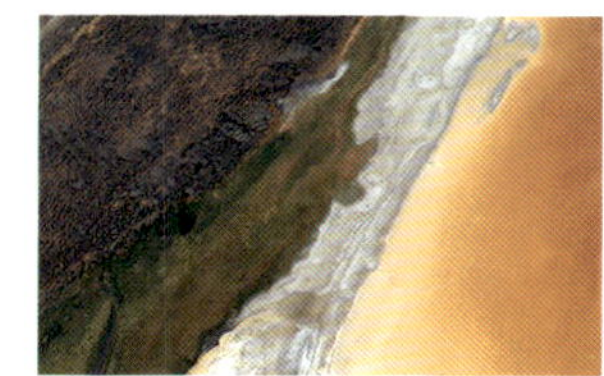

Maui's Triumph

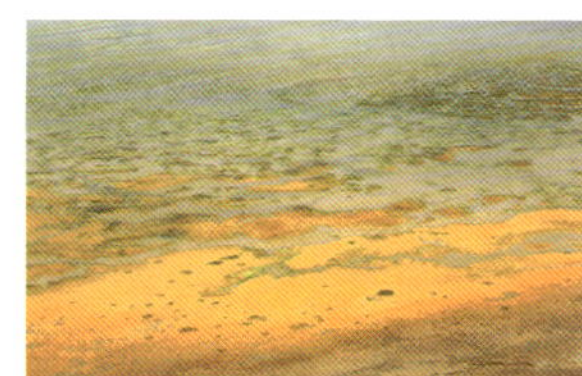

Breaking Out

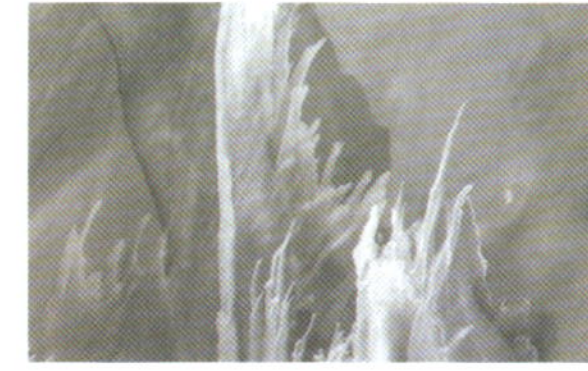

Extra Solar

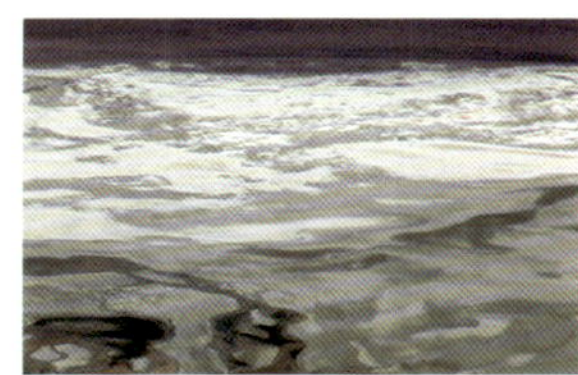

Seascape II

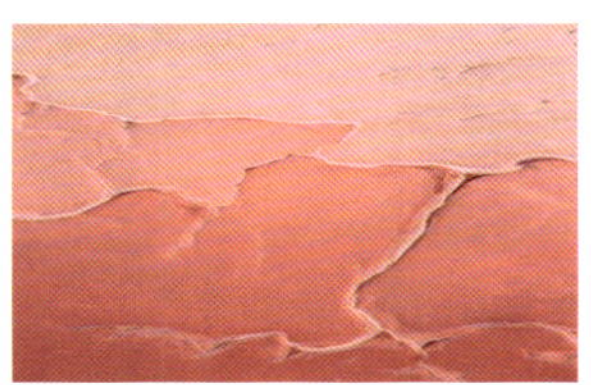

Song of Deborah

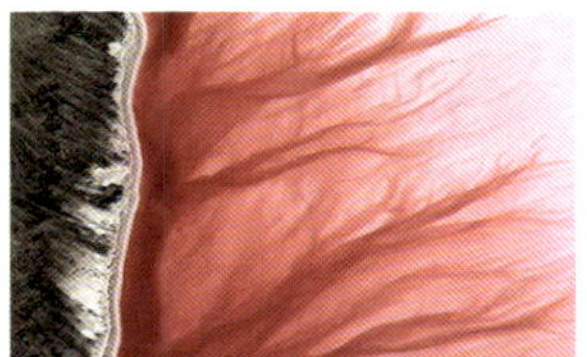

Birth of Aphrodite

Red Sea

Sun Tunnels

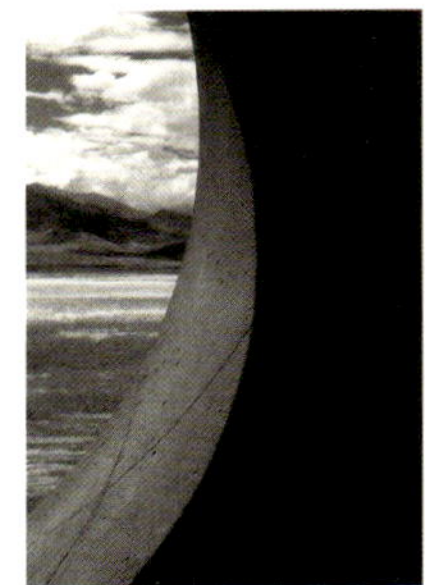

23

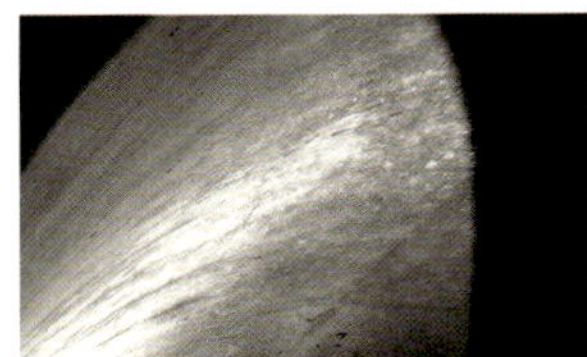

25

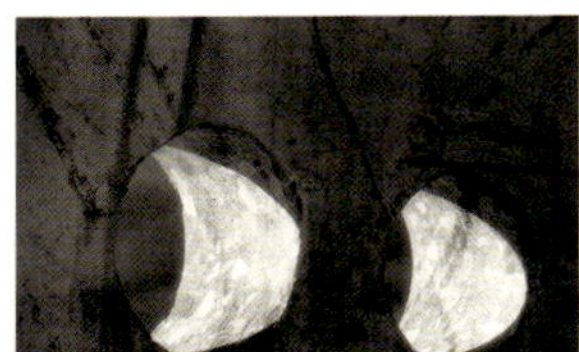

28

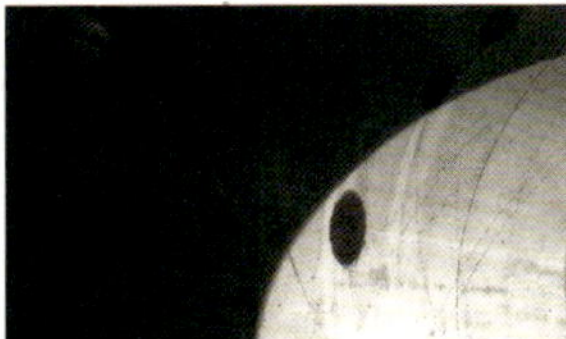

26

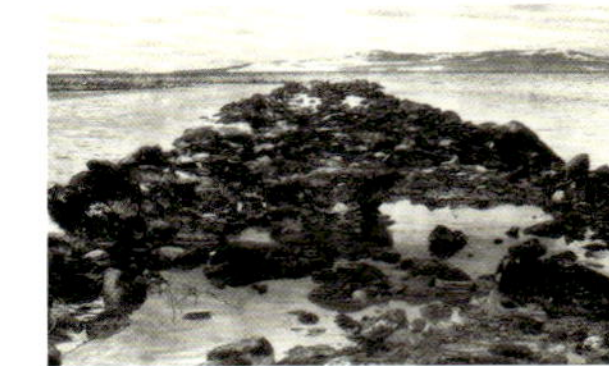

31

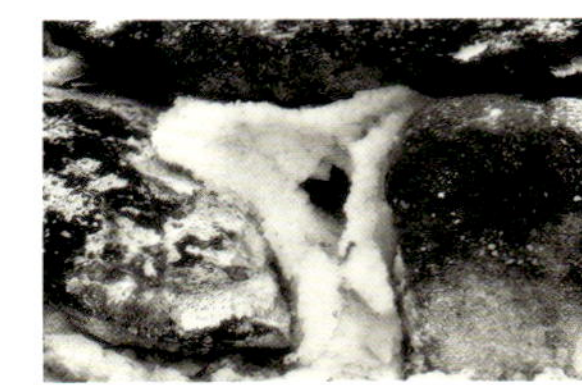

24

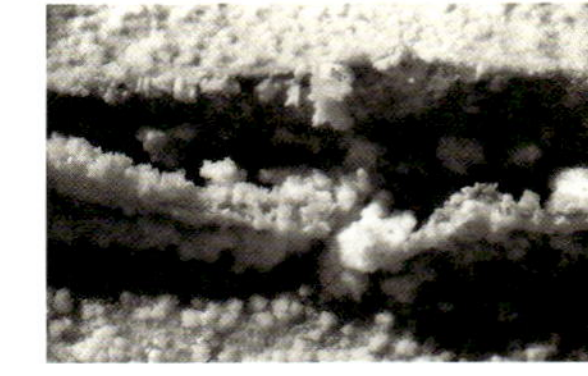

1

Spiral Jetty

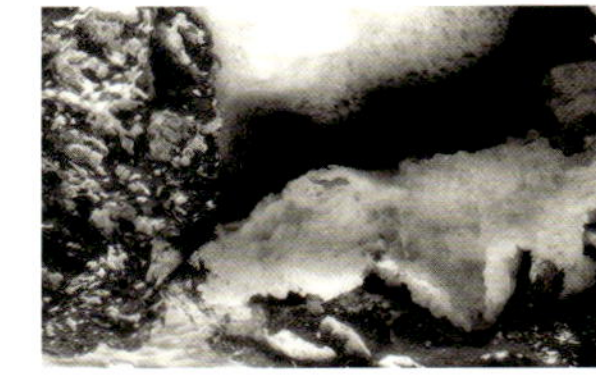

5

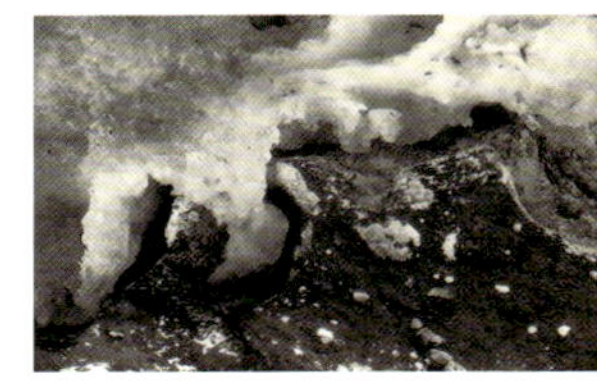

13

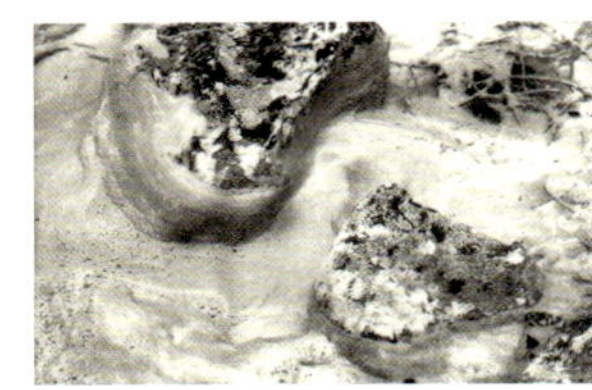

18

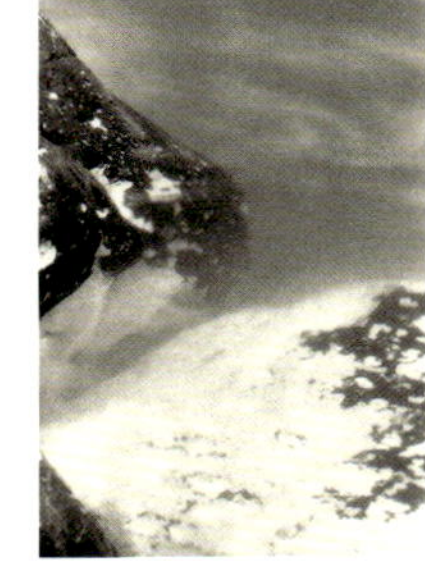

8

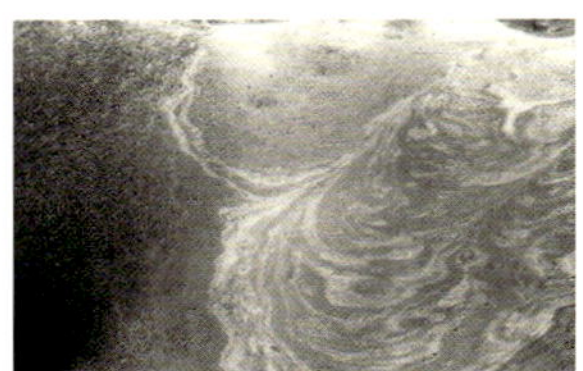

10

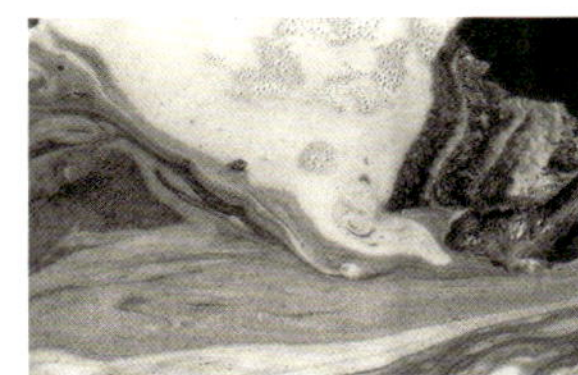

15

11

20

21